Africa of the Heart

AFRICA OF THE HEART

A Personal Journey

✿ ✿ ✿

JOSEPH HONE

BEECH TREE BOOKS
WILLIAM MORROW
New York

The author gratefully acknowledges the help of the British Broadcasting Corporation and the Virginia Center for the Creative Arts in the preparation of this book. Grateful acknowledgment is also made for permission to reprint lines from LES FLEURS DU MAL by Charles Baudelaire. Translation copyright © 1982 by Richard Howard. Reprinted by permission of David R. Godine, Publishers, Inc.

Library of Congress Cataloging-in-Publication Data

Hone, Joseph, 1937–
Africa of the heart.

(Beech tree books)
1. Hone, Joseph, 1937–   —Journeys—Africa,
Central.   2. Africa, Central—Description and travel—
1981–   . 3. Novelists, English—20th century—
Journeys. I. Title.
PR6068.049Z463 1986   916.75'1'043   86-8800
ISBN 0-688-04859-5

Printed in the United States of America

First U.S. Edition

1 2 3 4 5 6 7 8 9 10

BOOK DESIGN BY VICTORIA HARTMAN

The word "book" is said to derive from *boka*, or beech.
The beech tree has been the patron tree of writers since ancient times and
represents the flowering of literature and knowledge.

For
Tom and Ann
and for
Gerald Hanley

"Arriving at each new city, the traveler finds again
a past of his that he did not know he had:
the foreignness of what you no longer are or
no longer possess lies in wait for you in foreign,
unpossessed places."

Italo Calvino—*Invisible Cities*

CONTENTS

PROLOGUE

When I was a gun-mad schoolboy of ten, one bitterly cold Christmas, camping in a rather seedy London mansion flat not long after the war, my father suddenly announced: "We're going to live in Africa." My mother was appalled. I was absolutely delighted.

It was my godfather—a recently demobilized and dementedly optimistic Army major—who had given my father this bright idea a few days earlier, first of all proposing that they pool his army gratuity and my mother's savings to buy "a stake in Africa" and, when this financial notion failed to impress on the maternal side, going on to suggest that the two of them take up "positions" (they neither of them, of course, ever took up "work" or "jobs") with the British Government's recently introduced (and calamitously ill-fated) groundnuts scheme in Tanganyika.

"They're going to need people like you and me, Nat," my godfather said. "To get these groundnuts off the ground." There was a great deal of such vivid, arcane talk, I remember, throughout that freezing holiday of 1947 among these two very unagricultural men who had never been in Africa, about our coming life in the sun. We'd all be posted up to some Happy Valley, my godfather said, filling the dreary little chintz-filled drawing room with African romance, as he and my father ran imaginative riot through the dark continent, a safari whipped on by liberal whisky-sodas, while I listened spellbound.

"Of course, the great thing will be the hunting." My godfather reached for the black-market scotch he'd brought with him. "All the animals—not touched since before the war. Bound to be thick on the ground. There for the taking. . . ."

He took another large measure. "I still have my old Mauser. And I fancy, Nat, you would very soon pick up the knack again out there." The knack he referred to was my father's prewar habit of moving round the Dublin cocktail bars with a loaded .45 under his coat, where he had once blasted the tops off the brandy and Benedictine bottles in the Wicklow Hotel—target practice before moving on to the real thing in the Spanish Civil War, a campaign luckily frustrated when the plane he was piloting never made it beyond Biarritz, and he and the rest of his bibulous Irish Brigade spent a week at the Imperial Palace instead, ambushing the champagne, before flying back to Dublin.

But I knew nothing of this at the time. All I heard then was the talk of guns. There were going to be guns in my coming life, real guns, not toys: Winchester .375s for the lion and a hand-tooled Purdey .450 Express for the elephant. I couldn't believe my luck. I'd be in Africa by the summer, freed from my wretched prep school—in Africa, stalking the animals—and more: an expedition up from the steamy coast, across the cool blue plainslands, over the great lakes; and then the darker journey into the interior, through the dripping rain forests, toward the Mountains of the Moon, before a long and difficult voyage on the Congo river, down the far side of Africa, in native *pirogues*. . . .

Of course, I knew Africa in those days, even if my father and godfather didn't. During longer holidays with cousins in a large Victorian house in Ireland I had read all the classic texts: some bound copies of the *Boys' Own Paper* and the rest of an Edwardian adventure library, once the pride of an even more distant relative, where I had unearthed the dusty, empire-glorying books, from attics and playroom shelves, cleaning the covers, the gaudy colored pictorial boards with their Union Jacks and blood-red images of derring-do—so that the young lieutenant's scarlet tunic, white pouch-belt, pith helmet, and lanyard on the front of Captain Brereton's *With Wolseley to Kumasi—A Tale of the First Ashanti War* came to shine mint fresh, as the intrepid officer pushed his way through an evil mangrove swamp, service revolver at the ready.

Before that cold winter holiday in London I had traveled the blistering Somali deserts with the same Captain Brereton, seeking revenge against the lesser breeds in *The Grip of the Mullah*. I had been in search of Prester John, too; risen over the animal-choked plains of East Africa with Jules Verne for six weeks in his balloon—and journeyed with him to the center of the African earth. Above all I had gone with Allan Quatermain to *King Solomon's Mines*—and Gagool the Witchfinder was never really dead for me. She lurked, half-crushed, yet still half-alive, in the broom cupboard at the bottom of the back stairs, or more certainly in the old laundry on the way to the yard where there was a malign Victorian device—a thundering linen press that worked on rollers, pressed down by a moving coffin-like half-ton weight—a mangle that had caught the witch in its huge rolling jaws but had not quite extinguished her evil flame.

In the morning room of this old house there were other more exact, supposedly factual African accounts, which I sought out and browsed through during the long, rain-sodden Irish days: bound, late nineteenth-century copies of the *Sphere* and the *Illustrated London News*—which made Africa blaze and spark more than the crackling fire, where the artists, suggesting even color by the stark and detailed horrors that they concentrated into their line engravings, brought the blood of Africa right onto the morning-room carpet for me—that dark, savage continent that the Victorians always wanted to see it as, so that they could save it with all sorts of missionary and military endeavor. For them, in their high-minded libraries and studies, Africa was a relaxation, a fantastic, long-running adventure serial—as it became for me, sixty years later, a child thumbing through the same illustrated magazines.

Here, in the final desperate defense of Khartoum, I saw the Mahdi's troops advancing on General Gordon standing on the Residency steps with a Bible in his hand—and later his decapitated head which the wicked infidels flourished aloft on a spear. Poor, brave General Gordon. I felt like Queen Victoria. I had a defective Diana air rifle in those days and there was a clump of bamboo to one side of the house—the nearest approach, I thought, to rampant African conditions which our mild Irish climate allowed. If the rain stopped before lunch I would go there with my rifle, push through the dripping greenery and exact a terrible vengeance on all the mad mullahs.

In those days, even the cold, dark granite church on the edge of the estate I made over into one of Livingstone's baking equatorial mission huts. And in place of the interminable hymns, prayers, lessons, sermons, and squeaky harmonium music I set up a faith in the African rite, so that the sounds of that low church on its rain-streaked, northern hill were replaced by hot murmurs, savage words and music: tribal chants, war cries, tom-toms, black magic at the altar—with the chance, when the collection plate came round, of making a conciliatory peace offering. Though this was rare, for the black man in me was angry then. And it was Livingstone himself, rather than mild-mannered Canon Bradshaw, who spoke from the pulpit—confronting an unruly, unchristian mob, where Aunt Susan and Uncle Harold over from Bagshot had gone native and were getting restless, only waiting my command to attack the Canon for his long-windedness, transfixing him with the assegais I had conveniently to hand in the shape of the dripping, steel-tipped umbrellas and walking sticks left in the church porch.

Above all, I knew from these adventure books, Africa had a certain haunting, unmistakable smell: a sweet smell of decay—decayed vegetable—and of leprous flesh, too: a mix of burnt cow dung and exotically perfumed flowers as I understood it. So that one summer, out on the yard manure heap, I set fire to a dead crow and some rotting turnips, the funeral pyre covered with June rose petals stolen from the pleasure garden. The resulting odor was thrillingly unspeakable.

I grew up with Africa on my mind, if not in my veins. For me it was a place of pulsating, ultimate adventure, of liberating space and freedom from the confines of a restricted, almost Victorian childhood: a world of dos and don'ts, of nannies, governesses, and tears-before-bedtime—which I had to invent every sort of release from, so that when my bedroom candle went out, I spoke to myself in a variety of imagined African tongues, heroic dialogues, full of wet labials, snorts, and strangled gutturals—the routine secrets of childhood normally shared, but here turned in on myself and transformed into heated native debates. Sometimes the darkness of my bedroom ideally mimicked an impenetrable African night; or, when the rain fell outside my window, the patter on the Virginia creeper was the happy sound of a torrent in a tropic forest. At other times the walls and ceilings dissolved, giving way to starlight on the plainslands, infinite space where the lion roared. Here, before sleep, round the fire of my mind—the sheets monkey skins, the eiderdown well tucked up as a zebra shield beneath my chin—here in the warbling speech of equatorial river tribes, I planned battles against rival clans and surprise attacks against the white man. In these nights I gathered around me, like toys or teddy bears, all the loose fictions of a boy's Africa—witch doctor's masks, long barbed assegais, poisoned arrows, old black powder Martini-Henry rifles—which I then brought together in cliff-hanging serial adventures: a boy's world—imperfect in fact, without other boys or real games—but perfectly realized now, in thought and speech, where I could play all the roles: friend or foe, black or white, where I could as easily impose victory or defeat—where, in the safety of my bed, I could imagine all the most dangerous games. So that when I dreamed later—in those dreams when I escaped Gagool, at least—I found myself in a continent of light, not of darkness: a child of the country long before I ever set foot there.

My father and godfather, those cloudy whisky-soda travelers, never managed to get to Africa. The groundnuts scheme sank with all hands as, in due course, they did themselves. And that chintzy mansion flat in Battersea, where I thought the "call" had at last come for me to leave for Africa, has long since collapsed in rubble.

But Africa remains for me, in Graham Greene's phrase, an "Africa of the heart"—a world which I must make good: my father's Africa, a dream of colonial escape, where he might win with one last throw of the dice; my godfather's imagined Happy Valley. There were those books, too: *Blackie's Story Books for Boys*—Henty's *The Dash for Khartoum* and *With Kitchener in the Soudan*—where the lovely beckoning jackets had to be made flesh. And of course, above all, there remained that long journey for me to make, started by the morning-room fire over the *Illustrated London News*—that great expedition up country, from the ocean mangrove swamps, across the deserts, up onto the plainslands, over the great lakes and into the pygmy interior, before native *pirogues* bore me swiftly down the Congo to the Atlantic on the far side: Livingstone's great journeys, where he was lost—and found—and where Stanley was finally triumphant. This, one day, had to be my journey too. There were all these debts to pay to the dream Africa of my childhood. And of course there was the reality itself.

BOOK ONE

CHAPTER

1

Invitations to the Voyage

"*W*hen will Africa start? I wonder—that first image, taste, smell. Or even some hint long before I get there which will rescue me from the limbo of trains and airport lounges. I feel like a surgeon, gloved and masked, waiting to start an important operation. I long for the first glimpse of the body.

"Coming out of the Gents' in the transit lounge at Brussels airport I saw her standing there, straight in front of me: a tall Congolese woman with great white rounds to her eyes, a mammy figure in a mammy cloth—or rather, since she must have been some rich man's wife, a very sophisticated version of this: a complexly tucked and folded swathe of black polka-dot print, with a bustle, running up to a carelessly but in fact artfully contrived hat like a French cockade in the same material. Here was the body: the high cheekbones, broad forehead, the splendid protuberant lips, rolling over, white-flecked waves on the burgundy dunes of her chin. Her skin had a purply phosphorescence to it: dark but one felt it would glow in the darkness. On her wrist a man's gold oyster Rolex, with gold bangles, like curtain rails, musical chimes, sliding up and down each arm. Though her toga betrayed no real shape I sensed a whole new anatomy beneath the folds—bones and widths and lengths which Gray had never delineated. On her feet the skimpiest of flip-flop sandals, as if she had just left a river. Yes, she has the magnetic bearing of a naked woman risen from water and afterward released from a glittering emporium where all the rich cloths and gold trinkets have flown from their rolls and caskets and attached themselves naturally to her. If I touched this woman, lived with her for a week, I could invent the rest of Africa. I would never need to go there."

I went into the duty-free at Brussels to buy some scotch and cologne to take with me upriver—the first a palliative against boredom, the

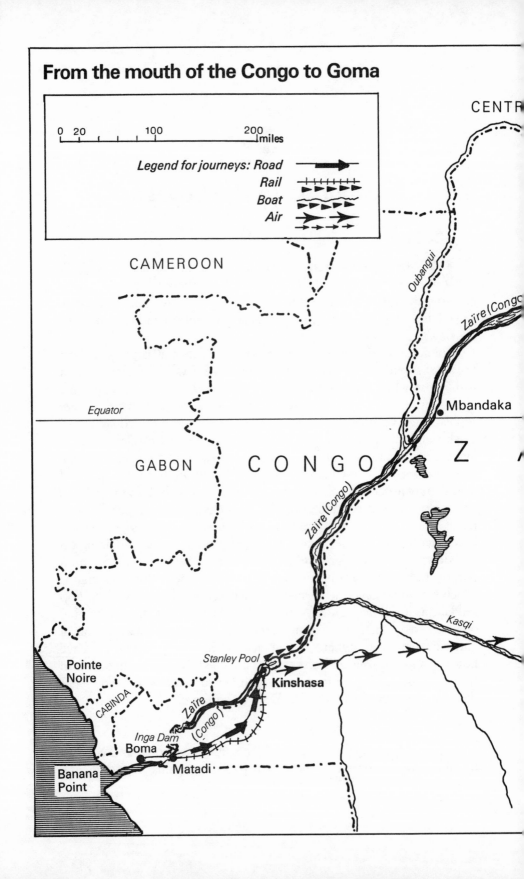

From the mouth of the Congo to Goma

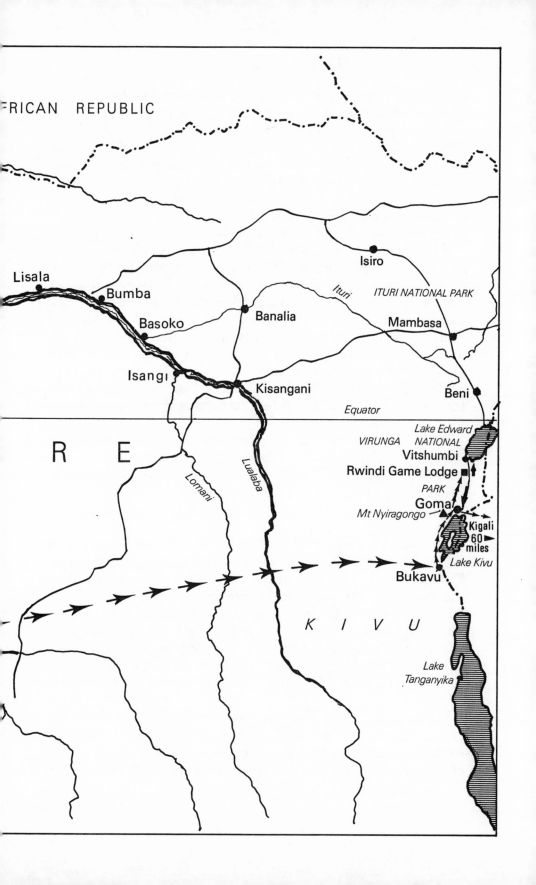

second against the heat. And suddenly I remembered I'd forgotten the playing cards and the poker dice which I'd left out at home as other necessary diversions for that long voyage up the Congo river—drinks with the captain at sundown on the water; an evening's mild gambling, with matches or old Belgian francs as counters, among the other unlikely first-class passengers: a Belgian priest, a swarthy Kurtz-type trader, a saturnine Congolese. I, at least, had it all planned—as I had to, for no one knew anything about these river boats in London, even after months of inquiry, at the Zaïrean Embassy, the airline and several travel agencies. The best I managed was some hints from an agency in St. Albans. But their river timetable, they admitted, might have applied to the colonial era in the Congo. I had even written to the British Embassy in Kinshasa more than two months before I left, asking details of these river boats, and getting no reply had tried to telephone them. The international operator told me it took at least forty-eight hours and usually a week to get through to the capital of Zaïre. So I traveled hopefully, with the Johnny Walker and the Monsieur de Givenchy, but without the cards or dice. An omen? But of what? Certainly I wasn't the first traveler made uneasy by all the queries hanging over the great river. That was the only consolation.

When I paid my bill at the duty-free checkout I noticed the minute tidewrack of white paint round the edges of my nails—legacy of a few days spent decorating our bathroom the previous week. Will I ever be free of home, I thought? Will I ever get to Africa?

I went on with my notes then. "I come to live suspended—exactly fulfilling the dreadful purpose of this arid, air-conditioned transit lounge. The Kinshasa flight has been delayed. They're waiting for something or somebody. And like a prisoner I either sleep, or, when awake, I look for signs—searching for the blue sky or a sparrow from a cell window. The lovely Congolese *maîtresse* was one such indicator, her whole body pointing to Africa. But the remnants of white paint beneath my nails, like forensic evidence found on a murderer, tell a different story: my alibi here, en route to Africa, is broken. I am still at home. I have never left there."

I dozed in the plastic chair that molded my backside perfectly, but gave no support anywhere else. I slept momentarily, though the dream seemed interminably long. I was edging nervously down the sheer sides of a black marble cliff—carved, like the stone effigies on Mount Rushmore, in the shape of a vast human face. I was looking desperately for grips, footholds, without ropes or pitons. It was raining heavily, the rock face slippery in any case, and I knew I must fall into the valley, a long flat tawny yellow plainsland where the sun shone brilliantly far beneath me. It was an African valley, for I could see the flat tops of acacia trees, anthills, white-rumped gazelle: a paradise without people, black or white, a vision of Africa before the fall. Then I fell, willingly releasing my grip, knowing that I would die. But there was a lovely sense of spinning vertigo, a free-fall happiness at least. Suddenly I was surrounded by voices, by pandemonium.

"Je vais téléphoner ma soeur! Je dois téléphoner ma SOEUR! . . ." I woke. Two skinny Congolese youths were being manhandled through the transit lounge by a pair of huge Belgian *flics.* We were all of us on our way now, moving down the covered ramp toward the plane. But the *déportés* refused to go into the great mouth of the ramp, kicking, struggling violently, one of them still shouting, *"Je vais téléphoner ma soeur. . . ."* He fell on the sloping rubber floor, only to be picked up by his shirt collar and dragged forward. The collar tore. The *flic* took him by the back of his jeans then and lugged him forward, sack of potatoes-style. The two Africans had no other clothes and no luggage. Their cries filled the ramp and none of us did anything. *"Je vais téléphoner ma soeur!"* The younger of the two boys—they were hardly more than that—kept repeating the phrase, a desperate, tear-choked shout, like a child being tortured in his lessons over a French phrase book. But finally they were brutally forced on through and ahead of us and hidden somewhere in the great belly of the plane, for when we all got to our seats there was just the Muzak—a medley from *My Fair Lady*—and the smell of cheap cologne. I complained to the Belgian steward when he came round to see if my seat belt was secure. *"Mais—ils sont des terroristes,"* he told me, adjusting the air flow on the nipple above. "Judge and executioner—are you?" I asked him suddenly, speaking in English now. "With your plane acting as the tumbril? Is that it?" The steward looked at me grimly but said nothing.

I was pretty certain I knew who these boys were. They were Zaïrean students living in Brussels—on scholarships, or with their parents in exile perhaps, two among thousands: students who had protested against President Mobutu's corrupt and vicious régime at home, who had demonstrated in Brussels for several years past now. But Mobutu had sent his secret police in among them, as *agents provocateurs,* to prey on them, with the help of the Belgian Ministry of the Interior and their Deuxième

Bureau. Together they had trapped many of these students, planted subversive documents, incriminated them. Those were the ones who were sent home, like these two, with just the clothes they stood up in. But that wouldn't matter. Their likely fate was one where clothes and baggage would be entirely superfluous.

The Muzak stopped. The big DC10 thudded clumsily down the runway, a minute of increasing pace, suicidal, land-bound—then a sudden silence as the wheels were free, the vibration stopped and the plane lifted into its true element like a great whale, nose up, searching for life, Africa-bound. Still I hadn't left. I heard the words, the sobs in the transit lounge, the cries all the way down the ramp: *"Je vais téléphoner ma soeur! Je vais téléphoner. . . ."* This was my invitation to the voyage. But we'd been hijacked, not invited to Africa: Baudelaire's sweet poetry of departure turned very sour. *"Mon enfant, ma soeur. . . ."* How did it go on?

> Le tout n'est qu'ordre et beauté,
> Luxe, calme et volupté . . .

I wondered. The omens told against—especially since the beautiful Congolese woman had disappeared way up front, into the armchairs and free champagne of the first class. Hers was the ordered opulence, the pleasure, peace and elegance: mine the thin, arse-aching, knee-stubbing seat, hemmed in by two *gros Belges* all night. I didn't sleep. Part of me traveled in the mind: I was taking a late train home from Paddington. Another part, a stranger, was flying to Africa.

2

No Exit

I met Harry Jupiter on my second morning at the Memling Hotel in Kinshasa. I was late down for breakfast. The cafe-terrace at the end of the lobby was crowded so I had to share a table with him. It was the luckiest meeting I had in Kinshasa—apart from Eleanor.

It was the dry season. There was no heat in the city and the terrace was set back in an almost cold shade under the roof at the back of the yellow-stained lobby. So Harry wore a pullover, a big one for he was a large man. The only unusual thing about it was that it was a cricket pullover, long-sleeved, in white wool, with the colored lines—red and green bands round the collar and waist—of some English cricket club. He was reading a French paper, not from Kinshasa, but from Brazzaville, the twin city, capital of the old French Congo on the other side of the river. A French paper and a continental breakfast: coffee and croissants. I was hoping for something more substantial.

"Omelette au jambon," I asked the woman when I'd finally caught her eye and willed her over to me. The woman sighed.

"You have to mark the card up." The man opposite spoke for the first time. "You mark out what you want," he said.

The waitress got me a card and I ticked right down the list. I was hungry. I ticked the croissants, too.

"There aren't any," the man said. "I bring my own when I breakfast here. There's a good *boulangerie* right behind the hotel, on the way to the Grand Marché. You can only get croissants for breakfast up at the Intercontinental."

"Thank you."

The big man must have been in his late fifties, with a faded American accent, from the deep south, I thought, but with distinct French intonations: the r's rolled easily and he hit a fine high Norman croak on the *é* of Marché. An old French-American from New Orleans? He folded his newspaper. "I see Mitterrand is on his way out here—a shot in the arm for all the ex-French territories up north. A little of the old *mission civilisatrice.* I doubt we can expect the King of the Belgians here, though."

He took a cheroot from a small leather cigar-case in front of him, offered me one. "I'll wait till I've had some food," I said. He laughed then, for the first time, a throaty, gravel-in-a-barrel laugh. "You'll be waiting half an hour for what you ordered. Have some of my coffee. You can use the other side of the cup. I'm Harry Jupiter."

I introduced myself. "Only got here yesterday. From London."

"Yes. I heard something of that. With the BBC, I think? I listen to your World Service every day. I get your magazine, too: the *Listener.*"

I was surprised.

"Oh, I have people out at the airport. You have to have—else you'd never get out of the place. Never get anything in either."

I was still surprised. "How did you spot me?"

"One of my boys did. He's a good boy, Alain. Speaks English well —I've taught him. That's one of my jobs here. Very few British people come to Kinshasa. And those that do—well, there's only two or three real flights in here a week from Europe now and I always have someone up there when they get in."

I took one of Harry's cheroots. They were small, chunky, wedge-shaped: tarry and unappetizing-looking. But they smoked well—a slow, woody, blue-whiffed smoke.

"They're from the Kivu region, way out on the eastern borders here. Though they get them in from Rwanda now. They don't make much of anything in Zaïre anymore. Gas is running out."

"Is it? I was hoping to do a lot of traveling in Zaïre."

"You were?" Harry's eyelids lifted, a sharp blue glint in the pupils. He licked his lips, as if he'd just spotted a long-odds winner in the paddock. "Travel is an interesting thing in this country," he said.

"Yes. So I've heard. I'm making for the coast first, down to Matadi and Banana Point. Then back up here and on upriver—on the big boat to Kisangani. Then I wanted to get into the Ituri forest, see something of the pygmies. And there's the Kivu region you mentioned on the eastern border—the lakes and volcanoes. . . ."

Harry's eyes were wide open now. "I think you misunderstand me," he said. "Travel here is interesting—because you can't."

"Oh."

"Oh indeed." He laughed, the gravel barrel tilting a little in his throat.

"Well, I was going to see the tourist people here this morning."

The barrel tilted some more. "They closed down the Ministry of

Tourism here two years ago, Mr. Hone. Didn't they tell you that in London?"

"No—just said I couldn't come into the country from the east; that I had to come in via Kinshasa. I was to have done the whole trip east to west, in the 'Footsteps of Stanley' sort of style. Now I'm going to have to reverse it."

"You're going to have to do a deal more than that, I fancy: you're going to have to get *out* of Kinshasa first—like a prison break. That'll be your first concern."

"Why should it be so difficult?"

The gravel barrel in his throat tilted right over now. "How were you thinking of managing it? You got a lot of native porters with tea chests, half a dozen armed askaris? There may be no other way out of here."

"No. I don't have much equipment in fact. I gave my son a compass for Christmas. He lent it back to me. I've got a map of equatorial Africa, though the scale looks a bit small to me. And I brought some tinned salmon and crackers, a bottle of lime juice, and some Johnny Walker Black Label—as well as all the usual malaria and dysentery pills."

"That's hardly enough to see you out to the suburbs here."

"But I'm going upriver by boat. I brought these as extras, a few goodies. I'd like to have gone across the continent with bearers and tea chests and old Lee-Enfield rifles. But it's not on these days."

"No, indeed. Only trouble is that nothing is on here these days. I'd revise your itinerary—or cancel it. Hang around the city here a bit. You'll have to, I guess, anyway. Apart from the transport, they don't much care for inquisitive foreigners nosing about out of town at the moment. Never have, in fact. Besides, Kinshasa is a country in itself. All you need is money to discover it."

"Well, I have a little of that. Not much, this is radio I'm doing. . . ."

Harry leaned forward, a real gleam in his eye, speaking with gravitas now. "Money is another very interesting thing here. Inflation makes it just like it was in the old Weimar Republic: you have to carry a lot of it around, in a wheelbarrow, ideally. There's no coin here at all now. It's all in old notes. 5-Zaïre notes usually. One of those used to buy you a whole night on the town. Now it won't even get you a beer."

"Oh."

"Your ham and eggs—when you get it: that'll be 50 or 60 Zaïres in this palatial establishment. Nearly fifteen dollars at the official rate."

"Is there another rate?" I asked cautiously.

Harry took a second cheroot from his little cigar-case. I noticed a Star of David inlaid in silver on the leather.

"Yes," he said, sighing with gratitude. "Indeed there is another rate. None of us would be here otherwise. The Parallel Rate." He uttered the phrase with a hushed twinkle in his voice, looking cautiously over the end of his cheroot, like a comic confronting the Holy Grail.

"The parallel rate?"

"The unofficial rate. You can get three, four, five times as much for your dollar on that. Dependirg on the priests, if they need things from Europe for the missions; or on whether it's holiday time for the *gros Belges*. Back to Brussels on the Sunday Rocket: well, they need the dollars then. And that's when you can move onto the parallel rate. That's when you really start to lead the life of Reilly here, Mr. Hone," Harry went on with enthusiasm. "Puts a whole different complexion on things: fresh radishes and *sole bonne femme* flown in from Brussels twice a week: a Mercedes, two chauffeurs, a dozen boys, and a big villa in the old Belgian residential quarter by the river. You really start to move here—on the parallel rate. And of course you can build yourself a wall then, too."

"A wall?"

"A big wall, round your villa. You'll see when you get about town. They're all building walls furiously right now. It's the smartest thing of the season. The bigger the better."

Harry looked up just then. There was a disturbance, an excited flutter at the end of the lobby. A magnificent middle-aged African in a dazzling, multicolored *bubus*—a sort of loose hanging nightgown affair—was making royal progress through the hall, followed by a scatter of obsequious attendants, supplicants, and hangers-on.

"That's General N'Gongo," Harry said. "A minister, a *Commissaire* last year. But temporarily in eclipse right now. He's building a wall— the biggest in Kinshasa, I'd say."

"On the parallel rate?" I suggested.

"I wouldn't speak too loudly. In the good old days here the General—he was a sergeant then—had people like you for breakfast. And that's another thing to bear in mind here, Mr. Hone, if you're white: keep a low profile. And don't talk French if you can help it. They might think you were Belgian, and that's not so good. The Belgians caused some trouble here, over the years, to put it mildly. Old King Leopold and his friends especially, when they had this whole country as their own private ball game, used to chop all the black hands off everywhere upriver, if the rubber wasn't coming in quick enough. So talk English," Harry advised me firmly. "They like that. They all want to learn English. That's why I'm here. Though of course I teach American. And I tell you—they like that even *better!*"

Harry grumbled and hawked with laughter: the skin in his cheeks and jowls vibrating. His face hadn't fallen yet, but it wouldn't be long, and when it did he would be a wonderfully complete Buddha, where age would really swell and toast the half-burnt ivory of his complexion. In name a supreme God, his body was that of a demigod already: rotund, juicy, like an inverted pear about to drop, with large dewy eyes, the lids drooping a little now with the sunstruck years, so that quite soon the wry, candid gaze would be pleasantly, comfortably hooded. Although there would never be anything of the hawk in Harry's expression; no sharp queries, unease, no suspicion, no devious intent whatsoever.

Harry, as I was to discover, had learned and survived so much deception in his life, absorbed and expelled every trickery and deceit, that he was guileless now—a great balloon hanging over the city: seeing, understanding and pardoning everything. Though perhaps at ground level the image of a huge bath sponge is more appropriate: Harry absorbed and released information like water. Or like a plant—better still: he lived by osmosis, drawing in all the gossip, the life of Kinshasa like sunlight. A balloon, a sponge, a plant—all that. And though I would probably have met him anyway, at some point in my rambles about the city, I was luckier than I knew that morning in meeting him so soon. Harry became most of my city, gave me all my entrances and exits there.

For a long time we drove round the edge of the African Cité in Kinshasa—the old native quarter in what was then Leopoldville. It was a vast area, marked simply by a huge rectangular blank space on the only map I'd seen of the city; two miles long and a mile wide, with well over a million people living there, I'd been told. Even if the crippled taxi hadn't been falling apart—splitting, tearing at the seams, tied up with string—we could never have driven through the Cité. There were no real roads, just endless mud-caked alleyways, narrow gullies that led to the mysterious interior, first among the grander breeze-block beer shops and garages that formed an outer ring to this *kasbah* before the tracks were lost in the huge mix of tacked-up buildings beyond: corrugated iron, flattened oil drums, discarded wooden pallets, circular windows framed in old tires, sacking, polyethylene, mud. The building materials stretched away to the horizon, each man his own Le Corbusier, restricted only by what seemed a regulation height—for the top of the Cité was flat, running away forever with the roofs at more or less the same level, set at little more than a man's height, flat as a warty bandaged hand. Bricks and scaffolding for a second story were things beyond the dreams of avarice in the Cité. It was gold enough to get one roof over your head here.

The beer shops were open. There was the throb of Congo reggae, taped out at 100 decibels, coming from behind each gaudy colored pub, where local artists had dreamed up their comic strip signs in brilliant acrylic housepaint. A huge green bottle of "Primus" beer exploded above one beer hall, where the gunpowder was a woman at the center, a black, slit-skirt Marilyn Monroe kicking the glass shards. Another sign showed two Africans, with white faces and black lips like Negro minstrels in reverse, sitting under an umbrella, gold rain descending all round them, as they quaffed a bile-green beer. A third panorama showed a whole family drinking merrily round a tomb where the departed, an old grandfather and mother, were set up in effigy above it—miniaturized people who appeared as waiters waiting to pick up the empties when the party was finished round their tombstone table. I wondered if this was a funeral parlor. I asked my driver. First he shook his head; then he nodded it. A combined operation, beer shop, and undertakers in one.

The really strange thing was the lack of people. There was the music and these tremendous comic strip invitations—but no people. Then, stopping at a junction, the window open, I heard a faint roar coming from all over the Cité, a bee's nest sound, a soft murmur set like a canopy over the whole rubbish-dump landscape. They were there all right, invisible, a million people under the sacks and wooden pallets, adding up the honey of their lives together in a million different ways. But I couldn't imagine how. I wanted to imagine their thoughts. But I couldn't.

When you come to the strangeness of a new city, you try and look through the buildings, into the rooms, searching the interiors, imagining the domestic intimacies, inventing the familiar as a silken thread through the labyrinth. But here, my mind reaching out over this great scrofulous, ulcerous, suppurating body, I could feel nothing, sense nothing except the crazy notion that everyone in the Cité was hidden around their ancestors' tombs just then, flooded in gold rain, with Marilyn Monroe dancing on the graves, the bottles exploding while they lowered the pea-green beer.

Beyond this real Cité we came to another: Cité de la Voix de Zaïre

—the new radio and TV center in bunker-style concrete built by the French a few years ago. Again, the place seemed almost totally deserted—a great skyscraper to one side, a long complex of sound stages and studios to the other. An African walked from one of the stages carrying a wheelless bicycle. Another followed with a big paint-brush. They set the bicycle down in the middle of the forecourt and the second man took his brush to it. But then—the problem: there was no paint. I was in an empty waiting room by then and I got up to look at the action, for presumably this was being filmed and I hadn't seen the cameras. There were no cameras. But the man was really painting the bicycle now, dabbing away at it. Were they rehearsing an act?—or just rehearsing the painting of the machine? I couldn't decide.

After twenty minutes I was called upstairs. I was sorry to leave, for by this time, having finished their imaginary painting, the two men had taken the bicycle to bits and were trying to reassemble it, without success. Just as I had to leave for my appointment, a third man arrived, a more severe-looking fellow, carrying a big tin of paint.

In a very grand office on the top floor of the skyscraper I met the Press Councillor, the *Citoyen Commissaire*—a tall, beautifully dressed man of the utmost sophistication, with perfect English. He wore a silk Kaunda suit in soft Windsor gray with the half-opened bud of a red rose nestling just beneath his throat. In front of him an untouched glass of fresh orange juice sat on a pile of newspapers, *The Times* and *Le Monde*. I could imagine this man's life all right, his thoughts, his domestic sur-roundings: a man of effortless, affable style, a welcome addition to any African reception at the Elysée Palace or 10 Downing Street; a man of the world, though not this world, I felt, for his present office was strangely mute, as the corridor outside and all the adjoining offices were: no sound of typewriters, teleprinters, telephones. And no people. The *Citoyen Commissaire* perched like a splendidly feathered rooster at the top of an empty hen house where everything, and everyone but him, had been struck by a power failure.

I told the *Commissaire* of my hopes in Zaïre. He listened carefully. "Not a political series," I assured him. "In the 'Footsteps of Stanley' —that sort of thing. I'm going coast to coast, west-east, from the Atlantic to the Indian Ocean. Color material. . . ."

"Yes, of course. Though didn't Stanley come into Zaïre the other way round, *from* the east, downriver?"

"Yes, but I couldn't get a visa—to come the right way round—from your London Embassy. They said I had to come into Zaïre via Kinshasa."

"Of course. We still have a few problems on the eastern borders. It's
lot advisable—for your own safety."

"Well, here I am anyway. I thought I'd spend a few days in Kinshasa,
then go down to the estuary, to Matadi, then out to Banana Point on
the Atlantic. Then back up here and upriver to Kisangani on the big
passenger boat—I think it's ten days on the river, you don't happen to
know the times of the boats, do you?—then into the Ituri Forest. I was
anxious to see something of the pygmy tribes there."

"Yes, indeed." A small secretary came into the room just then and
the tall, wonderfully dressed *Commissaire* spoke to him, standing up
slowly, where he seemed to go on standing up for some seconds. He
signed papers. Then he turned back to me. "An excellent itinerary.
Now, could you put all that down in writing for me? It's the usual
paperwork thing here, I'm afraid. Bureaucracy." He gestured round the
paperless room.

"Of course."

"And send it to me at once. With the heading of your BBC company,
on the notepaper." The *Commissaire* lifted up the glass of orange
juice—and I saw then that it was a trick glass where some oily, yellow
colored liquid had been sealed into the sides of the tumbler: an imagined
glass of orange juice where the idea stood for the substance.

"Certainly. I'll send the itinerary round tomorrow morning."

I was about to leave. He held his hand up, but not to shake. "There's
only one point," he said suavely. "We're holding local government
elections all over Zaïre at the moment." Then he added most pleasantly,
the one thing obviously following quite naturally on the other: "No
foreigners are allowed out of Kinshasa for the time being."

The secretary came in then again and I heard the name "Mitterrand"
exchanged in hushed tones between them. When I got downstairs and
out onto the forecourt again there were the remains of three or four
unpainted bicycles lying on the ground. Bicycles? I needed a boat, not
a bicycle anyway. Despite Harry and the *Commissaire* I was going up
the Congo come hell or high water. And the sooner I made a start in
that direction, the better. . . .

The riverboat timetable I'd finally got hold of was the most elaborate
collection of promises I've ever seen. Its forty foolscap pages gave com-
prehensive details of every trip you could possibly take—up, down or
off the Congo river. With its dozen routes and major destinations

throughout the great river basin, its hundreds of stopping places and its tempting collection of symbols denoting "De Luxe Cabin," "Dog Kennels," and "First-Class Restaurants"—it clearly offered the ultimate in African travel, particularly on the ONATRA company's main line— just where I wanted to go: the thousand-mile journey upstream from Kinshasa to the port of Kisangani on the great bend of the river in the heartlands of the continent.

Mbandaka, Mobeka, Lisala, Bumba, Isangi, Yangambi, Kisangani. . . . The names of the provincial capitals and smaller river stations conjured up just the sort of dramatic litany I wanted: a fabulous mix of African fact and fiction. Stanley had literally fought his way down this river just over a hundred years before: an astonishing journey in commandeered war canoes, with thirty-two ferocious pitched battles on the way, beating off an endless collection of cannibal tribes. The Belgians had taken over shortly afterward—with hippopotamus-hide whips, obscene brutalities, mass executions. Conrad had come this way a few years later—to his appointment with the evil Mr. Kurtz in the heart of darkness. André Gide and his boyfriend, Marc Allégret, had followed him. And long after that Graham Greene had followed them, taking the Bishop's boat in search of his character Querry, the stricken architect maimed by civilization, finally placing him among the genuine lepers crawling along the forest paths of the interior in *A Burnt-out Case.*

Savagery, mystery, primeval darkness—these were the real images, the real destinations hidden behind the bland facts and figures of the timetable. And now I was in Kinshasa myself, waiting to get on that boat, another traveler about to be named in this fantastic passenger list of men who had journeyed to Conrad's "dark places of the earth." Or was I about to be named?

"That will be 3000 Zaïres, first-class, one-way, inclusive for the ten-day trip." The important African loomed over his huge, empty, glass topped desk. We were in the vast ONATRA building in downtown Kinshasa: the biggest office block in the city, air-conditioned, built by the Belgians just before they ran from the country twenty-one years before. There had been an air of ponderous efficiency in the lobby and on my way along corridors to see this Great God of the riverboat company—a government monopoly with a necessary efficiency, I thought, since I was well aware that river transport is largely the only transport throughout Zaïre. Without boats everyone and everything came to a full stop in this country. I was just about to hand the money over—a stiff £300 at the official rate—when I hesitated.

"The boat still leaves Monday morning, nine o'clock?"

"No. Thursday, in fact. It's late coming downstream."

It was only my third day in Kinshasa. But already I knew enough about the crazy bureaucratic life in the city to put my money away. "I'll come back," I said. "Fix things up with you after the weekend."

I walked back up the main boulevard then—the Trente Juin: a straight two miles carved right through the heart of the city, a slummy Champs Elysées, before it curved at the top and ran out into the suburbs for another three miles. I tacked sharply away from the crippled beggars on their stumps and trolleys outside the Post Office, making for me on their pram wheels like raiders in war canoes. The sky was the usual suffocating blanket of gray above me. After only three days I was longing to be out of Kinshasa. But Harry Jupiter, when I met him at the Memling Hotel bar that lunchtime, maintained his original grave doubts about my ambitions.

"They're lying down at ONATRA," he said. "Or else they're blind. The Kisangani steamer is here right now, in port. I saw the funnel this morning."

"Maybe that's another steamer." I bought Harry a vermouth. We were in the little cocktail bar in the small corridor on the way into the restaurant. Harry didn't drink beer in the dry season.

"Listen," he said. "About the passenger boats: they don't work, they break down, they can't repair them, there's no fuel. The local boys cannibalize them, then sell the stuff as spare parts. It's all a dream—traveling upriver now. I've tried it myself."

I showed Harry the elaborate timetable then. He was amazed. "I've never seen one of these before." He looked at it carefully, handling it like a rare manuscript. "Lisala, Bumba, Basoko, Lokutu, Yangambi, Kisangani," he intoned. "Just names," he added finally. "Words, not deeds. You haven't realized that yet, have you? In Zaïre now, if they put something in writing—especially if they print it up like this—it stands for the deed. You don't actually have to *do* the thing then. It's a neat trick: timetables like this absolve them from taking any further action." Harry laughed, a generous rumble.

"Oh, I'm learning," I said. I told him about the glass of trick orange juice on the Press Councillor's desk. "Yes," he agreed. "But you're really only on chapter one."

On Monday I saw another more junior man at the ONATRA building, in the operations room this time: short, portly, officious. He was sitting in front of a huge wall plan of the whole river network, where little sliding colored buttons represented all the company's boats on stream at that moment.

"Ah yes," he said very confidently. "The Kisangani boat has been delayed—until the end of the week. Repairs. Come back tomorrow and I'll be able to tell you the position."

The next day the fat, confident executive had disappeared. Instead a thin, unconfident clerk was in his place. He looked at the wall plan for me, mystified, considering it like the Rosetta Stone. He tried to move one of the little colored buttons. But it was stuck fast. He consulted a big ledger instead.

"Kisangani?" He was equally perplexed here, thumbing nervously through the pages. But finding nothing to suit his purposes in the book, he suddenly looked up, and grasping the words out of the air, said sharply, "That boat is not leaving Kinshasa until the seventeenth." This was ten days away.

"What's the problem?"

"No problem." The clerk was affronted now. "The Kisangani boat left here yesterday. The next one isn't until the seventeenth." Triumphantly the little man closed the ledger. This boat business was obviously getting on top of these people, I thought—boats hithering and thithering up and downriver apparently at random; yesterday, today, tomorrow, the end of the week or not at all. I produced my famous timetable then, pointing out that the Kisangani boat was supposed to leave not yesterday or on the seventeenth, but every Monday at nine o'clock.

The clerk took the timetable from me gingerly—viewing it, like Harry, with some amazement. Indeed, he was speechless, turning all the wonderful pages, pondering the remote places, the exotic destinations, the clever symbols. He'd obviously never seen this fantastic document in his life before. "Lisala, Bumba, Basoko," he chanted reverently. "Lokutu, Isangi, Yangambi. . . ." He was spellbound by the majesty of it all. I left him at it.

Harry laughed again when I met him later that morning. He rolled in the aisles. "You're certainly getting the hang of things here," he said. "And maybe you can't blame them too much for it. You see, the white man is prey in Africa now. Fair game, to be stalked. They like to play you on all sorts of hooks. It's their revenge—just as we preyed on them. They do it very politely, you think you're playing straight. But what they're actually doing is tying you up in knots—and they're *pleased* to. Remember that. It's our turn for the slavery now. We're at the sharp end and there's nothing much you can do about it. Except money. You could try hiring a private boat, or hitch a lift on a cargo barge."

I went down to the port that afternoon, noticing how the old Belgian residential quarter had been built away from the river, turning its back on it, as one would on a malign presence. No one had ever really *liked* the river here, seen it as a friend—that was the obvious, interesting thing. The waterfront quite lacked any happy life, native or European. There was just a long run of dirty wharves, crumbling warehouses, stalled cranes and endless lines of rusting or sunken ships, old paddle steamers and barges, a few bows and funnels poking up through the vast brown sheet of water, broken hulks, the remnants of a once vibrant river transport system here which had long since disappeared. Stanley's "murderous river" had won this anti-colonial battle hands down. There were no boats at all to be seen out on the stream. The waters coursed through these narrows just as they had before Stanley discovered the place more than a hundred years before: untouched now as then.

Later that day Harry sent one of his Zaïrean boys down to the docks to enquire about cargo boats for me. The man had been promptly arrested. "As a smuggler—or what?" I asked Harry next morning.

"No. He was just the wrong tribe. Not a river tribe. He's from the Shaba region in the south. They're very fussy about who they let out on the river these days."

"*Fussy?* They don't seem to let anyone out on it."

"Yes. But maybe you're going about the whole thing the wrong way. You're asking them questions they can just give a yes or no answer to. That's fatal here. You're sort of saying, 'Does the boat leave for Kisangani today?' What you have to do is shout, 'What have you *done* with the boat for Kisangani!' You might get somewhere then."

"I see."

"Maybe I can still fix you up with something," Harry relented. "If you insist. But it'll take time. You might as well get accustomed to Kinshasa. Or maybe you could take a trip across to Brazzaville while you're waiting. Things tend to work over there. There's a little French restaurant right on the port. . . ." Harry bought me a vermouth this time—a large one—and consoled me with all the delights of Brazzaville.

Across the river you could always see Brazzaville—the chic French architecture on the city waterfront and the low white cliffs to either side, which reminded Stanley of Dover when he first came here, down the Congo river, to this western end of the Pool, just over a hundred years ago.

You could see Brazza if you leaned far enough out of my bedroom window in the Memling Hotel. And you could see it without any effort at all from most of the side windows upstairs in the Chancellery at the Embassy. You could see the other city from almost every tall building in Kinshasa, just as you could gaze at it from ground level, *en clair,* from any point along the ramparts on the southern bank, or from the port downtown, which gave straight out onto the hulks of rusting dredgers and decaying paddle steamers abandoned in the vast gray stream. Brazza was with you all the way along the riverfront, on the Avenue des Nations Unies, where the huge colonial villas and embassies looked down on the empty water, great mauve-green clumps of water hyacinth the only traffic, floating down like giant sprouting broccoli, torn out from the riverbanks all the way far up into the interior. You could see the crowded little ferry, too, morning and afternoon, plying across the mile of pewter-colored water that lay between the twin cities.

But you couldn't get to Brazzaville.

And you couldn't get up river because all the passenger boats had broken down or run aground in this dry season. You couldn't get downstream either, of course, in any sort of boat, as Stanley had discovered, for there was nothing but rapids and wicked cataracts and high falls from just below Kinshasa for 150 miles all the way until you hit open water again, on the neck of the estuary, at the port of Matadi.

There was a narrow-gauge, single-track railway from Kinshasa to Matadi, built through the tortuous Crystal Mountains by King Leopold and his murderous Belgians in the 1890s ("A black for every sleeper"), where the town guide now advertised "Train No. 50—First Class Only" leaving for the coast every morning. But I had been to the empty station at the bottom of the Boulevard Trente Juin on several mornings. It was a station in name alone: a stationary station, where once more the title sufficed for the purpose. And even if there had been trains, the fuel was running out in Zaïre anyway, which meant that cars were difficult too. Few people would drive you beyond the suburbs of Kinshasa—let alone out onto the few roads in the interior. So you couldn't move upcountry that way.

You could take a local Zaïre Aero Service flight out, to one of the many airstrips in the interior which the Belgians had built so that their paratroopers could control the whole country in the old days. You could go this way, if you had the cash and the temerity to bribe and fight your way out after a week waiting for a seat at Kinshasa International. Or you could hire a small plane and fly out privately, if you were very rich. And of course there were always rumors of other escapes. A Catholic mission boat from somewhere far upstream would be in town on the nineteenth—or a little Cessna from one of the fifty-seven Protestant missions was expected in Kinshasa the day after; or there was a private cargo tug you might hitch a lift with, leaving for Kisangani, a thousand miles up on the bend of the river, next weekend. But the rumors always died at the last moment, when you were on your way down to the port with your baggage or had finally made a deal with a taxi to the airport. The rumors died and you cursed as you looked across at Brazzaville, where things apparently worked.

Davidson had told me, with deft superiority, that afternoon at the Embassy: "I go to Brazza every month or so. There are a few British over there. But it takes me my diplomatic pass and four other ministry and customs chits to get on that ferry. It might take you a lot more." He looked at me unhelpfully. "Why do you want to go there anyway?"

"I hear things work over in Brazza," I said.

"Well, comparatively speaking. It was French. Mitterrand is keen on doing well by all the francophone countries now. And they used the African franc over there, a convertible currency. So, some things work. The telephone for example."

"Locally?"

"And overseas. They've a satellite link."

"I could phone home from there, you mean?"

"You might. You'd certainly find that difficult from here." Davidson tried to smile. "But why Brazza—when you told me last time you wanted to get upriver? To Kisangani and so on."

I smiled now. "I've been trying for over two weeks to get that boat: the big passenger boat. Monday mornings at nine o'clock. That's what the timetable says. But all I get are excuses, lies—I don't know what. There's no boat."

Davidson craned his neck round, looking out of his window over the river. "I think I saw the Kisangani boat in this morning," he said. "It was late coming downstream. Think I saw the big funnel."

I stood up and rushed to the window. "I can't see it. That's the funnel of the hospital boat, isn't it?"

There was no sun on the river. There had been no sun in the city, not a moment of it, since I'd arrived. It was the dry season.

"I don't know. Why don't you go down to the port and find out?"

"I've been down. I've been living in the port. And the ONATRA building. I thought while I was waiting I might go over to Brazza. I think I need a chit from you for that—to begin with. A certificate of good conduct or something."

"I tell you it's very difficult. I can give you a chit all right. But the rest of the papers will take you up to a week or more. Why bother?"

"I hear there's a French café-restaurant on the riverfront in Brazza, run by some cantankerous old *colon*. But decent food. He does grilled *telapia* and a good *steack-frites*. The wine is drinkable, too, I'm told. And the meal doesn't cost you £20, as it does here. And there are real newspapers in Brazza, aren't there?—from France. As well as a local one. And television and real taxis. And Bic razors and lighters in the shops. And telephones. I thought if I went to Brazza for the day I might feel a little at home," I said desperately.

CHAPTER
3

The Dry Season

*T*he Grand Marché, some way behind the Memling Hotel, was truly grand. It seemed to cover an area almost as big as the African Cité that lay immediately beyond it—except that here, over the center of the market, vast sloping concrete roofs had been set up against the tropical rain, so that walking toward it from a distance, with the roar of thousands of voices, there was the clear impression of a football stadium and a wild game somewhere immediately ahead. And when you passed beyond the cheap hotels, the heavily barred windows of the Greek and Lebanese shops on the Avenue Bokassa, when you got to where the streets ran out beyond the Avenue du Commerce, on the very edge of the market, you stepped into a warm black sea of humanity—water filled with dazzling colored sails, rising on wooden masts and booms from all the cotton print stalls that ringed the edge of the market.

Here were the paradise-bird fabrics, on rolls or temptingly hung in the air, in hundreds of different neon-hued patterns, flags of desire for every woman in the city, country bumpkin or wife of a *Citoyen Commissaire,* for there were few real shops at all in Kinshasa and certainly no formal African haberdashers: Queen or clown, you came here to this outer ring of fire in the market for your *bubus,* togas, mammy cloths.

I put a foot in the water and was at once borne away into the middle of the stream. The men were catered for at one end of the cotton print stalls. And soon, as the only white and trousered man on view that morning, I was being offered braces for every purse, in every material, cut and color, from plain canvas buttonhole to natty elastic clip-on jobs in blue or red pinstripe. Another stall displayed hundreds of brand-new white towels, electric purple ankle socks and dozens of strobe-light shirt lengths, Congo-Hawaii style, that made your eyes blink. The towels were going fast, a thrusting crowd round them. I managed to pick one up. Clearly woven into the deep pile was the logo and the legend of the "Intercontinental Hotel Kinshasa."

Caught in a slow-motion whirlpool I was gradually sucked and elbowed into the heart of the place—past the up-market grocery stalls, filled with the pilferings of white kitchens, I suspected, where a variety of very ordinary single tins of food were royally displayed on paper doilies like exotic fare in Fortnum's: Smedley's Baked Beans, small bottles of Belgian ketchup, French tinned prunes, and hundreds of different-sized cans of powdered milk, the larger ones clearly marked "US AID—NOT TO BE RE-SOLD."

The next vast circle of stalls held the basic staples of the country: palm oil and cassava. The cooking oil was sold in old jam jars and bottles of every conceivable shape and size, and clearly the contents of all the white dustbins in the city had been put to good use, so that for 10 Zaïres you bought your oil in an open Coke bottle; for 50 in the larger stoppered glass of a Dimple Haig. The cassava was offered in every manner as well—from the raw rude warty roots of the plant, to the tuber neatly rolled like salami in a banana leaf, or the nude, white powdered variety like grated coconut, and the sticky, jaundiced, sump-sludge paste form in which the cassava was mixed with the palm oil. These staples led to the more expensive side-dishes: bananas, sorgum, yams, and the tiny red peppers that had already burnt my mouth off, as *pili-pili* sauce, in the Memling restaurant.

At the center of the market was the Holy Grail of flesh—animal and fish: scrawny, tattered red lengths of frail muscled beef weighed out like gold; suppurating, heaving, bulbous mounds of offal; small steaks of hogfish; and above all, the greatest luxury, the dried out, black-crusted, burnt-glazed, ruby-brown carcasses of bush meat: monkeys and mongooses from the rain forests, crucified little bodies, the torn limbs transfixed on cross sticks. Here was the caviar and smoked salmon of the country.

To one side of the market, westward toward the Avenue du Marais, lay the flea market and the junk collections, bits and pieces beyond counting or identifying: battered Le Creuset ovenware, moldy French textbooks, and split bamboo furniture, remnants left behind by thousands of fleeing Belgians over the years—alarm clocks without hands, gutted art-nouveau radios, prewar oil fridges, tattered oleographs of the Christ King and Gothic-lettered Bible scrolls from the walls of abandoned missions, sepia-tinted photographs of Edwardian Bruges and

Ghent, cheap sun-stained reproductions of Breughel snowscapes, old mosquito nets, broken brass bedsteads and bidets. And beneath this lumpy rubbish an endless array of smaller domestic items were set out on trays: trinkets, buttons, brooches, paste jewelry, darning needles, empty cotton spools, along with forgotten airmail letters and picture postcards of the beach at Ostend. Here were the unconnected, incoherent shards of a thousand colonial lifetimes, dead luxuries, forgotten *billets doux*, desiccated memories of home—treasures that had sustained the Belgians in their great civilizing mission in the Congo for nearly eighty years, now scattered down the road like the bits and pieces from some terrible accident in which everyone has died.

Further along a pyramid of black tin trunks were piled high—the sort that wretched English boys used to lug back to prep school—freshly painted, a snip on the market. And beyond that, laid out like farmyard rubbish on the ground, were the fantastic ingredients of the witch doctor's trade: dried snake skins, chicken feathers, cloudy potions, evil-smelling roots and herbs, old teeth. It was here that I first saw Eleanor, with an older couple, two hippies, picking among the debris on the dusty soil, pondering a snake skin, smelling some wicked mandrake root. And she was still there half an hour later when I happened to come back the same way and saw her alone, one of the great tin boxes precariously balanced on her head, staggering off in long trousered strides back toward the European city. You could spot Eleanor a mile away, with her considerable height, her great helmet of blond curls—and her trousers.

When I got back from the market I saw Harry among a crowd of people gazing intently into the SABENA airways window just off the main boulevard, the Trente Juin. They were all absorbed in a chalked notice which had just been set up inside, just beneath the holiday posters of the Grande Place in Brussels—and the beach at Ostend. It gave the latest expected arrival and departure times of flights to and from Brussels. Harry, studying these departure times, no doubt, looked up a little guiltily when he saw me. "I was expecting some textbooks in," he said. "There are so few damn flights in or out of here these days."

But later, over a vermouth in the Memling, Harry admitted the real problem. "It gets you, this place, especially in the dry season. I long to be out of it. But somehow I can't. It traps you—a sort of mental coast fever. You find yourself haunting the SABENA window at this time of year—that's the first symptom. Then you start shouting at your boy. The drink usually comes next, or a woman you don't need, followed by a punch-up at some diplomatic party. And then you're on a stretcher to the airport for that midday Sunday flight: the Brussels Rocket. Red hot Caesar," he murmured. "Heap big mischief." Harry seemed in for a bad dose of coast fever right then. "Fact is," he went on. "Unless they carry you out, you're not likely to get out of Kinshasa any other way."

I thought Harry was exaggerating although I had to admit I was finding Kinshasa a pretty depressing place myself just then. It was certainly the dry season—the three months of Congo winter when the cleansing tropical rains and brilliant blue skies disappear completely to be replaced by a permanent gray: lowering, dust-filled, dirty clouds that come to crouch over the city, day in, day out, so that everyone, native and white, becomes restless, edgy, congregating outside airline offices, in bars or in bed.

There was nothing to suggest the great liberating spaces of Africa here, no fierce sun, rampant fruits or vivid colored blossom. Kinshasa in this winter world was a city besieged by the gray weather, feeding on what little it possessed of its own, so that all its flaws stood out, bones on the skeleton. The native poverty was all the more evident, while the few remaining trappings of Western "civilization"—the odd smart bars and hotels, French restaurants, pizza shops, airline offices and Belgian delicatessens—these had less point than ever in the all-embracing gloom. Usually deserted, they were like forgotten way stations in an old colonial march, memories of so much discredited European adventure in these parts. It was the dry season indeed, the juices of the city everywhere squeezed out by the crushing weather.

Harry said, "In the dry season I see a lot more of my friends, and we drink a lot more vermouth: the only good thing about this time of year—we tend to cling together." I hadn't yet met Harry's friends. But I'd learned a little more about him meanwhile. He was from the American deep south, all right: his grandmother French-speaking Bayou. He'd gone north, to college, he told me, and studied medicine for a bit. But he'd quit that and gone through the war with the US Army in England, and after D-Day in France, using his good French. He didn't elaborate on his postwar career, although I gathered he'd stayed on in the Army for some time, in some intelligence capacity perhaps—and I suspected this might be still part of his job in Kinshasa. Officially, though, he ran a language school in the city.

"You remember I told you about General N'Gongo," Harry said, after a second vermouth.

"The ex-Minister, temporarily in eclipse. The man who was building a wall round his house?"

"That's him. Well, he's trying to get back into the sun again, by standing as town councillor in these local elections. He's giving a party. Shall we take a look-see?"

"Splendid." I was keen on taking an opportunity of observing the democratic processes in Zaïre. "But a party?" I went on. "At ten in the morning?"

"Why certainly. The General's parties usually last a week. This one only started yesterday."

Outside the Memling, in the exhausted slate-gray light, the local tarts looked equally drained and listless, stumbling in their high heels over the open drain where the telephone cables had been exposed in a tatter of loose ends ever since I'd arrived. This was real cleft-stick Africa: the telephones never worked. Harry smiled benignly at the girls as if he'd known them all a long time ago, when they were children. And it was the children, the ragged boys looking after the cars, who crowded around him as he moved toward a huge peach-colored Cadillac that I hadn't seen before, a Sixties model, but in good trim, with a dimpled mock-leather roof. Harry kept a pocketful of old makuta coins, the ones you could never use now in the city for anything but a single cigarette, and the children jumped for them like porpoises round the car. They were Harry's children. Harry had told me: his wife lived in the States; he had two grown-up daughters. But they wouldn't brave the horrors of Kinshasa anymore—where, for family, he only had these bright raga-muffins.

One of them kept offering me a surprisingly well constructed little toy—a bicycle made from bits of wire where a stuffed rag man with lollipop legs moved the pedals in jerky steps. "I have a collection of those," Harry said. "Runs into hundreds."

Harry drove off down the shabby main boulevard, where the intended grand new buildings in the middle—permanently incomplete, so they were already old—soon gave way to the remnants of prewar white-washed, single-story colonial shops, stores, and garages, memories of a recent time when Kinshasa was Leopoldville, still an attractive jungle-fringed garden city with a population of only 50,000 instead of the three million or so who burst its seams and shanty towns today.

Huge, sixty-foot palm trees edged the end of the boulevard here, while the pavements soon ran out into sandy red soil cracked with broken storm drains, open sewers, and excavated telephone cables where the wires stood up now like abstract metal flowers. Trucks had taken over from the few buses for transport, filled with dour-faced workers, swaying about, packed in like meat carcasses. These were the lucky ones, Harry said: most people, when they got out of bed at all, had to walk these days.

On one side we passed the Greek Orthodox church in whitewashed brick, an incongruous Byzantine cross on the domed top. "My friend Naxos goes there," Harry said. "Noxious—the dentist. Maybe you'll meet him—we have a sort of Rotarian lunch once a month, at the Restaurant du Zoo. Sometimes once a week in the dry season. Keeps us in touch with reality—like that church does. I sometimes go there myself—same way you'd go to a movie: all that incense. And the Greek chants. Suddenly you're not in Africa."

A mile further down the boulevard we turned off into the old Belgian residential quarter—a grid of lovely tree-filled avenues and wildly overgrown cross streets, where the big prewar colonial villas nestled in their half-acre plots, all variously shrouded in bougainvillaea and mimosa, and surrounded beyond that by big dark frangipani and flamboyant trees: trees in their dull winter plumage now but which still arched right over the long roads, so that the huge car glided beneath them soundlessly, a magic barque floating through a tropic woodland.

"Mostly embassies and residencies here now," Harry said. "And a lot of the local boys made good, of course. You can spot their houses: they're the ones with the new walls."

I could indeed. Half the gracious old villas here had ugly new walls right round them, prison walls, each competing with the next in height and grandeur, built in every shape and material, from cut stone to breeze block—many of them being built at that very moment.

"There were no walls here in the old days," Harry explained. "Now it's the only sort of public work you see in the city. They're all at it. And it's not for robbers—just status. A new Mercedes used to fill that bill. Now you need a wall as well."

We came to a great open space then, with an overgrown meadow in the middle and a splendid empty plinth in the center of that.

"The Place de la Republique," Harry said, circling it in a leisurely arc. "And that used to be King Leopold out there riding in the middle. Government buildings all round and the Parliament on the far side looking over the river. The Belgians got the whole place together twenty years ago—just before they took fright here and beat it. But nothing very much has happened since, as you'll notice."

We passed a soldier dozing on a chair just inside the gates of the Parliament. He was dressed in a perfect Ruritanian military outfit, a chocolate soldier in color and uniform, wearing a green double-breasted jacket crossed in lines of glittering braid, hung with red shoulder tassels, with pantaloons below that tucked into "Beau Geste" boots at the bottom—and a plumed, dove-gray pillbox cap askew at the top.

"A member of the Presidential Guard," Harry advised me in hushed tones. I gazed round the great meadow again, this splendid empty space which the Belgians must have seen as the crowning glory in their civilizing mission in the Congo, a legacy that would last a thousand years, of spacious, classic order, filled with all the exemplary totems of their own dour northlands: a mint, a treasury, houses of parliament with a great white chief in the center of it all, a savior on horseback. But the natives had found no real use for these western beads and trinkets. The King, long since, had been rudely unhorsed, the plaza gone to grass, the buildings emptied, so that only the sleeping chocolate soldier remained as living evidence of Europe here: a man dressed, appropriately, as if for some *opéra comique*. This, I was beginning to see, was the true Belgian legacy in Zaïre, the real form of life in these parts.

General N'Gongo's house must have been one of the biggest in Kinshasa—a vast, granite-gray colonial building by the river, not a villa, much more like a Victorian railway terminus. And his wall was a superb creation, an easy winner, a veritable Maginot Line in quarried stone topped with spiky railings. On the street side the mansion was fronted by a Versailles-style garden: formal borders, gravel paths, clipped hedges and lawns. Little of all this was visible when we got there that morning. The General's election party was gathering momentum. Long tables and benches covered most of the ground, interspersed with little open cookhouses, charcoal braziers, and mobile bars—in the form of wheelbarrows filled with crates of Primus beer which excitable servants pushed among an even more excited multitude of convivial electors—whole families camped about the ground for the duration. It all seemed very like a high moment in the miracle of the loaves and fishes.

We'd parked our car at the end of a long line of other equally exotic autos outside in the street and now we moved among the throng, disciples ourselves at the feast. It was the very merriest of occasions, the crowd *en fête*, in dazzling multicolored cotton print mammy cloths and togas, swaying about, some joined together dancing, snaking along the paths in tribal crocodiles. The smell of burnt kebabs and the bitter aroma of stewed cassava lay heavy on the air. Palm wine moved rapidly down many gullets, along with yams, steamed bananas and *telapia*, the tasty Congo hogfish. Harry explained the menu.

"But it's the beer they like best," he said. And I could see the truth of this. The big green liter bottles of Primus were being drained on a no-tomorrow basis.

"Isn't it all rather dubious?" I asked. "Buying votes. Or has the election already taken place?"

Harry snorted. "Votes here are counted in empties. I understand the present rate runs at somewhere between three and four bottles a vote —just like old Tammany Hall."

"Where's the General?" I wondered, after half an hour's merry-making. And it was only then that we learned that the poor man had died during the night. The festivities had continued unabated. We'd been attending the General's wake that morning, not his election party. And that was only the start of the comedy, an *entr'acte* in the long-running *opéra comique* of Kinshasa. A week later Harry told me that the General, shortly after his funeral, had been elected to the City Council—by an overwhelming majority.

Gradually—unable to move out of Kinshasa, to get up or downriver or into the interior—I retreated into my bedroom at the top of the Memling, making it over into some semblance of a cozy drawing room, littering it with all the familiar bits and pieces I'd brought with me in my big suitcase. There were two chintz-covered single beds, two similarly draped armchairs, two low tables, two small writing desks, with a big blown-up photograph above them of an old, wood-fired paddle steamer somewhere far upriver which I gazed on longingly. The room was large and comfortable enough, with a bathroom at the back where there was hot water if you were into it before eight in the mornings. But normally I stayed in bed then, the curtains closed, putting off facing the lowering gray skies outside for as long as I could, reading the paperbacks I'd brought with me, the ones that would speak of anything but Africa: Elizabeth Bowen's *The Last September*, Anthony Burgess's *Earthly Powers*.

No one ever disturbed me here. The telephone rarely worked. But that didn't matter. I had no one to call. And the room wasn't made up till some time way after midday, when I finally was out and about, arguing with the clerks in the ONATRA building or trying to get a coffee out of Davidson at the Embassy. You could have died and stiffened at the top of the Memling long before anyone found you. I spent a lot of the time organizing and reorganizing my clothes in the big *armoire* along one wall; hanging the safari jackets, pullovers, ties—taking them out, rehanging them; opening the drawers and settling my tropical shirts that I didn't need in the glum, gray weather; wire-brushing my desert boots where there were no deserts.

I stacked the top of the press, equally neatly, like a delicatessen shelf, with my explorer's kit and provisions: the sealed crackers and cheddar cheese and the Rose's Lime Juice—and made up the shelf beneath like a tiny display in a camping shop: my son's compass that I'd given him for Christmas and the map of equatorial Africa on too small a scale; the water-purifying tablets, the dysentery and malaria pills that I had to take every Monday. Was it Monday yet? No, it must have been Saturday. I counted the days out on my fingers. Yes, it was Saturday; my cricket team at home would be playing out beneath the trees at Moreton-in-Marsh that afternoon. It was Saturday. I'd pinned that fact down at least, for the names and numbers of the days had no meaning for me now in Kinshasa. The gray light got grayer outside my window, before I looked out and saw that the day was gone, turned off like a switch, and that it was night already. The hell with it—there was hardly any difference between day and night in Kinshasa now. I opened the Black Label and the tin of Swiss cigars.

The room was made for two—everything in it. But there was no one else here. I watered the scotch and looked across at the empty bed. That would have been more like it: a woman, a friend, a wife. But I had left all that behind me: relationships that worked and didn't work. Of course in the mind one travels much further, much more readily. I was with a woman—and an old paddle steamer for Kisangani would soon be leaving. The room was not neat but littered with clothes, tickets, passports, timetables: the haphazard debris of a shared hotel bedroom—pants, silk scarves, cold cream, sun lotions, a red bow-shaped smudge of lips on a paper handkerchief; a shoulder bag, its contents strewn over the bed—pills, keys, a checkbook—while the water warbled in the bathroom behind me. We'd be going out together in half an hour, for a meal in the Intercontinental or the Pergola, where we could smile at all the curiosities, the local color, black and white, sharing those naïve travelers' remarks that never survive print, before bed that night and a taxi that worked next morning down to the big river steamer in the port.

Women—women I'd known over many years—came and went, in and out of the steamy bathroom, dressing by the other bed, as I looked for my own clothes for the evening: a cream shirt with cuffs and the gold links and my freshly laundered linen tropicals. I sipped the scotch. The room became a peopled world—filled with a succession of dashing travelers, different women with a different man, but always making a pair, ready for every great adventure.

I went downstairs and had the *Farcies au Riz* by myself in the corner of the restaurant. Later, back in my bedroom, I drank a good deal of the Black Label, writing an incoherent letter home, an imagined lifeline. There was a party of some sort going on in the room next to mine now: the sound of a bad guitar, mad garrulous laughter, glasses breaking, European voices. Or were they? Tense, frenzied, drunken. Half an hour later, the scotch well depleted, I could stand the noise no longer: I'd shut them up—or join them.

The door wasn't locked. There were three people in the room, though it had sounded like half a dozen: a youngish, bearded man in jeans sitting on one of the beds, an ill-kempt girl next to him in a cheesecloth smock dress, caressing him as he whined through some Woody Guthrie ballad, very badly, on the guitar: hippies, aging flower children. On the bed opposite, against the wall in the same position as the empty bed in my own room, sat another, younger girl, feet up, cradling, covering her head in her arms, a splash of blond curls flowing out over bronzed skin: crooning to herself, oblivious of the others, the floor a wreck all around her with the bedclothes and pillows strewn everywhere. They all looked up at me. But they didn't stop—the crooning, the mumbling ballad, the caressing. Their eyes were glazed, white-eyed, staring, with drink or drugs.

"I'm right next door," I said. "I'm sorry—it's a hell of a row." They said nothing—and I knew this was no party I wanted to join.

"Screw off," the bearded man said. "Take your fuckin' ass outa' here." American. His girl friend spoke then. "Wait—maybe he's got some drink." I shook my head, about to leave. The other girl on the bed was still looking at me, still crooning. She said nothing. But I recognized her. She was the trousered girl I'd seen in the flea market that morning wobbling back to town with the big tin box on her head, the girl with the helmet of blond curls. She had a young, outdoor face, broad and open like a sunburst, barely mature, but given a quirky distinction by a straight, nearly bridgeless nose set up between her cheeks like a ladder: a creamy, tennis-playing sort of face, bowed lips and blue eyes—but all smudged and washed away now. She had athletic legs, too—long calves, thighs and splendidly sculpted knees—bent up beneath her on the bed now, in red pirate pants and a check cotton shirt. Though she was young enough—in her early twenties, I thought—she didn't have the air of a hippy at all. She was just blind drunk. She blinked at me, smiling sweetly beneath her great tatter of blond curls, a sad and empty smile, as if she had just lost something vital in her life minutes before but had quite forgotten what it was. She was trying to see me through her clouds: then another slighter smile which failed completely, a forlorn attempt to connect.

Hours later, long after I'd finally got to sleep, I woke with the knocking on my door. When I opened it she was standing there, practically naked, shivering, just a towel draped round her waist: the same girl with the tossed gold curls set tight around her head.

"Will you make love with me?" she demanded. "I can't pay my bill." I was surprised, not least by this imperious request, but by the accent: the purest tones of old stockbroker Surrey. It was a prewar voice somehow, from a forgotten home counties class, touched with unconscious hauteur—a tiny drawl in the syllables, the pointed vowels still clear as a bell, even in drink: a voice which had lost currency years before but which here still automatically assumed a natural order in things—of demand and supply.

4

Eleanor

'*T*ony?'

She moved forward hesitantly into the small hallway of my room. I was awake. But I was still speechless.

"Tony—can I have a bath then? It doesn't work—next door." Her voice was slurred. She was very drunk. Yet she only swayed a little, just her head, like a flag on top of a mast, keeping some miraculous balance—on her strong feet: those long sturdy legs, splendidly proportioned knees and thighs which held her up now, staking her naked to the floor, as the towel fell away from her waist and she stood there, a woebegone, shivery Venus risen from nothing, sunk in drink.

"It's four o'clock," I said, looking at the alarm. "And I'm not Tony."

"No." She paused. Then she moved forward down the hallway, stumbling on the edge of the carpet, past the bathroom door. I caught her arm as it fell across my face. It was damp. She was wet all over. She shrieked slightly then. "The bathroom's in there," I said. "You're going the wrong way. Besides, you must have just had a bath. You're soaking."

"That was Charlie. He douched me."

"Christ," I said. "That rotten guitarist? Where's he now?"

"Gone. Thank God."

"I see. Who's Tony?"

"I—don't—know." She dragged the words out, sighing. But then she said, quite sharply, "And who are you?"

"I'm Branigan, the detective," I said, suffering the slight euphoria of a hangover myself. "You remember—I came to see you last night."

"About—?"

"About midnight."

"Was there a crime?"

"A little. You were all kicking up the hell of a row. This is a hotel—"

"*An* hotel," she interrupted. Then she started to retch. "Oh *God. . . .*"

"Yes. You were lowering the drink, all of you, as well."

"What about tomorrow, though—if I feel like this now?"

"It's tomorrow already. It's Sunday."

She moved forward into the room—and then she collapsed suddenly, right across my bed, face down, buttocks shining damply in the faint light. It was chilly in the early dawn. "You'll catch cold," I told her.

"You're not Branigan—are you?" she groaned into my pillows.

"No. I'm Joe."

"Can I get into your bed then?"

"Yes, if you're able to. What's all this about money?"

"I haven't any, seem to have lost it—or else those creeps next door stole it. If I sleep with you, will you—" She tried to lift her head round to face me, but failed miserably.

"Yes," I said. "Shut up for God's sake, and get into bed. I can use the other one."

I helped her into my bed where she flopped around like a slippery seal before I got a towel and rubbed her, making her a bit warm. "What's the matter—really?" I asked after a minute or so.

"I don't know. I was cold."

"And?"

"I don't know."

"I know. You're sloshed—out of your mind. But why? You don't look the sort, not like your friends. But you're a real soak all the same, aren't you?"

"No, I'm not. I'm Eleanor. Thirty-three, from Camberley. I'm *called* Eleanor, I mean. My real name is Smith." She was on her back now, lying quite still staring up at the ceiling with a fixed concentration, as if trying to solve a very difficult problem.

"That's your surname, you mean? Well, at least we're getting our names right. Or are we? Everybody's called Smith."

"Do you sing?" She suddenly turned to me stupidly.

"No. I'm on something else at the moment: crossing Africa, coast to coast, a little promenade—if I can get any sleep."

"But you bought us all drinks last night—after you were angry."

"Did I indeed."

"Yes. 'Indeed—you—did!' So sucks to you. You're a soak, too. Hey-diddle-diddle, the cat and the fiddle, the cow jumped over the moon, the little dog laughed to see such fun and the cat ran away with the spoon. So there."

"A history of old nannies somewhere," I said.

"Yes, long ago and far away." I finished drying her, tucked the sheets up over her breasts beneath her chin, and she seemed to settle. I got into the other bed then and turned the lights off. We lay in the darkness, the vague sounds of morning gathering in the streets outside.

The rest of the night passed.

Around ten, she spent half an hour trying to wake up. I'd given her a glass of water. But that had come up straight away in the bathroom.

"God, you must really have been drinking," I said when she came back.

"I have. For weeks out here. And that's what I need now."

She didn't get back into bed, but started to move about the room now, restless, giddy, opening the cupboards, looking for some drink. But I'd hidden the remains of the Black Label. She found some of my African books and notes instead—looked at them with horror before throwing them on the floor. Then she put a towel round her shoulders and went into the small hallway, stumbling on the carpet again, making for the door. But the door was locked and she couldn't work the catch. "Bugger!" she said. She didn't swear with any relish: the word was like a sour taste in her mouth which she wanted to spit out. She turned and made for the phone next to my bed.

"That's all right," I said. "It doesn't work. There's no room service here anyway."

"Singer, detective." She started to shout. "You're some bloody writer!"

"No—take it easy." But she didn't. She aimed a great swipe at me before I caught her arm. She fought viciously.

"I *know* about writers. For God's sake—let me go!"

"What do you know?" We were swaying round the room, bumping together in an ugly dance. But I held on to her. I thought she might do something really rash.

"They put you in books!"

"I wasn't thinking of putting you in a book—"

"You're all the same. I've read about you writers: you all have problems. . . ." She had another awful retch coming, I saw then. She sped to the bathroom again. When she came out she looked like death, a bad case of the shakes. I'd got some of my own clothes out for her meanwhile, a spare pair of pajamas, a pullover, some socks—for it was still chilly with the usual gray blanket of cloud outside all over the city, the weather bearing down like a horrible load.

"So you really want to take me over?" she said. "You've got the costume and all."

"Come on—put them on. I just want to stop you catching cold. Put them on, get back into bed." She was shivering now. I had to help her into the pajamas, the socks, the pullover. They were all too big. She looked clownish in them. But she wouldn't get back into bed.

"I want to walk. Walk, walk, walk. It's the only cure." She started to pace to and fro across the room then, before she fell over the edge of the carpet again. I picked her up. I was beginning to get a little worried.

"Listen, if you get back into bed—I'll get you some aspirin, some water, some coffee downstairs." She finally agreed. I sat on the edge of the bed and talked to her. I felt that might be one cure. "Eleanor, apart from the money—"

"I don't need it now," she said defiantly.

"What about your friends last night?"

"They couldn't pay either. That's why they must have taken my money—before they went."

"But you're not living in the Memling, are you?"

"Only on credit—that was the idea. They threw us out of the Amethyst Hotel down by the Grand Marché. Couldn't pay there either. Money from home hasn't arrived."

"Well, we can fix something up there I should think. Your things are all next door?"

"No—at the Amethyst. There till I pay the bill." She sat up, starting to retch again.

"You're going to feel worse before you feel better. Might as well accept that."

"For Christ's sake! There you go again! I 'might as well accept that.' Why in hell should I accept it? I don't, I can tell you. I don't want to feel worse. I couldn't anyway. With a drink I'd feel better. Can you get me one? You must have some duty-free hidden away. Get me some— then I'll feel better."

"Listen—either you let me try and deal with you, or the Embassy people will be round here in half an hour, or worse. You're surely not a real drunk. But you've got a real future there."

"What's this then? Samuel Smiles and Dale Carnegie—how to make friends with people under the influence? Listen—if I got involved with you, where would it end? I know your sort—I told you: a year from now you'll have me in some book or travel article: 'A funny thing happened to me in Kinshasa last summer.' And I'll be still here, nits in my hair, still trying to get upriver but floating on drink instead."

"Upriver? That's my problem—"

"Mine's worse. I've a friend upriver somewhere. He could help me. You can't."

"Who? Who have you got?"

"Robert. He's a Belgian. He's my friend. But I can't find out where he is—and I can't get a boat up. He's an engineer. But he moves around—I don't know where. There's no post and no telephones and I can never hear anything on the company's radio. They all shout in French. But he could help me."

"Okay. So you don't need help. How much do you owe—to get your things out of hock?"

"660 Zaïres. The last two weeks for the room."

"When you're better—we can go round, fix it up." I wasn't going to just give her the money—for another blinder. "And if you want to walk," I went on. "Well, we could walk round the Zoo, have lunch there, there's a good restaurant, I'm told. That's another therapy: food."

"God—I couldn't."

"Not yet, later—"

"Not *ever*. Jesus. . . ."

"You will, you will."

"I'd prefer to hate you a bit instead. Can I?"

"If it does you any good." I sat down on the edge of the bed again. She looked at me, her eyes all puffy, a fright.

After a moment she said, "I can't—I can't." She was in despair now, crying, about to sob, the ultimate morning-after depths.

"Yes, you can," I said. "Go on—hate me if you want." I touched her on the nose.

"I'll try. I really will."

"Of course you don't have to. You've just got a bad hangover, Eleanor. That's all."

"And I used to think about the poor in Africa," she said. Then she really started to sob, shuddering, sniveling. I put my arm round her, ruffled her blond curls gently.

"Cry then."

"Oh God," she wailed. "I'm so drunk. . . ."

"If you had no money where did you get all this drink?"

"The money I didn't spend on my room, for Chrissakes," she

came back very sharply. "And buying things at the flea market."

"Those tin trunks I saw you with?"

"I was getting ready to go upriver. I've been getting ready for over a month now. So I spent all my money on *not* getting up the bloody river—and then on drink." She looked at me closely—her face all liquid, like an uncooked egg. "Stupid. But lovely when you're at it."

She lay back on the pillow then, exhausted. Her eyes closed slowly as I looked at her. She slept, for about five minutes. Then she stirred. I was shaving in the bathroom, the water running. At first I thought she was singing.

"Hate, hate, hate!" Her voice rose above the gurgle down the pipes, like the repeated "Alleluias" in a hymn. I put my head round the door. She was lying, a Crusader on a tomb, arms crossed over her breasts, eyes closed. But she was awake.

"Listen," I said. "You know why you drink? Just for fun, I think. And maybe you're something of a lazy bitch as well: won't fight, won't face it—whatever it is. Because you're certainly no fool. I've never seen a clever girl so drunk. So what's the problem? You must know. So let's face it—"

"God, my head. It's itching inside, with colors." She'd been sitting up in bed but now she fell back like a log.

"Sounds like the start of the DTs. Another few drinks and you'll black out. You want that?"

"No. But I still want to be drunk."

"For God's sake—"

"Give me a chance." She looked at me rather desperately for a second.

"Fine. But not a drink."

"You self-righteous shit!" She leaped from the bed—or as much of a leap as she could manage—and started staggering round the room looking for a bottle, opening the drawers and cupboards. But I'd hidden the Black Label under my suitcase—under the bed—and she couldn't find it. Meanwhile my pajama trousers had slipped off down her legs. She stood in the middle of the room and shouted, "I just want to be drunk, fuck you. Why can't you accept that?" She stormed toward me, grabbing a pillow on the way, just like a schoolgirl, debagged, in the middle of a dorm riot.

"Let me tell you," she raged. "My father's a judge."

She aimed a great blow at me with the pillow which I ducked, so that she missed, tripped, and fell, lying out like an accident on the floor, my pajama top way up over her midriff. I picked her up.

"We lived on a hill," she murmured in my arms. "The Old Rectory, Sandy Wood Lane, Camber. . . ."

"I see," I said. Then she stumbled again, on the corner of the bed. But she picked herself up this time. "Look," she said. "If you don't want to have a drink with me—why don't you just let me go?"

"That's a good point. I'm thinking of it. Except you've got no clothes here—and no money and you haven't paid your bill. And I've never seen anyone so cut in my life, so I don't think you'll get far. But I'm considering it."

I walked down the hallway to the bedroom door, unlocked it, then opened it. "I've considered it. You can go." She stood at the end of the bed, shivering a fraction, looking vacantly out into the corridor, bags under her eyes, all done in. "Can or must?" she said at last.

"Can." I shrugged my shoulders.

"All right—I'll stay for a bit," she said rather more gently now. "And I won't need a drink."

"I'll go downstairs then—see if I can get you some coffee, some breakfast. That's the first thing. Then maybe we can go for a walk, see if we can settle your affairs."

She climbed back into bed. And I realized, as I left, that there were, at least, now two people in my room; a room built for two—and so appropriately filled at last. Appropriately? I'd imagined another woman with me all right, the previous evening—the haphazard debris of a shared adventure scattered over the floor, the lipstick and paper handkerchiefs and lotions. But here was something rather different: a naked drunk, hove-to like a seal in my bed, owing £70 round the corner somewhere, seemingly quite lost, nutty, pickled in drink: not the chic companion I'd imagined—me in my linen tropicals and gold cuff-link. . . . But Eleanor—in what? Just my pajama top. I suddenly saw the two of us walking into the Intercontinental for dinner that way. I smiled— imagining Davidson's face at the Embassy when he heard about it: "God—that BBC chap. I knew there'd be trouble." And suddenly, as I walked down the long gloomy corridor, I thought: Yes, Davidson— I'd like that trouble for you. I felt brisker, almost happy, for the first time since I'd arrived in Kinshasa.

Harry was on the café terrace in the lobby when I got down, having a late Sunday breakfast. I joined him, telling him the night's news. His belly rumbled and a laugh emerged.

"But who is she?" I asked. "Do you know—have you seen her around?"

"Yes. I've seen her around—with a group of hippies. They hang out at the Amethyst or the Universe, by the Grand Marché. You get a few of them out here every month in Kinshasa: optimists—they crash about town for a bit, on the booze or grass. Then they try to get upriver. Or up-country anyhow. But they can't, even if they had the money, which they've spent by then. Zaíre's too tough for hippies, far too tough. They never make it. The embassies have to ship them out home in the end. It's quite a regular business here."

"Yes. But this girl's no hippy. Just a drunk."

"A lush. Yes, I've heard about her. She's the same woman the Reverend Mustard told me about. She went to see him."

"Who's he?"

"Missionary—of sorts. Has a crackpot church in a roofless room in the Cité. Calls it the Church of All Sinners. A frustrated missionary. He's been trying to get upriver, too—for months. But the other missions won't touch him. Won't help him with a boat. He's not kosher. So he deals with the riffraff, black and white, on the edge of the market. She met him. It must have been her—big girl with blond curls?"

"Yes. English. Very English and very drunk. She wanted to get upriver."

"That's her."

"But why? She mentioned something about a Belgian engineer—a boyfriend."

"Yes," Harry nodded, remembering something new. "Yes, that's it. The same woman. She came out here—oh, a month ago maybe—to marry him. But when she got here, he'd beat it—upriver. Said he had some urgent job. In fact he'd just changed his mind. That's the story, I think. Though I've not met her."

"She's quite something."

"Drunks usually are—when they're drunk."

"Yes. I wonder what she's like sober."

"Well, you'll probably have the time to find out. I heard this morning—all the river boats are finished right now. The two big ones stuck upstream somewhere. The channels narrow, the levels drop—in the dry season."

"Well, I can't leave her naked upstairs in my room."

"No. She doesn't sound a gift horse—does she? You'll have to bail her out. Oh, and talking of bail I think I can get you onto the parallel rate. A friend is leaving for London in a few days. He'll take any dollars you have."

"Well, that's something," I said. "Thank you."

"For nothing. Looks like you may need the money."

"Maybe you'll meet her."

"Fine. And maybe you'll start surviving here yourself now."

"I need that, I can tell you. I was halfway toward the drink myself last night. Might have ended up like her."

Harry nodded. "That's not at all difficult here," he told me slowly, gravely. "That's *easy*," he added with a laugh which for him was somewhat restrained.

"So you went to see the Reverend Mustard?" I said later when I'd got back upstairs. "Extraordinary name." Eleanor was testing the breakfast I'd managed to get for her. I'd gone into the chaos of the next bedroom, too, and rescued her clothes, her baggy red pirate pants, check shirt, and sneakers.

"I thought there might be some croissants in a smart place like this." She picked up the hard sliced *baguette*.

"What about this man Mustard? He couldn't help?"

"How do you know I've seen him?"

"I've friends here. At least—I've one."

"Lucky old you."

"Met him downstairs just now. Harry Jupiter. An American. He knows Mustard."

"Mustard's mad," she said.

"Who's sane? That's more like it here. Or was it just that he wouldn't lend you any money?"

"I've lots of money. At home. They don't seem able to get it to me here. But my real problem is not seeing Robert. I told you. Puts me all off balance." She spoke with total conviction, with no hint of Harry's belief that she'd been dropped by this man. Perhaps he was wrong. Perhaps it was just a failure of communications. Sobering up now, she looked so little like a wild goose chase type. She looked much more the sort of woman who knew herself—just as she would the nature of her lovers or fiancé. Yet she didn't seem to know about her drinking. There was some flaw there she was unaware of.

"Well, why couldn't he have got in touch with you then?"

"Moving about all the time, I told you. He's on a survey project, for a Belgian company in Brussels. A new dam they're planning, up beyond Kisangani somewhere."

"Didn't he leave a message for you here—before he left?"

"Yes. Just to say he'd had to leave. Urgently. That's all. And I spoke to him afterward on the radio here. But I couldn't hear him properly. He said something about being back in Kinshasa—last Monday, I thought he said. But he never turned up."

"Why come all this way? If you weren't sure—"

"My business." She looked at me sharply. Then she relented. "Why do you think? Not to play Scrabble."

"And not to get blind drunk either, I fancy."

"You 'fancy,' do you?" She sensed my doubts about her relationship with Robert, but wasn't going to admit it—like the drink. If Harry was right, then the two factors were connected: she had her doubts about Robert as well and so she drank. That seemed a simple enough equation.

All the same—I couldn't follow it. There was so little of the drunk in her. She was so much more an orange-squash type: the open, unmarked face of a tennis-playing girl from the home counties.

"What do you do?" I asked her. "When you're not—out here."

"Gathering material?"

I didn't spot the query in her voice. "On what?" I asked.

"No. I meant, isn't that what you're doing—on me?"

"I'm just trying to get out of this town—like you."

"Just being polite then, were you? Passing the time, considering my welfare, good health? Either that—or you're being curious. 'Curiosity killed the cat'...." She had moved back into her aggressive, childish mood.

"Well, what do you expect? It was you who burst in here at four o'clock this morning, remember? Who wouldn't be curious?"

"I'm nervous—of people," she said.

"Didn't seem that way, last night—stumbling naked in here."

"No. But I am."

"When you're sober."

"I have a vision of life. Other people don't always share it." She spoke without any pretension, stating a casual fact.

"That's what brought you out here? Robert, this man: he has the same vision?"

"A hope," she said. "It's a hope I have." She had an expert way of avoiding any issue, any direct question. Was this the drink still working in her—or just real character?

"A hope of life here—with him? Or in Brussels? There's usually some facts in hope."

"A definition, yes. But doesn't that ruin it? When you have that?"

"Well, you've certainly come to the right place in Kinshasa: there are no facts here. No deeds at all. Only hope."

"Yes. Perhaps that's why I like it."

"But you can't. You're just inventing a life—with drink. You said you were thirty-three. But you don't look it. Or near it."

"No."

"You're not thirty-three?" She shook her head. "And your father's not a judge either, then?"

"Oh yes, he is. But not professionally."

We were getting nowhere. But suddenly she perked up. "I'm going to marry Robert," she said very firmly. "When my money comes through and I can get out of here—take a boat up river to Kisangani." She was pure child again now, believing in everything, not yet touched by life.

"I've been trying the same thing here for the last two weeks," I said. "But the boats are all sunk, smashed up, or grounded. And the fuel is running out anyway. We're stuck. That's the horror of the whole place, don't you see? We *can't* get out. Though Harry said he might be able to fix me up with a boat."

"We could go upstream together then."

"We'll be lucky."

"I have a boy here who's helping me: he's looking for boats, too. Maybe he'll find one. You could come on that."

"A boy?"

"Well, a man. A 'youth' if you prefer it—you know what they call them here—a local fellow. Dibwe he's called. Or Sammy. He prefers that. He's crazy about me."

"I'm not surprised." I looked at Eleanor sitting up against the pillows: a blond Venus recovering in a pajama top—with red pirate pants to come: an eye-turner in Bond Street, let alone Kinshasa. Sammy would certainly be running about like a wild thing looking for boats, though with no more luck than I'd had, I fancied. Boats were as rare as girls like this in Kinshasa.

"Anyway," I said, "I'm going down to see the ONATRA people again this morning—one last try. I'll let you know when I get back. Meanwhile, finish your breakfast, take a bath. Then we can go over to your hotel and settle things up."

"Thanks," she said. And then, underlining this and as if she really wanted to confirm her basic good sense and sobriety, she went on, "Thank you *really*—an awful lot. And I'm sorry I've been so shitty."

When I got outside on the gray streets I realized it was Sunday. The ONATRA building would be closed. The boats could be postponed for another day: I could still pretend there'd be a boat tomorrow, another twenty-four hours to feed hope, postpone reality.

I met Harry again, half an hour later, when I came back into the lobby of the Memling, a Brazzaville paper tucked under his arm, a half-burnt cheroot in his lips. He seemed in excellent humor, wearing a faded linen sports jacket over his cricketing pullover and what looked like an MCC tie: Harry dressed to kill.

"Well," he said as I came up to him. "Bailed her out yet?"

"No. She's still recovering. She was really stoned."

Harry looked at his watch. "Listen," he said. "I didn't tell you at breakfast. Today's our little monthly lunch at the Restaurant du Zoo. A few friends—Chillerjam, Noxious. And Mustard's coming too. Why don't you both join us?"

"The girl? She's not up to it. Drunk enough already."

"For Godssakes, Hone!—don't be so British and puritanical. Bring her along."

"I'm not so sure—"

"Let her be the judge . . ."

"She's in no condition—"

"What is she?—a racehorse?"

"I'll see."

"Well, I'm meeting Chillerjam in the cocktail bar," Harry said. "Make up your own mind, if you won't let her make up hers. This is our big day of the month. No one should lose out." He moved off to the bar. I didn't share Harry's good humor. He was fighting gamely against the odds, I felt, that was all. Drink and merry parties weren't a way of getting out of Kinshasa: afterward it only made the place so much worse. My foreboding was confirmed as soon as I opened the bedroom door upstairs.

Eleanor was swaying about the room, crooning. She had her red pirate pants on now, but nothing on top. She'd found the last third of the Black Label in my absence. The bottle was empty on the bed. She seemed to have had another bath. Her arms and shoulders, at least, were damp with water. She waved her hands about vaguely, a conductor trying to catch up with some silent music. "The water so soft—and the sky so gray," she crooned. She was right there, I thought. This was one of the peculiar qualities of the tap water in Kinshasa. It had a wonderful softness to it: silken rainwater filtered all the way down the great river from the interior. When you washed your hair in Kinshasa it went all fufsky-pufsky afterward.

"All right," I said. "Well, that's the drink finished at last. Now we can start afresh."

"Yes!" Eleanor turned on me decisively, derisively. " 'We—can—start—afresh!' Isn't that simply wonderful!"

"I'm going out," I said. "I'm lunching with Harry and some friends. At the Restaurant du Zoo. You can do what you like. Stay here—or come with us. But I'm not hanging around this damn bedroom any longer."

She stood in the middle of the floor, arms dropped to her sides, vacant, bedraggled all over again, drunk. I walked out, making a half-hearted attempt to slam the door.

CHAPTER
5

Children of the Country

"Mrs. Kirkpatrick arrived in town last night," Harry told me eagerly in the cocktail bar. "Went straight from the airport to see Boots."

"Who?"

"Mobutu. El Presidente. Mrs. K—straight from the UN."

"Maybe Reagan thought Mitterrand was getting too much of the African limelight out here."

"No sir! Reagan thought Boots was pocketing too much of the annual $60 million US aid they get out here. The House Foreign Affairs Committee cut it down to half a few weeks ago: Boots said he wouldn't accept any money at all in that case. Of course that was for public consumption. He wants every cent he can lay his hands on—in cash, of course. So Mrs. K came out here to smooth things over. Mrs. K— and half a dozen technicians from Chubb safes." Harry groaned. I knew he had a good bit coming.

"Why? Why the mechanics?" I gave him his cue.

"They'll give Boots the money—if he agrees to keep it in a new safe, where the Ambassador here has the other half of the combination: so he and Boots can only open it together. A fail-safe device—like a nuke missile."

Harry looked up from his second dry Martini. He'd moved off vermouth for the holiday. A thin, small, very neatly dressed Indian had just opened the door into the cocktail bar.

"Dr. Chillerjam I presume." Harry introduced me. "Mr. Hone— from the BBC. The good doctor tends us all out here—till he gets his visa for Britain. How are things that way, Vijay? Ready for the prison break yet? Good and ready?"

Dr. Chillerjam looked terrified. He was immaculately dressed, I saw now, in a dark, synthetic suit, where only the dazzlingly white cuffs gave an air of sartorial impropriety by protruding too far, almost covering

66

his tiny hands. His face was a strange oblong shape, the jaw lines and both sides of the forehead cut almost at right angles so that, when you looked at him straight on, his head seemed to have been produced from a mold. I thought his tan complexion rather darkened now as he produced a curious trick of rolling his eyes so completely that both pupils disappeared entirely beneath the lids and he appeared sightless. "Now Harry, I'm perfectly happy here," he said. "Perfectly. Quite at home, I may say, without further contradiction. No problems." His voice was wonderfully sing-song—so that I thought at first he must be parodying Peter Sellers's Indian accent in *The Millionairess*. He continued—when he looked at me at all with his roller-coaster eyes—to look at me nervously.

"Don't worry, Vijay," Harry told him. "Mr. Hone's only doing color stuff out here, background. He's not checking up on your qualifications."

The doctor took no notice of this last sally. "Have you been in India?" he asked me suddenly.

"Yes. New Delhi, Simla, Calcutta, Bombay. But that was years ago."

Dr. Chillerjam seemed relieved to hear this, as if I might have spotted him there, out of all India's teeming millions, spotted his nameplate above a doorway in Calcutta—'Failed MD" or some such—and possibly reported on some unethical behavior of his.

"What'll it be, Vijay?" Harry asked him brusquely. "A Sidecar? Whisky Sour? White Lady? Or a Harvey Wallbanger? Vijay's a great cocktail man, Mr. Hone. Little bar here wouldn't survive without him."

The doctor cast his eyes down, like a wise virgin. "You're too kind, Harry. Too kind. A small beer would be—entirely acceptable."

"No, it wouldn't. You'll take something a little stronger. I can see it. The dry season. It's getting you down, Vijay. You'll take a large Bloody Mary. They've got some real tomato juice in."

Harry turned to the barman who was laboring, as always, over a vast collection of unpaid chits by the till.

The doctor sipped his drink, distancing himself from it, like nasty medicine. "I don't believe we have had one fellow out here from the BBC before," he said. "You must be perfect in talking. Perfect. I am so lucky."

The doctor beamed, losing his nervousness and taking to his drink now in a much more friendly fashion. The cocktail bar gave immediately out onto the Memling restaurant: on the far side was a door leading to a back street. A man had just come through it. The other two, sitting opposite me, hadn't seen him. But I suspected he was soon to be part of our group: the Reverend Mustard—I would have laid a bet on it. Not that there was anything about him which even hinted at a holy calling—no dog collar, meek surmise or air of Christian heartiness. It was simply that the man who had just come in looked like a rummy from the word go: a nice one, but definitely in the remittance man department, on the run from Acacia Road, South Ken: very English-looking, with a pipe, an old elbow-leathered, tweed sports jacket and baggy, crumpled trousers. He looked around him now, among the few diners, with an expression of awful shock mixed with abject apology— a guilty man, on the run, cornered at last, in a fit of absent-mindedness. Then he made for us, as if toward a lifeboat.

I'd have won my bet. It was Mustard all right. He joined us, breathless, exhausted for some reason.

"Rough morning, Reverend?" Harry asked him after we'd been introduced. "No takers for the Church of All Sinners this morning?"

"Lord," the Reverend Mustard said, invoking the deity straight away. "There were too many—too many altogether."

He wasn't from South Kensington, I realized. The accent was soft, lowland Scots: a Scots missionary—that seemed appropriate. But just like Eleanor, the accent didn't fit the dress, as neither of them fitted the country. Harry bought him a beer without asking him. Mustard had very good eyes, I noticed now, big gray-blue orbs which he leveled at you—unblinkingly, unnervingly—for seconds at a time before they took fright and changed direction. Having quizzed me in this manner, he now turned his attention, like a laser beam, to the froth on his beer. Then he suddenly took to it, like a diver, slugging down half the glass at one go. There was silence as we watched him. This seemed something of a ritual.

"First today!" Vijay said to him, seeming to offer him, wanting to remind him, of the appropriate cliché.

"Lord," he said again. And then he added in a somber voice, " 'Be thou my vision, be thou my breastplate.' " Then he drank the other half of lager straight off. There was further silence. I wondered if this whole business—these swift drinks and invocations—had something to do with his curious faith, if they were part of some sort of transubstantiation or communion ceremony for him.

"Tell me, how are things out in the Cité and Grand Marché?" Harry asked Mustard. "What's the price of cassava this morning? Natives getting restless at all?"

Mustard answered him promptly, like a grocer. "It touched 200 Zaïres a sack yesterday."

"That's tops, isn't it," Harry commented, more to himself than to us. "Boots is going to need some hard cash pretty soon all right. Every cent. Saved by the bell. Good old Mrs. K." It crossed my mind then: I was amongst a little informal intelligence group that morning in the Memling bar. Mrs. Kirkpatrick—and the American Ambassador fiddling with the new Chubb safe—would have all the latest market prices and gossip in Kinshasa before the day was out. Zaïre really belonged to the US House Foreign Affairs Committee and was run on their behalf by the CIA. Well, why not. The Belgians had been far worse—and the Russians were never a pleasant alternative. Of course, there were the Africans themselves, the Zaïreans, who might have run the place. Now there was a point. I'd have to consider that later.

We all got into Harry's peach-colored Cadillac. He wasn't driving this morning. He had his boy in tow, doubling as chauffeur: Alain, a frisky overeager young man dressed in a dark Kaunda jacket with a smart green cravat. "Green is the color of the country," Harry said as we sped off, with a great "W-r-r-u-m-p-h!" into the gray day. "Isn't it, Alain?"

"Yes, *sir*." Alain had an American accent, when he wasn't chewing gum.

" 'Green grow the rushes, oh . . .' " Harry sang out joyfully. "When you get up-country, in the rains," he told me, "you'll see—it's all green, not gray. Just one great big carpet of green—where man never put a foot."

"And never will," Mustard added. Mustard, with a few drinks on board, was less nervous: he was almost cheeky. "What are your feelings, Mr. Hone, about sin?" he went on. I was going to say that I was against it, but I held my tongue.

"It's not an African concept," Harry said. "That's for sure. Just part of all the nonsense we brought to this continent."

"Every man is a sinner, black or white. But each has the possibility of grace." The Reverend Mustard spoke in a small voice now, the still small voice in the wilderness.

"Goddamn it, Reverend, the blacks had that to begin with here, till we came along—"

"If they did—they weren't aware of it."

"A sin to let them know then. I'm all for the happy savage, aren't you, Mr. Hone? Rousseau's Man: innocent, uncorrupted."

"Yes—but I suppose it's too late."

Harry nodded, ruefully. "Most of the missions have given up trying to save souls here anyway—save them from what we've done to them, in fact. They're back to animism here. And Kimbangoism—and Mobutuism, of course. Boots saw himself as the Congolese Christ some years back. And why not? Fired the local Cardinal and told all the Protestants to amalgamate. There were fifty-seven different Protestant sects here—can you imagine? A real gravy train. Now they're all one—except for the Reverend here. I'll give you that, Reverend: it's quite a pitch you're making on your own. Trouble is the Catholics still have a head start in Zaïre: the Pope's legions—and there's only one of you, in a church without a roof. But I'm on your side. Christ started with less."

"Thank you, Harry," Mustard said, "I appreciate that." And he meant it.

I hadn't been to the Restaurant du Zoo before—and we wouldn't have got in without booking, for the long, low building just before the zoo gates was crowded with prosperous, barrel-fat *Kinois,* some *en famille* with their wives, nannies and children—all the younger women with the most fashionable Zaïrean hairstyles, in the antennae mode, where the hair was brought together and tightly plaited so that it stuck out all over the scalp like the firing pins of a mine. Though some of the grandest of these courtesans went a step further in their coiffure: the hair, forced into these antennae, was then further built up—the strands connected and woven together into little hirsute baskets and birds' nests standing inches clear above their heads.

Harry remarked on these startling confections as we went in. "All part of Boots's 'authenticity' campaign. No European names, clothes or hairstyles allowed in Zaïre now. Quite right, too. It's one of the few real successes Boots has created out here. He's no fool, of course. Used to be a journalist—like you, Mr. Hone. Giving the people back to themselves. What better?"

Harry maintained his high good humor. But the Reverend Mustard seemed not so keen on this spread of authenticity about us.

"Men from the Ministry out in force as usual." He spoke sourly, looking at the courtly African banquets, while a waiter led us through them into a further room at the end of the restaurant—a long table looking out on the terrace and car park beyond, filled with vast, cigar-like cars, all surrounded by raggedy children, each car "adopted" by separate groups of these vagabonds who, as Harry had explained, would come into their due reward in a few hours time when the clients left.

"It's all part of the code here," Harry had told me on the way in. "A mysterious code. Those kids out there are just the tip of it. I still barely know the score after five years here. But everyone has their place and price in Kinshasa: a precise cash for the job rate—from those kids to the government ministers. You have to know *exactly* what they want—not to let the air out of your tires or to get a shipment of textbooks in here. They're surprisingly honest about corruption: a few cigarettes, a crate of scotch or a $1000 cash—no more and no less, else they take offense. And you have to know *when* to pay—just as important: before, in the middle or afterward. Or all three. All part of the code. And that's what visitors don't realize—think they're just dealing with a lot of creeps, dumbbells or shysters. In fact, more than just cash, each African is an entire crossword puzzle here. You have to work your way through the clues—and get them right if you want anything from him."

Two other men were already seated at our table—a young man and an elderly one. But before we met a voice—a raddled croaky voice— came from behind.

"Bonjour, Monsieur Harry! Comment vas-tu, chéri?"

I turned. A tiny, ancient woman had come up behind us, dressed in a wispy, *thé dansant* gown, a shipboard romance outfit from the Thirties: a sharp, deeply creased, sunburnt face with a thin fuzz of hair above. She looked a cross between Colette and Edith Piaf in their last years. Harry spoke to her effusively in French for a minute.

"Madame Yvette," he explained as we sat down. "That's her portrait over there—fifty years ago when she first came out to the Congo. She still runs the place." I looked up at the large, amateurish chocolate-box portrait on the wall: a young, blond vivacious woman—dressed and styled straight off a Paris street, the Rue du Faubourg St. Honoré. . . . The picture bore no resemblance to the woman I'd just seen. But suddenly a sense of history moved in me. Here was an identifiable, living image of history in Kinshasa; the sense that people from a European world I knew had lived out whole lifetimes here, were still living it, had not gone yet, leaving all their broken bidets, old radios and alarm clocks behind them in the flea market. For the first time it became possible to contemplate a European life entirely lived in this city, with a sort of happiness, I supposed, because it was your town and you had no other. You were a real child of the country. The place was yours—as it would never be mine—and you loved it, as I never would, because you knew it as I didn't, knowing nothing of the code.

I sat down then with a feeling of envy and hopelessness. I was neither tourist nor inhabitant. I couldn't survive here on tourist color and I would never be here long enough to savor all the real messages and intimacies of the place: the change in seasons and in people, in oneself. Madame Yvette and Harry and the others knew the place and I knew really nothing about it at all. It was as simple as that.

The elderly man opposite me was Naxos, the Greek dentist, except that he wasn't Greek. He was Albanian. He made this clear to me at once when he heard I was doing things for the BBC.

"I listen to your BBC World Service round the clock," he told me happily. "I could not be here without it."

"How long have you been here?"

"Many years," he said. In his thin hand he lifted the apéritif of chilled Muscadet that had been ordered all round to begin with. Then he ran a finger down through the condensation on the side of the glass, like a child playing on a clouded windowpane. "I came here with the Belgians after the war. I was never able to go back to my country, you see. The Communists took over. I am a Royalist." He raised his glass. Of course—I remembered: King Zog of Albania. It was a name you never forgot. I raised my own glass.

"I listen every day," he went on. "Though I cannot receive your Albanian service, of course. But your other news absorbs me." He spoke English meticulously, slowly, treading on thin ice with each word, testing them, intent that they should bear the full gravity of his thought. He was a very serious old gentleman.

"I'm glad you're such a fan," I said. "Many people say the World Service is the best thing about the BBC."

"Well, they have people, you see, in the right places," he said, leaning toward me with an air of knowing confidentiality. "They would certainly be first with the news."

"The news?"

"A *coup d'état*—what else? We are waiting for it: all Albanians—a return of the monarchy. It cannot be long." He was suddenly ecstatic.

"Yes," I said. "Of course." I had been about to say I thought this a most unlikely event, but stopped myself just in time. The old man was too deeply committed. None the less he saw the doubt in my eyes.

"You surely cannot support the present criminal régime in my country?" he asked tartly.

"No—of course not."

"I am surprised—given your own monarchy—that you would not support ours. I am really surprised." Naxos shook his head in astonishment.

"Well, I'm sure the Queen does support it. But as far as I'm concerned with the BBC, it's different. The BBC is not part of our government— or Buckingham Palace, you see. We have to be—uninvolved, not take sides."

"That is very strange," Naxos said. "You are the first BBC man I have met. I have thought for many years that you were on our side." He turned away now, pointedly, joining in on the conversation next to him, between Harry and Vijay.

Why couldn't I have lied to Naxos?—told him how we were all rabid Albanian Royalists to a man in the BBC; how a restored monarchy and the Macedonian question was ever on our minds if not on our lips? The truth had no place in Kinshasa, no meaning in this city—which was all fiction.

I'd wanted to ask Naxos about life in Zaïre, his own life in the country. But it was clear that he didn't live here. He lived in another world, a dead land ruled by the ghost of King Zog. And his lifeline to it was a radio—the BBC World Service, a Prince Charming that would one day wake him to the news of a restored monarchy and bring about his own repatriation, from nightmare to reality.

The young man next to me, Michel, was a Belgian—a journalist of some sort, a stringer for various European papers, he intimated. Though I suspected—from his expensive business clothes and his general air of success and extreme well-being—that there was private money behind him. Harry, indeed, had mentioned his family in the car before we'd met: one of the oldest and most powerful of the great Belgian commercial dynasties, the dozen or so families that had run the Congo ever since King Leopold had given the place up as his private estate in 1908.

Michel was a very go-ahead young man, swift, smooth, excitable. He'd lived in America, studied business management there. Everything about him, in thought and gesture, was searching, ambitious. And though he was certainly no *gros Belge* I couldn't fathom his place among us expatriates. He seemed far too straightforward, well adjusted and businesslike to have had a real connection with any of Harry's little clan. It was only much later in the meal that I discovered where his curious fictions lay. Meanwhile the Muscadet began to flow, interrupted with mouthfuls of grilled *telapia*—so that for long moments, if I didn't listen to the conversation, I could almost believe I was back in Europe, in some smart Parisian restaurant. But Africa was inescapably there whenever I did listen.

Harry was holding forth at the end of the table. "Downhill all the way," he was saying. "I *love* it! I don't know why you get so upset by African affairs, Vijay. All they're doing is regaining the life they had here—before we came: a few tubers to eat, a little bush meat on high days and holidays, a fire in the woods, the local medicine men and bonesetters to tend them. They're just doing you out of a job, that's all. Though remember, we brought the real illnesses here: tuberculosis, syphilis, measles, and the rest. And of course they had no natural immunity to them. So all you do is pump them full of Western drugs—"

"When we can *get* them—out of those crazy Customs," Vijay interrupted.

"So you save them—the few that ever get to a clinic or hospital, that is. And the rich, of course. But what of all the rest? All they get is a taste for aspirin. Then you have to pack 'em back to the woods, if they'll go. And they won't if they can possibly help it, because the witch doctors won't touch them then. And the missionaries can't—because the fuel has run out and the roads are all gone anyway. So they just die. And the children are even worse. You *know* the child mortality rate here, Vijay—up to half the kids here die now before they're ten years old."

"One has to help, do what we can," Vijay said. "A little—it is better than nothing."

"But that's what I'm saying, Vijay: it's *not* better than nothing. It's worse. Leave 'em *entirely* to their own devices—that way, someday, maybe they'll cure themselves, like they used to. You don't see it—but what we should be doing in Africa now is rescuing the people from *our* development, releasing them from it, not trying to increase it. Get rid of all these cockamamie notions of 'development'—aspirins and Mercedes. You know, there's only one thing saving Africa today—saving them from us: the fact that the communications here are all shot to hell. Twenty, thirty years ago—colonial times—you could travel all over the continent, west-east, up into the interior and down the far side. No real problem—there were river boats, lake steamers, railways, fairish roads. Now you can't get beyond the suburbs of Kinshasa without a private plane. So we just can't get to the locals anymore with our development. And that suits me fine. And what's more the fat cats in government can't get out into the country either—and that saves a lot of agony, too. Their writ runs out at the city limits now. Mr. Hone complains of the transport system in Zaïre. But I tell you—it's a saving grace. We can't *get* to them anymore, with our forks and Bibles or valium or video games or UN schemes—or little men with stethoscopes and white coats. With no transport, no communications, the Africans are very nearly free of that again: free of all our garbage. Don't you see?"

Vijay didn't see. But he didn't really mind. Vijay was just anxious to get to England.

Later in the meal, after the South African steaks, at the brandy and coffee stage, with our going to and fro from the Gents', we swopped places about the table and I got myself next to the Reverend Mustard. I wanted to see what he knew about Eleanor. He knew little—and nothing of any credit either. "One of the great unwashed," he told me grandly—and incorrectly, for Eleanor seemed to be always washing, one way or another. Mustard, now that he was firmly seated, fed, and watered, had dropped his vague, careworn role. He was all supercilious matinée idol—a man released by this good restaurant and the cognac fumes from the grubby cares and concerns of Africa. "We have girls like her out here all the time, though they never get beyond Kinshasa. Going's too tough," he went on, "so they hang around town 'till their cash runs out—in one of those Greek or Syrian hotels by the Grand Marché. Then they start looking for money from the locals. I try and avoid them. Just—bums." He hit the word vigorously.

"And she came and saw you?"

"Yes. I met her in the flea market first time. She was interested in the witch doctor's business there."

"The old chicken feathers?"

"All that—Africana, superstition. Wanted to know where she could get hold of some real Congolese masks and fetish statues. You know —the native voodoo business. Told her they were all gone in Kinshasa. Cleared out by the Belgians years ago. Though she might get some upriver, in the villages. Then she wanted money. I hate these amateur African fanciers," he went on, looking at me pointedly, the big gray-blue orbs drilling into me. "The women especially: their ideas of an incorrupt native nobility. You know what they really want from the natives, don't you?" Modesty forbade him a clearer explanation. But I knew what he meant.

"She doesn't want that. Just wants to get hold of her Belgian boyfriend—somewhere upriver."

"So she said: a hard luck story. I didn't believe it." Mustard set into his cognac again. "She won't get upriver anyway. None of us will. You heard what Harry said. Well, it's even worse than that, not just transport. Since the Belgians left, the forests are coming back everywhere, creeping in, every day a little more." Mustard was speaking with relish now—cradling, massaging the words. He leaned toward me confidentially. "Upriver," he whispered, "in parts, you know, they've started eating each other again." His staring eyes had a mad touch to them now, glittering with happiness. He was hearing the tom-toms already, contemplating, it seemed, in all this encroaching cannibalism, some really hard-won conversions in his proposed ministries upriver.

I laughed. "You can't be serious."

"I am. And they are. Food's running out. They're starving."

"What—missionaries for the pot? You must be joking."

"No. Not at all."

"Have you *been* upriver?"

"No. But the rumors are well founded. You'll see! The natives are basically corrupt. Oh, I don't mean corrupt so much in *our* ways—though they've learned that too. I mean they're a fallen people. Never risen indeed, for there was never any Eden here. That's another ridiculous European view—Harry's 'noble savage'! There was never any such thing: just animal instinct, mindless squalor, cannibalism—savagery in fact. We fool ourselves believing otherwise. You have to start from the premise of basic sin here, Mr. Hone—no matter what you liberal BBC people think about it. That's all woolly hope. Experience here will teach you quite otherwise."

"If I manage to get any. Though I still think you're talking rubbish."

"You believe in Harry's native dream, do you? That they'd be better off without us . . ."

"No, not entirely. Because at some point the Europeans were always going to bring their bullets and trinkets to Africa, whatever happened. But the wars we fought—and created—here were just the domination of a stronger tribe, which had been going on here before that since the year dot: a white tribe took over, where before it had been a black tribe—lording it over all the weaker ones. There was never any Eden here—I agree. But the whites are not innately better—or worse—than the blacks, as you seem to think. And God certainly doesn't distinguish between them."

I wondered—their views on Africa so opposed—what had brought Harry and Mustard together in the first place. It must have been just part of the whole crazy air of Kinshasa—where, for the lack of any compromising sanity, opposites readily attracted each other, making the most unlikely connections commonplace. Oh yes, in that way there was a certain charm in Kinshasa—a mood of the permanently unexpected and eccentric. I had the clear sense here—without mail, newspapers, radio or television, where the telephone never worked and there were no roads out—of living in a fantastic quarantine where all previous notions of health and efficiency had no meaning now whatsoever. I was exposed here to some heady, unpredictable fever quite unknown to medicine—where the symptoms of the disease appeared as either farce or tragedy. Certainly in Kinshasa there was nothing in between.

Here among the sumptuous colonial villas by the river and the tin huts of the African Cité, in the bars, casinos, nightclubs, and beer shops, in all the people and places—here was a late-sleeping, little-doing, chatter-filled, utterly inconsequential *dolce vita*. It was life in a decrepit, shoddy, poverty-stricken world, certainly. But one in which, freed from all Western ambitions and restraints, the human character, black or white, could emerge unfettered—freely expressing, glorying in every sort of nutty excess, each bizarre whim. So that Kinshasa, I saw, without its Belgian straitjacket, its old European ties, had become a circus of every sort of human folly and delusion, a honey pot for misfits. Here—as with Mustard and Vijay and Naxos—a man could live with the person he really was, freely expressing every preposterous whim, the dark or light sides, no longer having to put up with his boring, indeterminate shadow. Here, in Kinshasa, the sublime was the ridiculous—there was no journey between the two—and unless you recognized this and went along with it you were finished.

I was dreaming. But Mustard was talking to me again, something urgent and mocking in his tone. "Anyway," he was saying, "I'm sure I know what you BBC people are really out here for—looking for those monsters upriver." Harry had offered his Kivu cheroots all round and there was a sort of masonic fug in the air as gray as the weather outside.

"Oh—what monsters?"

"Don't pretend. Up in the swamps, between the Ubangui and Sangha rivers here: prehistoric beasts. Iguanadon or better. Long necks, vast bodies. There've been quite a few sightings over the years—and now this American professor is on the trail."

"I heard nothing—"

"Oh yes, I assure you. Quite recently—some of the pygmy tribes up there—two of them were devoured one morning, on the edge of this great swamp, place as big as Britain, animal came right up out of the mist and made a meal of them. Another group attacked it, poison arrows, killed it. But the body dropped back into the water."

"That's always the problem with monsters: people see them but never any hard evidence." I smiled. But Mustard was entirely serious.

"I'm not joking, you know. This American, from some university in Wisconsin, a natural scientist—he's been over here on and off for years chasing them. Gathered a lot of evidence. And Michel—he's thinking of organizing tourist trips up to the area." Mustard turned to Michel next to him. "Aren't you, Michel?—those monsters."

"Well, it's a good possibility," Michel agreed, equally serious. "Though I'm anxious to get the boat going first." He leaned over toward me. "There's a fantastic tourist market to be tapped here—if I can get one of the old paddle steamers working again." I could appreciate his problems here.

"Up the Congo—in the footsteps of Stanley and all that," he continued eagerly. "An up-market operation, of course—just like this new Orient Express they've got going again. Do it the same way: do the steamer up again—like it would have been in the Twenties here. Cabins all refurbished, air-conditioned: cane chairs, teak paneling, little art-deco candelabra. Small pool on the deck, movies at night, cocktail bar, piano, and some local folklore at each port of call. And the best French cooking, naturally. Get a chef from Europe." Michel licked his lips and Madame Yvette arrived offering more cognac. The scheme was practically airborne already.

"I think the monsters for the tourists—that's a great idea, Michel," Harry commented ironically. "They'll come running on that, no question. And I like the cocktail bar, don't you, Vijay? And the little piano. Maybe Vijay could be barman and I could hit the ivories, Michel. Would you consider that? And Mr. Hone here—why, he could do PR for us all in Europe. The BBC would surely take a little promotional material. And Mustard could be the padre on board and Naxos could look after the teeth. Why, we're a whole crew here, ready and willing—and you could play captain, of course. When do we start?"

Harry looked about him. Our glasses were recharged. I was very ready to join in the fun. The strange thing was that no one else was. Each of them round the table considered these ideas entirely seriously now, each seeming to ponder their coming shipboard careers. Naxos scratched his thinning hair quizzically with one finger; Mustard was lost in adventurous riverine thought; Michel's eyes sparkled, filled with detailed blueprints, while Vijay was blissfully dumb, seeing no cause here to repeat his earlier comment on Harry's "good jokes." All of them were on the rear deck of this old paddle steamer, moving off into a dramatic sunset, out of Kinshasa into the Pool, crates of scotch waiting below, the clink of ice in the cocktail bar, a Cole Porter number warming up on the piano, monsters and other folklore laid on for the morrow.

It was a wonderful fiction, of course. And as usual in this prison of a city, it was better and far more real than the dull facts which surrounded us all: the facts that you couldn't get beyond the suburbs here, were trapped in the place with nothing to feed on but your own fabulous or monstrous imaginings.

Then Eleanor arrived.

She pushed her way through the bibulous Africans in the front room and on into our further retreat: a slightly flushed, swaying, merry figure, her red pirate pants sticking down beneath the hem of one of my tropical linen jackets. She came to rest, glassy-eyed, standing above us all at the end of the table. The jacket fitted her well enough, for she was a big girl. All the same, she was a startling vision—something out of a Renoir picture, with her careless, candid abundance: lavish blond curls, cherry blossom cheeks, my white coat above the red exclamation marks of her pants and splendid legs—a vision in the cigar fug, come to disrupt all gray days.

"Ah—so *this* is where you all are. Merrymaking!"

But we weren't. Confronted by this living fiction, this dream made flesh, Harry's little band was speechless, their previous imaginings set at nought. But Harry saved the day at once—effortlessly, happily.

" 'Sit down, sit down, sit down—you're rocking the boat,' " he sang out. Eleanor sat down—mischief in her eyes. Or was it just vivid alcoholic expectation, a thirst renewed?

CHAPTER
6

Escape

*T*hough it was right next to it, the only window in the small white-washed bedroom on the third floor of the Amethyst Hotel didn't give out onto the Grand Marché. It gave onto nothing except the broken guttering, a valley between two slanting corrugated iron roofs at the back of the hotel, a narrow area which Eleanor had turned into a sort of hidden terrace where she had put out a chair and slung a clothesline between the roof peaks, with some of her shirts and pants still hanging limply in the dull air when we got round to the Amethyst later that afternoon.

I'd lent Eleanor the money to pay her account. Money was less of a problem now. Harry had put me on the parallel rate before I'd left the restaurant. And $400 had suddenly become the equivalent of $1200—mostly in grubby 5- and 10-Zaïre notes which I had with me now, like some old mattress-miser, in a huge brown envelope. The hotel was as crummy as I'd expected. But Eleanor's room, though it had no view, was a surprise. She'd been there nearly a month, all the more time, I thought, for her unhappiness to have resulted in some squalor about the place. Instead it was set out and kept almost like a new pin, with only two empty wine bottles, behind a curtain that gave into a minute cubicle with rickety shower and wash basin, as evidence of her earlier despair.

But more than just a tidy room, what Eleanor had done here—managing far better than I in the Memling—was to make the whole place over into a personal space, a room filled with her own bizarre choices, eccentric bits and pieces, reflecting the vision she had of herself as a woman, a traveler, where the decor had been studiously composed about her in a collection of quite unexpected objects, most of them obviously picked up from the flea market round the corner: knickknacks that gave the high-ceilinged, rather gaunt, corridor-shaped room a strange domestic intimacy now, a setting for a life years ago, in some long-dead colonial Congo, because Eleanor had filled the place with the discarded detritus, the household remains of Belgian families who had fled the country twenty years before.

Quite apart from the lack of any view over the city, Africa had been shut out more or less entirely here. The mementoes she'd collected were European, a jumble of dead, unrelated objects which she'd resurrected and built round her like twigs in a nest, transforming the room into an image, however transitory, of home.

On a table was an old, wind-up "Sonor" gramophone, complete with a dented, scalloped horn and a pile of seventy-eights—mostly French popular *chansons* from the Forties and Fifties: Piaf, Trenet, Guetary. On the wall above there was a set of small nineteenth-century steel engravings—Antwerp under snow, Bruges Cathedral, and the like; over the bed a tattered poster for the Brussels World Fair of '58; by her bedside an ancient servant's alarm clock with two huge brass bells on top; on another smaller table a lilac-blue china tea set, chipped but serviceable, the teapot rounded, bulbous, without a lid in the Thirties mode—the whole neatly laid out with butter dishes as if the cucumber sandwiches and hot water were expected at any moment.

But Eleanor wasn't having any tea. She'd collapsed on the bed—on an old vermilion counterpane that couldn't have been part of the hotel's equipment—almost as soon as we'd arrived in the room. And now I was looking around me wondering at this museum. There were some dog-eared paperbacks by my chair: a *série noire* collection—Simenon, American tough-guy translations—and a few unexpected literary texts: Céline's *Voyage au bout de la nuit,* Montherlant, Claudel, Gide. I opened a copy of *Les Faux Monnayeurs.* Inside was an old Brussels restaurant bill. Three large black tin trunks lay piled on each other in a corner. On the top one, neatly laid out on what looked like an embroidered altar cloth, was the only real evidence of Africa in the room—chicken feathers, claws, old tubers, thorns; a little collection of desiccated rubbish from the witch doctor stalls. Beside the trunks were two polished wood clothes horses, large upstanding objects for smart colonial uniforms or dress suits, but which Eleanor had made over as rigs for what I now saw was a vast collection of trousers—of every sort, shape, and color, right through the rainbow: pirate pants, Bermuda shorts, cropped denims, blue jeans, tennis shorts, jodhpurs, baggy golfing slacks, track suit bottoms, waterproof leggings, even *Lederhosen*—the equipment of

some sly trouser fetishist, it seemed, if one didn't know the girl concerned, know how each pair would transform her into a trousered
dream.

But meanwhile Eleanor slept, and I sat there, an uneasy guardian,
the huge envelope on my knee, stuffed with 10,000 Zaïres. I had a
problem to consider. After we'd left the restaurant Harry had taken me
aside and offered me the use of his school's minibus—it was the end
of term at his Academy—with his boy Alain as chauffeur and enough
fuel to get me down to the coast and back: to the port of Matadi at the
neck of the estuary and then to Boma near the Atlantic coast. A three-
or four-day trip. The problem was what to do about Eleanor. She had
hit it off with Harry, all right, but not so much with the others. And
Davidson at the Embassy was no use to any of us. I felt, having helped
her thus far, I could hardly disappear, leaving her alone in the gray city.
On the other hand, the liabilities of sharing such a trip, with such a
woman. . . .

Eleanor began to stir an hour later. "You can make . . . some tea,"
she murmured thickly. "There's a little boil-up under the table."

And so there was—a brass camping device that ran on some sort of
firelighter, with a tiny billy can on top. I filled it at the wash basin. And
half an hour later, the day ended, a real gloom outside now, she was
sitting up in bed taking tea—lemon tea for there was no milk—from
a cup and saucer out of the lilac-blue Thirties tea service. I turned the
light on, a single bulb in the center of the ceiling, where the shade had
been completely covered with a red scarf. It gave the place the air of
winter secrecy, a glow, a warm shade everywhere, so that Eleanor's fresh
complexion was transformed: she was pale red now, the tossed curls
pink; a fainter woman altogether, a wraith shrouded beneath the vermilion counterpane.

But after the tea she perked up. "That's marvelous—about your friend
Harry—the poppet," she said. "Offering us the minibus."

Harry had breakfast with me next morning, before I took over the
minibus, and I asked him at once why he'd involved Eleanor in the trip.

He humphed. "I guess she's not going to see that *Belge* again. Take
her mind off that."

"Yes, but—"

"A great 'Yes, but' man, Mr. Hone. I thought you were an old roving
correspondent: stopping the presses, holding up bars and girls from

Rio to Rangoon. No trouble. First with the news. Instead you're behaving like a—like a virgin! Here, take a few cheroots with you—and hit the road, Goddamnit."

Eleanor was waiting outside the Amethyst—a tall figure, made the more so by a tiny African in the most fanciful neon-colored shirt standing beside her, holding her bag. I was surprised. I didn't think the hotel ran to hall porters—and the youth looked just like a bellhop.

"This is my friend Sammy," Eleanor told me. "You don't mind if he comes with us? He can keep Alain company. He so much wants to. You don't mind?"

Sammy looked at Eleanor adoringly. I shook his hand, bending down in the process. Sammy couldn't have been more than twenty—in his young, scrawny, unfilled body. But his face was that of a much older man: a heavy pugilist's face, flat-nosed, pock-marked, with bloodshot eyes, a wispy beard ringing his chin and tight-cropped, curly hair round the top—an excited, eager, smile-drenched face. What could I say?

"He knows Alain anyway," Eleanor rushed on. "And Harry. Harry said it would be all right. He's at Harry's school anyway, he says. And there's plenty of room."

I sighed. Sammy busied himself with Alain fixing the bags into the back, among the two jerry cans of spare fuel.

"No, I don't mind," I said. "Why not?"

"Sammy knows the area, too. He comes from Bas Zaïre. It'll be easier."

"I have *got* maps," I said. "And a French guide book." I looked at Eleanor carefully. "How are you feeling?"

"Excited!" She beamed—whether wilfully avoiding the real implications of my question or not I couldn't tell. Certainly she showed no signs of drink—or even a hangover. The orange-squash girl seemed entirely in charge here: a complete recovery. She was young, of course. At forty-five her sort of drinking would have kept me in bed for a week.

"What about Robert—upriver?" I asked.

"Oh, Sammy's left a message—round at the firm. We'll be back in a day or two anyway, won't we?" She cocked her head to one side, curious, intent suddenly, running her hand quickly through her curls in a nervous gesture. I shrugged my shoulders.

"Anything's possible—as long as we can keep off the drink."

She straightened her head, smiling. "Oh—the drink!" She laughed outright. "That was only being stuck in this dump, Joe. Drive you to all *sorts* of sin. Look, I found my camera."

She held up a little Kodak—a new slim-line model with a foldaway handle that came out at the bottom. She held it up to her eyes now like a duchess with a lorgnette. "See! I'll be able to show Robert all the snaps."

She was wearing a pair of brushed navy denims, perfectly creased down to her county casual shoes, with a sleeveless Puffa jacket over one of her Viyella check shirts, a slim gold choker round her neck, and a smart leather shoulder bag—something straight out of Badminton Horse Trials. She looked like the most unlikely drinker in the world now.

We hit the road five minutes later—the two boys in the front, us in the back, widely separated on the bench seat, by the windows to either side. We went west up the grand boulevard and out of the town past the Presidential Domain and through another shanty suburb beyond before we came on to the Matadi road. It wasn't difficult to find. There was no other road west out of the city. The day was gray as usual. But the feeling of relief in leaving Kinshasa at last made everything spectacular, each dull view a vision. And it was dull enough, in truth. Though Eleanor was enchanted—ecstatic over the least thing. She either talked too much, I'd learned, or held her tongue in a clamp. Now she let fly.

"*Look* at that incredible art-deco bungalow! See the moldings—the curves—there: at either end of the terrace. And *that*!" She spied a larger house, a prewar Belgian villa set back from the road behind some frangipani trees, with elaborately angular designs and panels set in the brickwork. "Must be by Horta—the Brussels designer. Stop! Stop!" We reversed for a closer look.

"What's that? . . . And this! . . . And why?" Eleanor was a descending angel that morning, lighting on every shabby view and touching it with gold.

Further on, the hills to the west of Kinshasa were dotted with shacks and other impromptu homesteads as far as the eye could see: a dry eroded scrubland littered with rubbish, a vast tidewrack of congealing slums lapping at the boundary of the city, where apart from a few cassava and banana plots scraped out of the hard stony ground, almost every scrap of natural vegetation, all the trees, had long since been cropped or burnt. Not a bush survived—just groves of blackened tree stumps now and then—as if the forests had been all shelled away in some war years before. But the grim landscape hardly mattered. We were off, down to the sea, the sea: released at last.

The shacks and the rubbish land ran out as we rose into the bare hills, up to the top of a long rise. Beyond, running away all round us then, lay the Crystal Mountains, a long jagged range of steep granite, loose stone, and bare desert that cut Kinshasa and the interior completely off from the Atlantic. The empty, narrow strip of old black tarmac ran up and down the arid hills now: roller-coasting, twisting, turning, making supreme efforts to force a passage through the cruel geography. Fifty miles north of the road the Congo river fell much more directly from Kinshasa to the sea, but in a series of deep gorges and terrifying cataracts that had always denied navigation here and had thus kept the world out of the Congo interior—from 1482 when the Portuguese first discovered the river mouth until nearly 400 years later, in 1877, when Stanley's great transcontinental expedition, coming from the east and discovering the dark heartlands, had dragged itself, more dead than alive, through these same mountains to the sea.

A few years later this road had been hacked out into the interior—and then, as another bypass to the rapids, the Belgians built their narrow-gauge railway, running along beside us most of the way now, 250 miles up from the port of Matadi to Kinshasa. It had taken them eight years—a black for every sleeper, as the likely rumor had it. That was the long Congo tragedy, the start of King Leopold's so-called Congo Free State, of the rubber boom in all the virgin rain forests upstream and the fearful atrocities committed by the Belgian administrators and their brutal African "Force Publique"—a situation which the Irishman, Roger Casement, then British Consul at the old estuary capital of Boma, had finally exposed in his famous report of 1904. And now, in search of Stanley and Roger Casement and of the Atlantic itself, I was traveling the same rough paths. . . .

Of course, it wasn't quite like that. The path was smooth enough and I was no lone traveler. There was Eleanor—and Sammy and Alain: people just as much a foreign country to me, I realized, as the jagged hills, the nothing country, all round. Normally, on these BBC journeys, I always traveled alone—avoiding any filter, any other human presence that might come between me and the landscape, which might influence, soften or alter my own opinions on it. I had always avoided the luxury of another person's company—where there is the temptation to relax one's hold, one's perceptions, to hide from the harsh realities, running for cover in shared jokes and chatter; where there are the preoccupations, the worry or concern for the other person: another person—in whom the sharp discomforts, the isolation and loneliness of individual travel can all be dissolved.

"You didn't want me to come, really—did you?" When she'd finished looking at the views, when the view became all the same—gray hills and gray sky—Eleanor spoke. I explained my feelings about this sort of travel—professional travel.

"Oh, I shan't get in your way." She turned and looked intently out the window again, as if to confirm this.

"It's not *you*. It'd be anyone."

"Your wife even?"

"Yes. She never comes on these trips. We go to Normandy instead."

"Funny. I'd love traveling—with someone I loved."

"Haven't you ever?"

"Loved or traveled?" Eleanor looked back at me.

"Both."

"Not far," she said. "Like this!"

"You'd be doing that a lot with Robert, I expect—when you marry: an engineer, moving about all the time."

"Yes! I wouldn't be in his way, of course. He'd be out at the site."

"And you'd be making tea at home, waiting. In a tent?"

"Oh yes, fancy free. We'd always be fancy free in his kind of job. Takes him all over the place. Any number of people like him—wanted all over the third world."

"How long have you known him?"

"A year. No—fourteen months." For the first time she answered a question directly. "I met him in London," she went on. "A friend—of a friend. An architect I know. At the AA."

"Alcoholics Anonymous?"

"No," she said, pityingly, wagging her head at me in a governessy way. "The Architectural Association. In Bedford Square. I'm studying there."

"Qualified?"

"No. Only my second year."

"Ah, these are great truth-tellings. . . ." She looked surprised. "Well . . . you said you were a Miss Smith the other night, thirty-three, from Camberley. That wasn't true, was it?"

"Twenty-two. And we live outside Windsor—just beyond the Great Park. But I *am* Smith. Sorry about that."

"Why are you so keen to marry—settle down so early? At your age, don't you want a bit more freedom?"

"What a dreadfully old-fashioned idea about marriage! Yours is a matter of bondage, is it?"

"No. But we've two children. Children bind you."

"Not if you don't have them. There are devices now, you know."

"Why bother to marry then? Why not just live with the man? Almost as common these days as the 'devices.' " She didn't reply. I looked at her carefully. She started to finger the gold choker round her neck. "It's you who used the word 'marry,' you know. 'Marry him' you said."

"Yes. That's what we've arranged," she said shortly. "I *like* the idea," she added sharply.

"Means more freedom?"

"Of course! It *is* freedom, being with who you love."

"I see. But the formal marriage part: that's just a piece of paper. Or a church. Are you a church person?"

"I'm not *not* a church person."

"We were married in a town hall—in Italy. But it's all the same thing, just a formal recognition, nothing to do with the real business of marriage. It's just these days, without children, people tend to live together. . . . But then, as you said, you have a particular vision of things. A hope, you said: you want to get to it."

"Don't you?"

"Yes. I want to get across this damned great continent: 'Coast to Coast,' and I haven't even reached the first coast yet." It was my turn to avoid the issue. After twenty years of marriage—this wasn't something I was moving toward anymore. I'd rather lost the trail there. Perhaps, I had thought, being in Africa, being away for three months, would help me pick it up again when I got home. Home? There was another thought: home was twelve weeks further on, and I was still traveling away from it, not toward it. This trip had all the markings of a sort of penance for me—a hundred days in the wilderness, a real one now, surrounding us, all the way to the horizon. And I had willed myself here, to this preposterous land. This was punishment for something, all right. At least Eleanor had come out here on a happy pilgrimage. I was running away from hope and she was making toward it. I hadn't come out to Africa to die, like Mary Kingsley. But in two weeks here I saw now exactly what she had in mind. Mary Kingsley had lost her father and mother; I had lost Eleanor's "particular vision," exactly that— merging lines of destiny and all the other happy human coincidences one hopes to move toward in life. I wasn't going to die in Africa, I hoped. But I wished I had something to move toward.

We were silent now. And I was glum. "There's really not very much to see," I said eventually to the boys in front, looking out at the razed landscape.

Alain stopped his chewing and turned to me brightly. "There is a Bantu proverb we have: 'The road does not enlighten the traveler as to what he may find at his destination.'"

"Yes, indeed," I answered, as the long, unenlightening road unwound.

The African was dressed in a tattered lounge suit and jaunty trilby hat, like a Forties spiv—an unusual, indeed an illegal outfit, I thought, in Zaïre. But what really caught my attention as we stopped by the roadside shop an hour later was the monkey the man held up. Its tail was arched back and tied round its neck—and he clutched it by the tail, like a handbag, its arms forked out in front, so that it appeared about to spring forward at any moment, struggling free of its captor. Then I realized the monkey was dead.

"Bush meat," Alain said, when he got back with a packet of cigarettes. "Very nice, very happy, very expensive." He looked at the monkey enviously. "When the Belgians were here," he went on, "one good meal every day. Now one a week—maybe."

"What would it cost?" Eleanor asked. The man had come over to the minibus now and was flourishing the monkey at the window. She didn't like it. But she didn't withdraw her face—anxious to confront every African experience head on, I supposed. The monkey's eyes were still open: a real little organ-grinder's monkey. It was strange to think of monkeys, not in a zoo, but available like this, in the wild; to eat.

"Many, many Zaïres," Sammy said. "A hundred Zaïres."

"*DEUX cents*," the man outside said anxiously. We drove off.

"Funny. But not funny." Eleanor closed the window.

"It's the caviar of the country. I saw them in the market. Tiny, black-glazed bodies. They smoke them, the carcass splayed out on a sort of wooden crucifix."

"Yes," Alain agreed, "and down here in Bas Zaïre they do it best. We will show you—there are many places in the villages."

Eleanor made a little grimace.

"This is Africa," I said. "Not Windsor Great Park. You must know about Africa? Mustard said you were looking for some of those Congolese masks. And those chicken feathers and old claws you have from the witch doctors' stalls. You like Africa?"

"I *love* it." She turned, enthusiastic. "But not the smoked monkeys, I think."

"Part and parcel."

"Yes. So I like part, not the parcel."

A little further on, coming down off a hill on the outskirts of a village, groups of matchstick children were stalking up the banks on either side of the road. They would hover like birds of prey—before pouncing on something hidden in the tufts of scanty bush. "They're looking for mice," Alain explained. "To eat—of course," I said, beginning to get the hang of these rural food supplies. Alain nodded.

An hour later we stopped at the big Protestant mission hospital at Kimpese, a whole settlement just off the empty road—long lines of old umber-washed, single-story colonial buildings surrounded by a ring of tents and shanty shacks, where hundreds of families seemed to be camped out on the withered grass. Vijay had told me about this hospital, recommending a visit: it was one of the few—one of the best—hospitals in Zaïre, he'd said.

A big, rubicund Zaïrean administrator, a boxer dressed like a banker, showed us round. He opened the door of the X-ray room with a flourish. A ragged African was writhing about on a chromium operating table, groaning in some deep pain, a look of terrible outrage on his old, white-stubbled face. He was surrounded by numbed relatives or friends—and a hurried, nervous woman in a white coat. She was trying to take his blood pressure, pumping up a rubber band round his arm. Meanwhile, as if from this pumping, the blood seeped from rags about his stomach, dripping over the side of the table. The Administrator closed the door. "A hunting accident," he told us blandly. "Looking for bush meat?" I asked. The man nodded.

"That man we saw in the X-ray room," I asked Alain as we left. "Do they *shoot* the bush meat here?"

"No, no," Alain assured me. "That was a row: a family fight—with knives. They fight here in the countryside, most often." He opened a new package of chewing gum, before adjusting his green cravat in the driving mirror. Alain was a city man; he drove a peach-colored Cadillac in town. These country folk, he clearly implied—well, they weren't civilized: how could they be? Sammy, on the other hand—more of a country bumpkin, from these parts indeed—was obviously most impressed by everything he'd seen at the hospital. "For you not well," he said. "I would be there—so many good beds, good people. I would be better there very quick." But all I had in my mind then was the look of the old African as he lay in the X-ray room—eyes wide, astonished, as his blood drained away in a little rivulet. It was his expression on the smart operating table—one of outraged, unbelieving astonishment, like an animal in a slaughterhouse—that stayed with me.

Later, coming in toward Matadi in the evening, there was a splendid granite railway bridge over the road, Stanley Bridge, where the legend, cut in big letters beneath, loudly proclaimed how this railway in 1898 had "Opened up the Congo to Civilization."

We got out of the minibus to look at it. "So this is your Stanley?" Eleanor said. "That you've come searching for."

"Mine? Yours as well. He was British after all."

"Yes. But hardly much to write home about—in these parts."

"Look," I said as we got back into our seats. "I'm not out here playing sides, you know. I'm trying to see *both* sides."

"Good for you. What time do we get to Matadi? I'm tired."

"I'm looking for Roger Casement down here as well," I went on, elaborating on my fair-mindedness. "And he was certainly on *their* side, the Congolese. He saved them, almost single-handed, with his report when he was British Consul here."

I told her about Casement. Surprisingly, she had vaguely heard of him: "The Irish rebellion? And wasn't he queer—or a German spy or something?"

"No. He just became an Irish Republican. But, yes—he liked boys."

"Doesn't seem like the Irish somehow, does it, being queer?"

Eleanor was tired—and nervous for some reason. It had become warmer now, as it darkened, coming down off the mountains, nearing sea level. She rolled her sleeves up and started to scratch her arms vigorously.

Later, when it grew quite dark, passing through the mud hut villages near Matadi, the driving—hitherto along an empty road—became more difficult. Long lines, whole regiments of people in Indian file, walked along either side of the narrow strip of tarmac—women mostly, their heads bent low in our headlights, carrying immense bundles of sticks in straps against their foreheads, the men walking like lords, empty-handed, ahead of them. And all were the same chocolate color as the night, so that we were often nearly upon them in our minibus, before either we or they had to swerve violently.

The little mud huts were everywhere now, on both sides, running back into the darkness of the bush, a few with unglazed windows where a faint candle burnt inside. There was no electricity. And it was all very strange to me. The people were like large dark ants emerging from these mud structures, walking endlessly in long lines with their great burdens, up and down the road. But what went on inside all these dark or barely lit huts, I wondered? That's what I wanted to know: what actually *happened* in all these little earthy cells during the long 12-hour tropical night? I couldn't even imagine the thoughts, the words, the style, of the humanity that lived here. This was Africa just out there. Not the Africa of the Memling bar, but the real thing. And I knew nothing about it, couldn't even imagine the human coincidences, the destinies of the people inside those mud huts. I might have been fair-minded—but just out of sheer ignorance.

This road, and the railway nearby that the Belgians had cut through these formidable mountains eighty years before, had certainly brought me no closer to these people. Had they brought them "civilization"? It seemed unlikely—and perhaps that was all for the best. But what was I doing here, more lordly than any of the local men, sweeping by in this smart minibus? They were eating mice further back up the track—and killing themselves with knives or in shooting monkeys. The people in these mud huts might have been Martians. My journey down that road seemed quite absurd. And I felt the awful dislocation of travel now—where all the objects in it, and of it, faded, disappeared, and the threads home were lost as well. I was free-floating, as we went down toward the lights of the city—desperately looking for moorings. Eleanor continued to scratch her arms.

The boys shared a room in the great six-story granite-bricked Metropole Hotel in Matadi, with a tiled interior courtyard and open terraced corridors, arched and pillared, all the way up to the top: a bit of Portugal set up here on a rise overlooking a neat, palm-filled public garden with the old colonial *Mairie* opposite, and the port down a steep hill at the back. Eleanor and I had separate rooms, next to each other, at the end of a long corridor. I left my bag in my room and scuttled down at once to the bar for a beer. Here was a mooring—a cold Primus, sitting up on a stool next to a red-shaded lamp—the wooden counter smelling of old gin slings, an advert for "Stella Artois" above the Ricard bottles: here was a world I knew, at least.

It wasn't that hot, for it was still the dry season down here. But it was worse than Kinshasa in a way, for the weather was close, a hint of permanent thunder in the air. I found I was sweating, shaking. The cold beer eased that a little. I wondered what Eleanor would do when she came down. Make for the whisky? The hell with it—if that was what she wanted. Though she hadn't much money left—just a few hundred Zaïres out of the thousand I'd lent her. But when she arrived she asked for a cassis: best behavior.

She sat up on the stool in a fresh pair of jeans and a white silk shirt, still moist after another bath or shower, and I told her how I couldn't seem to get my hand on the pulse of the country: how out of place and unnecessary I felt, how the mice and the monkey and the hospital and the long lines of ant-like people with their great burdens—how it had all, not appalled me so much as remained quite distant from me, things seen soundlessly beyond a double-glazed window, how unreal it all was to me in fact; only terrible in the abstract, when you thought about it.

"Oh, I didn't feel that. Just the opposite. It was all perfectly real to me at the time: I *felt* the awfulness then. But now, when I think about it, I feel nothing. What's for dinner?"

There was a menu on the counter. "*Côte de Porc Blackwell*" I said, looking at one curious item. "I wonder who he is, or was?" I remembered the Reverend Mustard's confidential news: "Upriver, they're eating each other now again. . . ." I told Eleanor of this hungry vision.

"So—we're eating missionary then tonight—the Reverend Blackwell!" She laughed nicely—and that was another mooring.

A rugged, weatherbeaten, middle-aged Belgian in a bush jacket joined our table halfway through the meal. The small restaurant was empty and the man—a big strawberry mark below one cheek—was looking for company, bringing his glass over with him from the bar. He'd had a few beers already. He was an engineering contractor, he told us in his thick colonial patois, down from Kinshasa—an "*enfant du pays*," he remarked with great assurance, involved in building the huge power line project, running from the Inga Dam just above Matadi to the copper mines in the Shaba province, a thousand miles away to the southeast.

"This country's a paradise," he said, getting into another beer. His English was more American, and colloquially fluent. He was no fool— though in every other way he had all the markings of a typical *gros belge*. "Europe's finished," he went on. "Damn great dirty cities, motorways, drugs, hippies. I never go there now, if I can help it. My boy looks after me here," he added thickly, appreciatively. "He really does. Anything I want. A good cook: steak, whatever I want."

"Where do you get the steak?"

"Up from South Africa. There's plenty of it."

"But the Africans round here are starving. Mice, monkeys—"

"Bullshit," the Belgian interrupted. "No one is really starving here. And they've always eaten monkeys. And mongoose, too. Great delicacies. You've heard too much mission talk—and UN aid talk. And read too many lying articles about President Mobutu. What do you want them to eat in the countryside here—*pâté de foie gras*? And you expect *democracy* here—your Houses of Parliament? They just need one strong man in Zaïre—that's the way it always was in Africa—and they've *got* him. Anything less and there'd be real chaos here, like in the Sixties— and don't you mind about mice and monkeys. I was *born* here—*enfant du pays*. I know what it's all about."

His was the common white attitude in Zaïre, common to all the Belgians certainly. The few of these old or new colonialists left in the country condescended to it now, excusing their plunder here by praising their servants; calling Zaïre a paradise allowed them to forget the hell they'd made it. And yet there was some truth in what the man said. Democracy here was hardly an answer, certainly. The lies rested in what he and most other white people here always failed to say.

"No. I'm not suggesting Westminster here," I said.

"What then? Apart from a strong man—Mobutu? Oh, he's not your sort, or mine. But he's *their* sort: and that's what's supposed to matter. Okay, so he's a mad paranoic. And ruthless—a little Hitler. Corrupt, extravagant. But you people—you're far too quick to foul-mouth African leaders, because they're not like your Mrs. Thatcher or Mitterrand, counting the pennies. Well, that's dead right, they're *not* like them. And they're not really corrupt in our way either. What you call corruption here—it's just life. Always was. A bearing of gifts—tribal tribute. Only now it's in dollars or a new Mercedes, not chickens and cows."

This wasn't new to me either. This was all just a little further along from Harry's view: "Let the Africans get on with things—in their *own* way." It was all part of the apparently encouraging "Why not?" view we took of Advice in the West—when what we really meant was, "Why should we bother?"

The Belgian called the waiter over then, paid our bill before I could stop him, and tipped the man heavily. Both of them were very happy. It was a perfect master-servant relationship. On the way out Eleanor asked him if he knew about the dam they were building up beyond Kisangani—knew the Belgian company from Brussels which her fiancé worked for.

"Hell, they're not going to build that dam. Not now: no money. I know the company, though—they were out here surveying it."

"You know Robert?" Eleanor asked him, giving his surname.

"Yes. I met him here, a month or so ago. Tall man, glasses, dark hair?" Eleanor nodded, eyes alight. "We met up in Kinshasa at the Intercontinental. Told me it was all over. He's gone back to Brussels."

CHAPTER
7

The Horror

"He's lying. Or else he's got the wrong man." Eleanor seemed quite unconcerned, happy, as we drove round Matadi next morning getting various permissions to visit Inga Dam and Vivi. Then we went down to the ferry. The city was built into the side of a steep granite gorge on the southern bank of the river, so that there were no straight roads anywhere, only narrow winding tracks up and down the slopes leading between shabby warehouses and some shops filled with nothing. In the center, around the hotel, the red-brick Catholic church and public gardens, the old colonial business quarter remained: a few white stucco buildings with long verandahs and steep red corrugated iron roofs: the *Mairie*, Customs and Excise, District Health Board, and such like. But the life had gone out of them. That sort of European business had disappeared in this little central area, no bigger than a village. Life in the city had become a matter of basic survival and that went on everywhere these days, in each household of its 300,000 inhabitants. There was no civic or administrative center any longer, around which people gravitated, gathered, looked for help. That was another discredited colonial concept. It was each man for himself now.

The port lay at the bottom of a steep hill below the hotel: a big port, but with only six cargo ships at berth and without any activity around them whatsoever. The only cargo I could see were hundreds of new Citroën and Renault cars all lined up on a quay: tribal gifts, I imagined, except that with the shortage of petrol, they'd be stalled there until they disintegrated in the ferociously damp-and-dry climate.

The river was the only interesting thing in Matadi. Though it was over a mile wide at this point—even at the very head of the estuary, and in the dry season—it none the less rushed through the wide gorge with the pace of a mountain torrent, a great gray-glinting sheet of water in permanent flood, where from the ferry quay you could clearly see the vicious twirls and eddies far out in the stream, rising up, curling over hidden rocks, leaving a trail of tossing whitecaps behind. It was a real monster of a river: there were no boats out on it, no bathers or riverside cafés—nothing of that sort. The water here, in its khaki tank color, seemed armor-plated—armed against you, out to get you: "Nzadi" in the local KiKongo language—"the river that eats all rivers."

The ferry came across as we waited—moving diagonally, pushing at full power way upstream against the current, before drifting back to our jetty. A few trucks, filled way over the top with green bananas and men camped out on top of them, drove off the boat—and then the foot passengers came, dozens of tiny old women bearing immense bundles of dry sticks on their backs, held by a single strap across their foreheads, bent double. They were like slaves building a pyramid. They never looked up, never faltered, and the men with them never carried a thing. Eleanor got out her camera and took some photographs as we went across. "My goodness," she said. "It's wonderful!" The two boys stayed in the minibus, heads flat out against the seat, eyes closed, nursing hangovers. After we'd left them last night at the hotel they'd obviously gone on for a real binge somewhere in town.

Driving up through a cutting in the rocky gorge on the far side and getting onto the flat land above, the countryside changed. It was fertile here, between the sea and the mountains: almost pastureland, with cassava and banana plots beside each breeze-block homestead on the roadside, and big forests just visible on the horizon beyond. Now, coming through a village, there were furniture shops on either side, right down the length of the road. Eleanor needed some furniture, she said. We stopped outside one of the larger emporiums, where there were whole suites displayed—garden chairs, beds, tables—mostly in white cane, Habitat-style and good-looking, too.

"But you haven't got the money," I said. "And we haven't got the room."

"That chair—those ones—if you put cushions on them: they'd be splendid in the garden. Or in my bedroom in Kin."

"Listen—you'll never get any of it into the minibus."

"They can send it on."

We were surrounded now—the first European shoppers here in years, it seemed. *"Trois, quatre, cinq cent Zaïres. . . ."* The African owner was jumping up and down with excitement, a tall man with a scarred face in a sort of kimono, thin as a rake. He would eat for weeks after this. "Listen," I said to Alain, taking him aside, "she doesn't really want any of this—it won't fit, she's no money. . . ." But Eleanor was sitting now in one of the grander chairs, an indoor model, elaborately carved in hard wood, high-backed, like a throne.

"*Cinq cent Zaïres!*" the African said. "*C'est rien! Rien!*" And such was the man's anxiety and enthusiasm now that he and two of his assistants picked up the whole chair, with Eleanor still in it, and carried her like royalty to the minibus, where they opened the tailgate and tried to push both chair and smiling queen inside.

"No!" I shouted, closing the tailgate. "We haven't the money, or the space. It's nonsense." I gave the man 10 Zaïres for his trouble and we drove off.

Eleanor was upset. "You are an old miser," she said.

"No. Just practical. And you're coming on this trip with me. I'm paying Harry for it. You can buy something smaller later on."

"Don't want anything smaller later on. I wanted that—those cane garden chairs. And who are you to—"

"Well, you *wait*—till you meet Robert: then you can go out and play homes and gardens with him. I'm trying to find Stanley's old house in Vivi, not set up house here."

Beyond the village, every few miles or so, carved out of the bush, were little roadside cemeteries: Christian burials, for there were crosses over most of the mounds of red earth. But these were only a minor part of the interments, I felt: polite gestures made to appease the local missionaries. The real native faith took over with the elaborately painted wooden tombstones and triptychs behind each mound, where the dead were set up as they had been in life, pictured in the most naïve manner, with shiny house paint, in their best suits and hats, or in togas and dazzling cotton print dresses. Some of the grander, larger graves showed whole families partying round well-laden tables while, in little embrasures and tabernacles set into these wooden backings, kitchen implements had been stored: knives, forks, dishes—the wherewithal to feast through eternity.

We'd stopped to take a closer look. Eleanor was taking photographs. The boys didn't like any of this, I could sense. They stayed in the minibus and looked the other way.

"Just like the ancient Egyptians! All these grave gifts and things: see them through the afterlife." Eleanor surveyed this mournful patch carved out of the bush with happiness and excitement—as if the dead were rising in front of her.

In one of the little tabernacles, at the back of the cemetery, she found the remains of an old, deeply rusted revolver. "That's a good idea: protect yourself in Hades."

"You'd be one up on your relatives certainly—and your enemies— if you could get the ammunition."

"But look!" She peered deeper into the recess. "They've left that as well." I bent down. There were several rusted shells right at the back.

"No fools, are they?" she asked.

"No. I never thought they were. Just, I find it difficult. . . ."

"Lot more sense in their lives, really, than ours. Makes sense—taking all these sort of things with you."

She was bending down over the grave, almost on her knees, her gold hair a splash of living color against the dead earth; vibrant life in this gloomy place. And suddenly a fit of mortality swept over me. I didn't want to be here anymore. Life in these parts was bad enough and death seemed all the emptier. "Let's go back." I said.

"Just a moment." She took a 5-Zaïre note from her bag and pushed it into the little cupboard, hiding it underneath the revolver. "There," she said. "For the shops in heaven."

On the way back to the minibus I wondered why Robert had dropped her—how anyone could drop such a woman.

A little further on we turned right off the main road to Boma and now we were on a rocky, desert track leading ten miles up to Inga Dam on the northern bank of the river. When we got there, on a steep granite headland, we looked upstream on a mile or so of continuous, withering rapids: a fantastic, tumbling flow of whitecapped water, the whole scattered with jagged rocks, like teeth which the current rushed at before flying up in great mist-spumed waves, then rolling away in deep troughs, corrugated, thunderous tides. The scale of the river here, high up on the headland, was difficult to judge. There were no trees, no houses or people anywhere to compare it with in the rock-filled valley where the water was. From this distance, 1000, 1500 feet above it, the river might have been an Alpine stream in flood once more. It was only when you looked downstream, at what you knew was a vast dam, that you could begin to gauge the size of the flow here, for the dam was insignificant, a garden wall built off the main torrent: a game that a child had set up at the edge of nature.

It was here, in 1877, just above these Inga falls, that Stanley lost his second-in-command and great friend, Frank Pollock, the Kent fisherman who, unable to move with blistered feet, had drowned in one of these same whitewater whirlpools, along with several Zanzibaris. Stanley's whole troupe had been on the brink of death at this point in his three-year journey in any case. There was no food to be had in these cruel hills. And it was obviously at a premium that day, in the same place, a hundred years later. Beneath the dam the few local workers made a real living trapping catfish and *crevettes* and selling them to visitors. And I realized now one reason for Alain's earlier enthusiasm about visiting the dam: we drove back with a great, slimy, whiskery catfish nestling in banana leaves behind us, the minibus soon smelling like a fish shop in the damp-gray heat.

On the main road again we started to look for Vivi—a village, somewhere nearby on the northern bank, where Stanley, sent back by King Leopold to open up the whole region, had set up camp, creating the first European settlement in the interior. His original wooden house was still there—kept as a small museum, Alain had said. But Vivi wasn't marked on my map. It was somewhere off the road, between the dam and Matadi. The locals would surely know. But they didn't. We stopped time and again. "Vivi?" They shook their heads. "Go back," one man said. "Back to Matadi. Then along the bank. You must walk. There is no road."

"But there must be a road. There's a museum there. Stanley's old house."

"Stanley?" They shook their heads. "You have some friend Stanley there?" We drove up a track that petered out. It was hopeless. On the main road again we met a very smartly dressed African: immaculate beige Kaunda suit, tiny beard, two-tone leather shoes, gold-rimmed specs, carrying a man's handbag. We gave him a lift. He was going back to Matadi, a high school teacher there. He explained the position: Vivi, by road, was thirty miles away, along an impossible track—or it was now. The only way to get to the village was to walk, along the river bank; there was a path cut in the rocks. You could do it in two or three hours that way.

"But why go there anyway?" the little man asked. "There's nothing in Vivi." Yes, he knew about Stanley's wooden house, the first European building in the interior, all that. But it had all been burnt down a year before—some children, a cigarette end, a bush fire. No one really knew, or cared less, obviously: the house had just disappeared. "But anyway," the schoolmaster went on in good French, much more eagerly now, picking his nose hungrily, bearding me as a vital contact from the great world. "What I'm interested in is international affairs. I have studied them. I wish to be a diplomat. You will help me there."

I expressed doubts about this, and he became indignant. He had an ambitious, hurt expression, the face of a frustrated intellectual: thin, querulous, dissatisfied—a clerk betrayed, where a rising tide of Third World expectations had long ago engulfed him. He waved his little black handbag about, bristling. "But why are you interested in this man Stanley?" he demanded. "That colonial robber?"

"I'm interested in the history here, that's why."

"Well, why not *our* history then? Why yours—which was just one of murder and exploitation here? Nothing but that."

The man had a point—just as the Belgian engineer had, about the irrelevancy of democracy and European values in Zaïre. And at that moment I felt further away than ever from Zaïre, from the concerns and attitudes of both these men I'd met: African schoolmaster and Belgian engineer, black and white. Here in Zaïre, I saw, there was no room for any middle ground, any objectivity. Black or white, you either loved or loathed the place. As a native you furiously condemned the colonial past, yet longed for escape into a sophisticated European world; as a European you conveniently forgot about King Leopold and tipped the waiters double. Inquiring strangers like me, vaguely archaeological, aiming for balance, had no place here at all. I was like a butterfly collector on a battlefield where the lines of attack had been drawn up years before, the war still raging. The Belgian would go on getting rump steak from South Africa and the children would continue to eat mice. That was the condition of things in Zaïre today, as it had been in the colonial state. Poverty and wealth were the only constants, then as now. History was irrelevant. Yet it existed here—somewhere—and I was determined to go on looking for it.

"Yes—I wish to be a diplomat," the man said again. "You will tell me all about that."

Paris, Rome, Vienna—I thought. We never got to Vivi, just as he would surely never get to these places. Longing for opposites, we would both be frustrated. There was no history for me here and no future for him in my world. There weren't First or Third Worlds here anymore, north or south: we were people from different planets.

We crossed back over on the ferry again and spent a second night at the Grand Metropole Hotel. The Belgian engineer had moved on and there was nothing to laugh at on the menu that night. Early bed —and the next morning, crossing the ferry once more, we drove on to Boma, the old capital.

* * *

"Well, bloody hell, Alain, *why* does nothing move anymore in this country? You produce your own oil. And that great dam we saw yesterday—only two of the six turbines are ever in use. You could light up the whole country here, end to end, with all that hydroelectric power—if you wanted. . . ."

We were all having lunch at the Mabuilu Hotel on the Boma waterfront. "We are finding our feet," Alain said at last, speaking French. "It takes time."

"But you're not. You're going downhill. I know copper is depressed these last few years on the world markets. But you still get a lot of money for it, one of the world's major producers. And uranium—something like half the West's needs are supplied by Zaïre. All our nuclear bombs. Where does all the money go?" I knew of course that, after Boots had taken his lion's share, it went to the Army and then to his ministers. But I wanted to hear Alain's ideas on the economy.

He was sharp enough, though. "Not here," he said, looking round the empty dining room. "Though I can tell you," he leaned forward confidentially, "about the oil. The refinery we built, beyond Moanda: it can't turn the crude into petrol. They have to send it out again—up to Pointe Noire in the French Congo. Then we have to import our own oil back, for hard currency: that's why."

"That's crazy."

Alain shrugged. "That's life. We have no part in the matter—you can see that." Sammy meanwhile, reveling in the Grand Hotel meal, was looking at Eleanor happily, adoringly, oblivious to our economic discussions.

"As for the dam," Alain went very correctly on. "We have to build the power lines first, before we can use all the power."

"But the dam was completed ten years ago."

"Takes time." Alain moved on to a seedy-looking *crème caramel* in the set menu. I shouldn't have tried to goad him. It was stupid of me. I would have learned far more if I'd let him speak in his own time. Casually, imperceptibly he might have told me some real truths then. Now he knew me only as one more bumptious, arrogant foreigner. I wiped the sweat from my brow. I'd been heated, annoyed, frustrated. But that was hardly an excuse. It was my job after all, to handle people carefully: the tactful reporter. All I'd done now was to scare a useful informant off.

"Have a beer." I tried to make amends. They both took another beer. But Alain was no more forthcoming. He'd clammed up about life in his country. Or else he'd told me all he really knew. "We have no part in the matter—you can see that." And I could.

After lunch, lying down in my bedroom looking out over the estuary, I thought I had a dose of coast fever coming on: I was dizzy, sweating, shaking. But I hadn't forgotten to take my malaria pills or the water purifying tablets. It was just anger and exhaustion. It was just the Congo, I thought. Harry had told me all about it—how the climate here was debilitating, an oppressive mix of damp and dry which always got you in the end: sooner or later, black or white, you'd come to suffer it. There were some places on earth not made for man—and this Congo river basin was one of them. It was as simple as that: the lack of fuel, the human chaos now—these were just incidentals. Here, certainly, was "one of the dark places of the earth." Conrad had seen the Congo perfectly, eighty years before. And there was no difference now.

There was a nothingness in the air, of this nothing country, which no human spirit could ever properly surmount. It wasn't Arab languor or a Mediterranean *dolce vita mañana* that slowed you down here: it was a malign aura set up against you, some active constituent in the atmosphere which continually irritated or depressed, so that there was no comfort even in sleep or sheer laziness. In the Congo, even in dreams, you couldn't escape the bug of unrest, unease, fear: a fear that you had trespassed out of man's domain, detribalized yourself, denied your human origins—and would shortly pay some terrible price for your betrayal. Here, in this empty country where one might at least have felt free, you were yet in chains; with no understanding of your surroundings, no foothold in reality, you were always aware of the implacable force, the vengeful aspect, something towering over you, looking at you. It was a world where you couldn't define the threat, lay your hands on the fear. That was the most frightening thing.

Later that afternoon we all went out, walking through the old capital of the Belgian Congo. It was like moving through a ghost town. The long line of ancient, wooden-framed, verandahed houses facing the wide stream were all deserted. Nothing moved on the empty dockside; a line of rail freight trucks lay permanently stalled beneath the silent derricks. A flotilla of decaying dredgers and paddle steamers rusted away in the smooth brown current that gave across to a mangrove-covered island and the flat alluvial delta land running away for miles beyond that. A single weather-yellowed, sun-stained cargo ship lay at anchor in the roads, lines of washing over the foredeck, rudder and screw high out of the water, an empty hulk, just an emblem of tides and travel now. Beyond it, upstream by the bank, the jagged prow of some long-drowned smaller boat poked out of the water, sunk there years before in the mud.

"There!" Alain said, pointing at this rusty protrusion. "That was one of Stanley's boats."

"Was it? Surely not—that would have been nearly a hundred years ago." Alain was trying to humor me, I felt. He knew of my anxiety to trace this man—and Roger Casement, too. Though no one in Boma had ever heard of him. We asked several people, including a local guide we'd taken with us. Half a dozen of the wooden buildings by the riverside were sufficiently old to qualify as his Consul's house. But no one had ever heard of Roger Casement, this savior of the Congolese people eighty years before. Stanley they knew about. The great hollow baobab tree on the riverfront which he'd camped inside after his three-year journey in 1877 was still there, a vast stunted growth with a dark space inside. I went in and tried to think of Stanley here in the gloom. But the place was dank, cold, dirty, reeking of urine: it had served many years as a *pissoir*. Behind the tree was a small brick hut with the word "Archives" on the door. I went in expectantly. But the room was used as an empty bottle store now, except for one dusty corner with a small bookshelf containing half a dozen French *série noire* novels, grandly stamped inside with the words "Belgian Cultural Centre, Boma, 1947."

Behind the riverfront was the wilderness of the old Belgian town, a grid of overgrown, tree-filled streets, once tidy boulevards, where the remnants of great imperial villas lurked in a tangled profusion of weeds, creeper, and long grass, the jungle taking over again. No one lived here now. The African town lay behind on the hills. To one side of this old central residential quarter lay what must once have been a public park, or perhaps a racecourse in the old days—a great swath of rough grass-land now, made over in the middle as an airstrip. To the south of this, behind a breeze-block wall, imprisoned in a rising jungle, lay other crumbling villas in a colonial Charles Addams style. But these had been originally set out, not on a street, but in acre-sized gardens, plots of land with outbuildings, almost farms.

We walked down a laneway here, pushing through great clumps of palm and banana trees, until we came to one of these ruined *manoirs*. The steep tin mansard roof was almost off, the first floor partly collapsed, the whole house subsiding now, about to be buried in a wild undergrowth. Squatters had taken over some of the outbuildings.

"This," our guide said. "This is Mr. Casement's house."

I was paying him, of course, so the man was determined to come up with some trumps—though the Consul's house, I was certain from old drawings, had been right on the riverfront. Still, I didn't want to disappoint him. We went inside, by a back door, where the building was still fairly firm. The first room we came to might have been a parlor or library once, for one could just see the remains of some old flock wallpaper and the marks of shelves. But the room itself was like a greenhouse now, where exotic weeds and saplings had grown up through the floor and hungry creepers come in by the windows—rampant moist growths in a tropical hothouse. I pushed gingerly through the damp, musty smelling blooms. I thought of bats and snakes—so that when there was a sudden scuttering over by some rubble in a doorway I nearly jumped out of my skin. It was a monkey, long-tailed, with a small, white-muzzled, quizzical face. It sat up on the rubble for an instant, chattering angrily; then it was gone. I retreated. Eleanor had found something by the back window, where the frame and sill had been tied up and held together with wire.

"Look." She plucked the taut strands: vague musical notes emerged. "Piano wire," she said. "Maybe this was the music room: Schubert duets and candlelight."

Our guide was very pleased. "Yes, piano," he confirmed immediately, proud of his English. "Mr. Casement—he was great piano player. Very good, *very* good. He play the piano here many often times. I hear him!" Eleanor plucked the strings again—somber, ironic twangs.

Going back toward the river, as it began to get dark, we came on the old European cemetery, only a few of the tallest headstones still visible above the hungry vegetation: a Portuguese nun and a Danish officer, one of the many mercenaries from King Leopold's deathly army. Monkeys rustled and scattered out of the long grass, scratching their backsides on the broken graves.

No one came to Boma now. But only seventy years before, in the rubber boom years, it had been the crowded gateway to a tremendous El Dorado upriver. And surveying these ruins all round me I had that feeling again, of the utter absurdity in all this vicious, useless Congo endeavor. In other countries, tracing such European arrivals and adventures, one had to go back hundreds, even thousands of years—and the adventurers were still there. But here, right in front of me in Boma, were the ghosts of a European presence that had come and gone in

little more than half a century—a country opened up, colonized, plun·
dered, and abandoned all in the space of a single lifetime. And what
remained—for black or white? Where was Stanley's "civilization" now?
It lay broken between an angry, detribalized schoolteacher who thought
himself a diplomat, and a Belgian engineer, praising the strong leader
who allowed him to eat rump steak while native children searched for
mice. It was absurd.

We walked down and looked out over the deserted river again, the
Atlantic only a few miles away: Stanley's "hateful, murderous river."
And I wished I could have taken a boat home from here, there and
then, just as Stanley had in 1877. Instead I had to turn back and cross
the whole of Africa, on the very edge of it now, night falling—still the
dark continent, where I had already clearly seen the shadow of Conrad's
Mr. Kurtz—and heard the echo of his words, "The horror! The horror!"
coming from somewhere far up this same river, in the heart of the
darkness.

CHAPTER

8

Amateurs

*B*ack in Kinshasa there was no news of Robert, and the two big passenger boats were still out of commission, grounded—or sunk, for all I knew—somewhere far upriver. Eleanor and I were confined to the city again, returned like escaped prisoners after a desperate break. And yet in some ways it was a pleasure to be back, among the few certain comforts of prison, the sure routines. Coffee and *oeufs au jambon* every morning on the Memling terrace was one of these, often with Harry, gossiping, swapping pages in the Brazzaville papers, pulling on one of his blue-whiffed cheroots—Harry in his cricket pullover: pear-shaped, ebullient, ironic.

I finally got round to asking about this pullover of his, the morning after we got back from Boma. "Oh yes—all part of the appropriate coloring: I'm a frustrated Englishman, ever since I lived there during the war. I had an apartment just off the Park, behind the Dorchester, Dean's Yard. I surely play cricket. 'Twelfth Man' they call me—good men and true—up at the American school odd weekends. I do it base-ball-fashion—great swipes. Fear of God stuff. Among the Indians here mostly; a few British, some Rhodesians. Vijay likes to umpire. And Mustard plays, too: bats southpaw, loses his temper, won't accept the decisions. He and Vijay had a real *bagarre* last time. The Reverend said he wasn't out—had to get the bar boys to carry him off the pitch in the end. Still a lot of things you haven't seen here, Mr. Hone."

"Maybe I could get a game?" I said, thinking of home again, those summer matches I was missing: sweet water, willow, greenswards beneath the flowering chestnuts and copper beeches, in Adlestrop, Chipping Norton, and Great Tew. Home: I never dreamed of home in Kinshasa because I thought about it so much in any case—the problems, failures, the delights. By the time I slept I had exhausted all the dreams of home.

"A game—why not? But will you be here long enough?" Harry smiled.

"Will I ever leave? I'm going to see the missionaries again. Try the Baptists this time. See if they have any boats going out. I'll give it another week. I can't come all this way to the Congo and say I've never been out on the bloody river. I'll have to get something."

Harry sighed. "There's a Frenchman I know. Works with Les Voies Fluviales, the government River Authority. I'll ask him—maybe he could get hold of one of their boats for you. They're supposed to keep the navigation open here." Harry laughed, the old eyes twinkling. "Dredge the channels, fix the marking buoys."

"That'd be great. I'll give it a week. If not, then I'll just have to fly out—up to Kivu, one of those cargo flights you told me about. Do the lakes and volcanoes up there, the National Park. Then on to Rwanda —if I can get into the country. They say the border is closed. Though not getting on the river. . . ." I shook my head.

"Plans, plans. . . ." Harry sighed for the lost world of plans. "And the girl?" he asked. "The lovely Eleanor?"

"I told you what the engineer in Matadi said: her boyfriend went back to Brussels."

"But she doesn't believe that?"

"No. I don't think so. I'm seeing her this morning."

"Problems," Harry said. "If she finds he's really gone."

"Oh, I don't know. She's off the booze. Not a drop in the three days we were away. Loved the whole trip."

"But she was traveling then, remember? Being stuck here is something different." Harry paused, draining the last of his coffee. "It's funny —a girl like her, everything going for her, holed up in that dump waiting on some creep who's dropped her. It doesn't figure. Must be something else behind it. She's smart as hell in every other way. And it doesn't figure either—your being here. Out of all the countries in the world—you *chose* to get stuck out here. You *chose* this crazy place."

"Oh, when I was a child I dreamed of crossing Africa—a great journey, coast to coast, like Stanley."

"So it's romance you're after—a dream?"

"Yes—originally. Except it can't be anything like the dream. And it isn't."

"But you really knew it wouldn't be—didn't you—before you started out?"

"Maybe. But there are other reasons: problems, running away from things maybe. There's that, too. Besides, it's just a job. I came out here to do a job for the BBC—that's all. I'm being paid for it. I'm lucky to travel."

"That makes sense. But not really *your* sense. You're not that sort of person: 'Just doing a job'. . . ."

"If there's any other reason—I tell you, I don't know what it is right now. I'm looking for a real reason—for being here—if there is any. Or maybe, I just travel for the sake of traveling, dream of leaving—even when there's nowhere to go and nothing to see."

Harry stood up. "Well, we should get you a game of cricket anyway. And Michel's throwing a party soon. Up in his big house on the river. Historic house—you'll like it. Used to be the British Consul's here, in the old days. You'd know about that—an Irishman, called Casement. Wrote a famous report years ago, about the slaves and the massacres up river."

I looked at Harry, amazed. "But that house was *downriver,* in Boma, not in Kinshasa. I was looking for it all the time I was down there. No sign of it, no one knew—"

"Of course not! It's moved up here now." Harry bent forward, his age-mottled knuckles on the table, making the most of this serious matter. "That house is up here, Hone, I tell you: a transport of dreams—the only sort that works here these days."

Upstairs in the Amethyst Hotel Eleanor was drunk. The window was open, giving out onto the narrow gutter between the two tin roofs and she walked now, in a loose-weave housecoat, between the bedroom and this makeshift terrace, combing her hair nervously with her fingers, scratching great red blotches which had risen along both forearms. Outside, beneath the chair on the guttering, lay a pile of letters, papers, a tipped-over wine bottle. The wind-up gramophone was on—some scratchy Parisian accordion tune from the Forties, the other old seventy-eights lying all over the floor. The room was no longer like a new pin. Clothes and trousers were strewn everywhere; a view of Bruges Cathedral lay smashed by the bed; two of the big tin trunks were open, half-filled like waste paper baskets with her other bits and pieces rescued from the flea market. Unhappiness had swept through the room like a wind.

"I'd been thinking," she said with false brightness, trying not to meet my gaze, "of going home." I picked up one of the records: Georges Guetary—"Une Boucle blonde."

"Home again, home again, bears!" she went on, the bright child again now as she returned to the terrace where she picked up some of the letters and papers, came back, and threw them on the bed. They were long letters, some still in their envelopes which had Belgian stamps, I saw.

"He's not coming back then," I said. "I'm sorry."

"Oh, even if he does—why should I wait? Why even forgive him— if he does!" she added, the prima donna now, a confident drama in her voice, ringing out over the Bal Musette music: *"Chaque samedi soir. . . ."* The singer made a meal of this last repeated refrain in the song, giving the dying fall, an air of impossible longing and regret.

"I don't know anything about Robert, of course," I said, "but it does all seem a bit curious."

"My wanting him in the first place, you mean?" The needle spun in its last groove with a hollow, empty sound.

"No. Just drinking over him. Being unhappy that way."

"I told you—I like it."

She wasn't as drunk as she had been on the first night I'd met her. She didn't stumble about. She was coherent. The drink was really only in her face, her blotched, baggy eyes that wouldn't look at you, in her lightheaded detachment.

"See if you can forget him without drinking. Don't let him go on taking it out of you, in that way, even when he's not here."

She turned away again. "I drank before. Before I met him. That's probably why he didn't come back."

"Why then? What's the real problem?"

I thought I'd take the first opportunity—to dive in deep for the truth, now that drink seemed to have released facts in her. But she clammed up, scratching an arm furiously. Finally she looked at me instead, silent, bleary-eyed.

"Do you have anything for your arms?" I asked at last.

"What should I have? It's a sort of eczema: goes away when I drink. It all came on when I went down to the coast and didn't have anything."

"I don't believe it—"

"What? It's true—the scratching all goes away, with drink."

"No—your hanging around here. There's no point. You'll come a cropper, drinking out here. So do something. Cable home. Get some money out. Then get home and drink *there*. Plenty of pubs and friends in Windsor. Drink at home, if you have to."

"Your best bossy mood again!" She swung round, more hopeful, one of the letters in her hand, waving it at me. But it wasn't one of Robert's letters. It had a British stamp. "Came this morning. They've sent the money out—a proper draft to the bank here—£500. So I can stay here. I don't have to go home now."

"Stay *here*? But why?" I must have looked very surprised, for she laughed then, a scatty, drink-fed trill, yet which seemed to release all the nervousness in her.

"Don't look like that," she said, coming over to me, gazing at me clearly at last. "You needn't worry—I don't have to sleep with you. Just want to kiss you." And she kissed me, on the mouth, before I could do anything about it, wriggling against me for an instant in a little dizzy spasm.

"I have to go see the missionaries," I said when she'd stepped back, and she laughed again.

"Oh dear—just for one kiss?"

"No. Just for a boat. See if they've got one going out anywhere."

"Can I come too—if they do?" She was anxious now behind her flush.

"But you said you were going home. You're half-packed." I looked over at the tin trunks.

"That was last night—before the letter came. And before you arrived. Seeing you. . . ." She stopped, turning away so as not to see me now. "Traveling with you," she went on finally. "It worked down in Matadi. It was fun. What's wrong with that?" She turned back with her most candid look. I said nothing. "And traveling with you," she added firmly, "I don't drink."

"No."

"It's only being stuck here."

"Yes. Well, of course you can come—if I'm going anywhere."

A bargain had been struck, a commitment made: another "Invitation to the Voyage"; another, but quite different, dream of escape offered.

> Imagine the magic
> of living together
> there, with all the time in the world
> for loving each other,
> for loving and dying . . .
> the suns dissolved
> in overcast skies
> have the same mysterious charm

for me
as your wayward eyes
through crystal tears
my sister, my child!

A missionary boat would take us both somewhere far upriver, losing ourselves from all our previous worlds, lovers beneath those overcast skies. A lovely, irresponsible dream of escape swept over me: second chances, happy journeys, vibrant life. But just then Eleanor started to tidy the room, picking up the records, straightening the chaos, taking her trousers out of the tin boxes and setting them all up neatly again on the clothes horses, reasserting a domestic propriety about the place. And I saw that I had offered her a different dream—not myself, but more a dream of order and competence which she saw in me, of realistic organization, successful plans—all the firm attachments to life that she believed I possessed, which would form a cure for her if she was with me.

"When I've been to the bank," she said casually, "I'll buy you lunch. At the Pergola." And suddenly it seemed as if I was in Europe again, where people made such friendly promises, ordinary businesslike appointments every day, where they could all be kept. Yet I think I wanted the chaotic freedom of Africa then, through her—wanted something of Eleanor's mad, drink-swept world, just as she needed my sanity. She found my seriousness attractive; I looked for escape in her irresponsible laughter. As I left she put on the Georges Guetary record: "Une Boucle blonde." It wasn't the sad accordion stuff, just the opposite—it was light operetta. It spoke of flirtations, summer evenings in Paris, a frothy romance, a blond kiss-curl, a skin-deep relationship: something entirely aboveboard and proper, at least. Surely that was all Eleanor wanted from me.

"I'll show you the only boat we have here—or the remains of it." We walked toward the riverbank, across the coarse, broad-leafed grass where an African was religiously hacking individual weeds out with a large panga. On a small bluff above the water lay an old boiler, a rusted barrel-like affair, but where the rivets in the plate were still firm, the Victorian ironwork intact.

"It's from the *Peace,* the first boat we had in the Congo," Owen Clark, the assistant general secretary of the mission, told me. "We got it in the 1880s sometime, not long after Stanley first arrived here. A rich Leeds merchant—the 'Miser of Headingley' he was known as—Robert Arthington, gave the mission £1000 to build it: sent out to the Congo in sections—carried up over the mountains by an army of porters from Boma, then put together here on the Pool: a little further down-stream, actually, where our first mission post was, where the Chanimetal boatyards are now. Must have been a wonderful boat: specially built. Steel hull, with only an eighteen-inch draft, special fold-out wire screens against the poisoned arrows—and this boiler was a new type then: you could raise steam in ten minutes to get away from the cannibals."

I touched one of the old steam cocks, the remains of a pressure gauge. And there was that nice, romantic feeling of touching history then—not in some museum, but here *in situ,* by the Congo river, just a few yards away from where that history had taken place: touching one of the vital mechanisms which had created that history. The rough fingers of some irascible Scots engineer, or some daring but mechanically in-efficient cleric—or even the Bishop himself: these hands had once moved across, lovingly tended, this bit of old cast iron—which had been a vital lifeline then, the wood furiously stoked in beneath this very boiler as the cannibal war canoes bore down on the little steamer, the same ferocious river tribes who only a few years before had seen—and some-times found—their lunch and dinner among Stanley's declining troupe.

Owen Clark must have felt something of all this, too, as we looked at the boiler. "Of course, that was the great age," he said. "Explorers —and missionaries you never hear of now. Only Stanley. But there were others, just after him, who did as much discovering this country. Baptists—but they were great explorers as well. George Grenfell—he was the man who really charted the rivers here. Not Stanley. And Thomas Comber with him. And Bentley, an extraordinary linguist: first identified and translated many of the river tongues. And Thomas Lewis at Kimpese. Do you know his book *These Seventy Years?*"

"No, I'm afraid not."

"They were all with the Baptists. The histories and journals are still in our BMS offices in London. Some wonderful stories. Of course, now we're all part of the ECZ: Eglise du Christ de Zaïre. Presidential decree some years ago. The Protestant missions had to amalgamate."

"Yes. I'd heard that. All fifty-seven varieties."

Clark nodded, smiled. "We were the first, though, down beneath Mount N'Galiema. We moved up here about 1900. We still own about ten meters of the riverbank here."

"But no boats?"

"No. The last one we had was the *Grenfell*—a small steamer in the Thirties. Long before my time."

We walked down right to the riverbank, through reeds, an overgrown path, the river no longer part of the mission—and the water itself quite empty in any case now, a gray, hurrying, mile-wide sheet in front of us where you could see the movement only in the endless passage of sprouting, mauve-green water hyacinth, clumps of endless vegetables, as if someone was carefully tending a vast market garden somewhere far upriver, but was then tossing every bit of produce into the water.

"Is it true?" I asked. "That some missionary, years ago, brought a bit of that water hyacinth out here from Belgium, just to plant locally in a pond—and it spread everywhere else afterward?"

"I don't really know. But it's the only real traffic on the river these days."

"But how do you manage—without a boat? Aren't you really a river mission?"

"Yes. We were, certainly. And we still have over 130 primary and secondary schools in Zaïre, as well as clinics, hospitals. Many of them upriver. But we've no money to build a boat the size we'd need, for cargo."

"I'd always sort of dreamed of a Bishop's boat here, a small paddle steamer, with cane chairs and an awning on the foredeck."

"Yes. Well, we had something just like that. But the *Grenfell* was the last of them."

"Do none of the missionaries have any boats now?"

"The Catholics have some. One or two. But they keep them upstream, on the middle river, for getting round the tributaries. And the Swedes have some boats on the big lakes. We only have a small plane, which we share. So I'm sorry—I can't really help you about boats."

We walked back toward the compound. Two old tin-roofed houses, on high metal stilts, with first-floor verandahs and mosquito-netted windows, lay to our right. Clark took me over to them.

"There—they must certainly be the oldest European houses in Kinshasa—nothing but a tiny fishing village then. The wood is Scots pine—prefabricated. They were brought out here in bits and pieces, too—set up in our first station; then moved down here. Made to last. Real Scots job. Look—do you see these little metal cups halfway up, set round each stilt? Filled with paraffin. The termites get up that far —then drown. That's one reason why they lasted. We still use them, of course. Most comfortable buildings on the compound, up high like that—nicely ventilated from beneath."

"They knew what they were doing in the old days, in the way of mod. cons—wasn't all 'heart of darkness' stuff."

"No. That was a very Victorian idea of Africa—home-produced, for home consumption. They'd heard all these tales of savagery, cannibalism, fever—which was all quite natural out here. But equally naturally the high-minded Victorians saw it all as a very dark business: eating each other. Though perhaps that was sometimes no more than good home economics: a useful food source. But I think it was the deaths out here in Africa, particularly in the Congo, that really made them see it as dark. You came out here—and almost certainly chances were you died. The mortality rate among the early whites was fantastic."

"But the missionaries didn't see it as 'dark'?"

"I don't think so: only in a spiritual sense. They were practical people as much as anything. Had to be. Of course, they had their problems—like all the Europeans here. Some of them, if they didn't die, had to be shipped home: unbalanced—became too much for them. Takes you that way, even now. The Belgians, I'm told, lost a lot of their administrators out here that way: a man would arrive at work one morning —find he couldn't even say *'Bonjour.'* Just seized up."

I looked at the two old stilt-houses again—steep-roofed with dark verandahs, quirky, haughty: solid Scots Victoriana set up on this Pool nearly a century before. And still here: sturdy relics. Yet they were alive, still lived in. For the first time I felt a real continuity of European history in the Congo, an image that I'd searched for in vain down at Matadi and Boma, in Stanley's village house and Casement's Consul's building: both destroyed now. It was this almost complete lack of any previous human creation, I realized, which disturbed me more than anything in the Congo. This was what was most malign in the air of the whole place—why you couldn't identify your fears here. It was because you couldn't see the past in this country, either African or European. You couldn't sense people moving, living, creating an existence in the Congo before a few years ago. You couldn't put bricks or mortar or even old grass huts round earlier lives in this world where all these structures had been destroyed or eaten up by the jungle again. There were no ghosts in this country—that was the real fear: the aura of man in history had been suffocated here, wiped out by the all-embracing nothingness.

Other people, much more than I, had felt the empty terror of this country: had come to name it, lived and died here. And just as some cantankerous old Scots engineer might have lovingly tended the boiler of the *Peace* so, too, serious, pale-faced young Baptist missionaries from the Scottish glens, Yorkshire dales or the puritan Midlands had climbed the open stairways of these same houses eighty years before—about to define their adventure, perhaps feel that first uneasy touch of fear. Behind the dark mosquito mesh, as I looked up at the verandah windows, I could see the shapes move: early Baptist clerics—the flash of a white Victorian linen jacket, a dog collar, an old pith helmet. . . . A black ancestral Bible brought by one of the young men to table at his first dinner, among his older hardened colleagues: the way, perhaps, he had hidden the book on the bench beside him as they talked, not of God, but of the mundane practicalities of their work: blackwater fever, malaria, early deaths. I didn't know the facts of the history in these two houses. But I could clearly imagine them. The facts were all there, if I'd wanted them, like a perfume in the old Scots pinewood. The houses were a marvelous reassurance to me, confirming my part in nature, placing me in history as I looked back out over the grim river which told me, gave me, nothing.

We walked back to Owen Clark's dark little office in the compound. An African was hammering away at an old, high-carriaged typewriter. A radio-telephone stood on another desk, with a notice above it, in French, stipulating that only "Government Authorized Users" were allowed to man the appliance. An ordinary telephone—dusty, unused-looking—lay next to the radio.

"Doesn't work, I'm afraid," Clark explained.

"I know. . . ."

"Oh, I think it would work—if we paid the *matabiche:* 100 Zaïres a month sweetener to the post office chaps. But we don't anymore. They have a nice line in the telephone business here these days. If you don't cough up enough, they bill you for other people's calls. Suddenly found we'd been phoning Hong Kong and Rio every day. The last bill was up in the stratosphere. We didn't pay—so there it is!" He looked at the telephone. "A museum piece! Like the boiler."

"But how do you run 130 schools—clinics, hospitals—from this headquarters without a telephone?"

He smiled. "Apart from the radio—rather back to messages in a cleft stick! That's how."

Owen Clark was a bright, friendly, informative, unafraid man—very far from any fuddy-duddy missionary image. For the first time in Kinshasa, in Zaïre, I felt I was talking to someone entirely sane, someone quite unaffected by the mental coast fever which destroyed all balance, all logic in the end and made everything a nightmare. Clark, though he'd been here quite a time, remained free of the infection; he believed—and retained a humorous hope as well. It was part of his missionary job, of course. But the man had to come long before the work in these parts—I saw that: a certain temperament, something fine and firm, was necessary for any real survival here. The job came later. Clark thought straight, was knowledgeable, aware of all the Congo's history, a part of it himself now. There was nothing of the barely controlled panic, nerves, the harsh irony, malice or the sheer dottiness, which gave an unhappy coloring to all the other whites I'd met here. And I saw how it was possible to survive as a European in Zaïre if you were honorable. Owen Clark had that gift. In the world of total corruption and misrule which I'd come to inhabit I'd forgotten that such people even existed. Clark would never be shipped home as a case of mental fatigue, a nervous wreck. But that could be my fate, I thought. I rather lacked the missionary spirit. Unless I could find some suitable cause or creed. What was there? Not much. As I'd told Harry, I didn't really know why I was out here. Oh, yes—to do a job, for the sake of traveling, because things weren't ideal at home. But there was nothing of the Holy Grail in any of these things. No, I don't suppose I even had the energy or the passion to seize up here and be carried out on the Sunday midday flight, the Brussels Rocket. I would always manage a dull *"Bonjour."* I said goodbye to Owen Clark at the gate of the compound—thanked him, envied him. What a dull thing it was, I thought: this lack of passion.

Eleanor, on the other hand, was full of beans at the Pergola where we had lunch—it was just behind the National Bank, where she and Sammy had spent most of the morning extracting her money, and now she very nearly flourished it in my face. Like me she'd obtained it in a huge brown envelope, stuffed full of old 5-and 10-Zaïre notes.

"I didn't take it *all* out," she said indignantly, when I'd commented on the dangers of carrying this bulky treasure trove about with her. "Just enough to pay you back, pay my room and meals for another week—and maybe hire a boat now. We could go fifty-fifty." She looked at me warily, stalking hope.

"The Baptists have no boats."

"So you said. But no need to be so depressed. If we both pay—well, we'll have enough to *hire* a boat."

"There aren't any boats for hire. One of Harry's boys checked that —unless for some astronomical sum."

We sat in the open, out on the empty restaurant terrace. Above us, as if to mock our talk of travel, the lovely fan-shaped leaves of the travelers' tree, a group of emperor palms, towered into the gray sky, the dry leaves creaking now and then, rustling vaguely in a breeze that would never be enough to move the blanket of cloud. Beneath our feet, creeping in through the withered border from the road, alley cats cried plaintively, paws meekly together, praying for titbits. I felt depressed. And I must have looked it, too.

"Listen," Eleanor said, putting her hand across, touching mine. "It's a start. Now that I have some money."

"To what?" I noticed the red blotches still running down her forearm.

"Well, we can travel—somewhere. That's what you're out here for, isn't it?"

Her eyes were still weary, still baggy with the remnants of drink. But nothing else about her suggested alcohol. She was back in her Renoir-riverside-café mode: candid, nervously flamboyant, a sun-dappled girl— if there'd been any sun. As before, she'd made a startling recovery, drinking nothing but mineral water. The idea of travel, I suspected, was the drug for her now—a need which I would have to sustain in her if she was to stay sober.

But still I procrastinated. "Yes," I said. "But I'm crossing the whole of Africa. The Kivu, Rwanda, Kenya, way up to Lake Turkana, the far coast, then Lamu. Another two months at least. You don't want all that."

She beamed, gave a small sigh. "I'd like to ... I'd like to do ..." she was about to say "all of that." But she compromised. "Well, maybe not all. But some. Why not? I'd love to." She looked at me—just as the cats did round our feet—with the intense, happy concentration of an animal about to be fed.

"I may simply have to fly out of here—it'll hardly be real travel. Up to the Kivu, then on into Rwanda, if the border's open. A plane from there to Nairobi. It looks like the only way. It's not real travel—all the boats and lake steamers and trains I'd meant to get. Like I told you—"

"Yes. You *did* tell me, but that's all right—we can fly! No fear of flying.

And maybe that's the best way for me to get back home in any case, via Nairobi: I can easily get more money there."

I munched my South African steak and gave a fatty bit to the most persistent of the cats. Then I gave Eleanor what she wanted. "Yes," I said. "All right—if you'd like that. We can do that."

And now she laughed, not the scatty, drink-fed trill anymore but a sober shout where you could sense the joy of a real person at last.

"What's so funny?"

"You! You look like God, so serious, up on a mountain. You know, you have problems, too, don't you?"

"What?"

"You stop doing things—before you've even started doing them. That's one problem."

"The old puritan ethic, I'm afraid. I should have been a missionary."

"Well?" she said.

"Well what?"

"Well—smile! Try it."

I tried it. Not a complete success. But not a failure either.

"Tell me, would your wife mind—my being with you?" Eleanor asked abruptly.

"I don't know. I shouldn't think so. That's part of the problem we have together: not knowing such things."

"I'm sorry. I didn't want to pry—"

"Oh no, go ahead. Marriages often come to be like that."

"I asked because—if I were her, I'd mind."

"But you're twenty-three—or something."

"That's not really the point."

"No. I suppose not."

Eleanor laughed suddenly, a poopy juvenile little splutter.

"What?"

"I thought you were going to say, 'I'm twice your age'—as you are."

"Maybe. But with you that's not really the point either—is it? You could be as old as I am in some ways."

"Yes?" She looked at me, trying to hide her eager fear, the fear of youth thinking itself too young, longing to be confirmed in the sophistications of age, when you would then be too old.

"When you said, that morning with the terrible hangover, that you were bad, nervous with people—but that you had a particular vision, a hope which others didn't share. That seemed the voice of experience somehow, not youth."

She was disappointed. "That was just hurt. Hurt can make you seem old. My parents divorced—oh, it's common enough, and I was in my mid-teens. But it still hurt. You see, I thought when I came here, to Africa, that I'd find the balance, control."

"Last place I'd have chosen for that. Drive you to drink—"

"Yes. But I thought there'd be so much to *do* out here: among real people, real problems. I thought I'd find the real thing here, be *busy*." She stopped suddenly.

"Yes, but busy at *what*, though? You're not a tourist or a missionary or a Third World architect yet. Or a tropical housewife. How would you have been so 'busy'?"

She paused, stumped again. "With things—I don't know." Then she suddenly identified the things and rushed on. "Well, yes, with African history, anthropology, art. Congolese masks, the tribes, ecology of the rain forests, the witch doctor's business with chicken feathers. And the languages—there are over 200 different river tongues on the Congo, did you know? And apart from all that—the wildlife: flora and fauna. Butterflies, moths, strange fish, strange animals—like the okapi: do you know about that? Half-giraffe, half-antelope—somewhere up in the Ituri Forest. And the people, too—the pygmies. All that—plenty to think myself busy with."

"Africa as a sort of undiscovered university and natural history museum for rich amateurs: the Victorian idea?"

"Yes!" she shouted with enthusiasm. "Just that. Why not? What's wrong with amateur interest?" she asked defiantly.

"Nothing," I said. "It's rare, that's all. It's not popular now. In fact, that's rather my line. That's why they don't much care for me up at the Embassy. Don't know why I'm here. Like everyone else about Africa these days: they expect a one-track response—just the hard stuff: mindlessly dull political interviews with some *Citoyen Commissaire*, or stories of African murder, loot, and rapine—disemboweling the nuns. A lot of people like that best. But, my God, they don't like the wider view, the amateur interest. And that's me, very much me. We're sisters under the skin there. Only trouble is we can't get out and about to express that sort of interest, locked up here studying the ecology of hotel bedrooms."

"We *will* get around," she said, happy now. "I know we will." And as if to confirm this the palms began to stir again above us, the trunks creaking minutely like doors opening. "And I'm glad you think it's all right—being amateur. Not trying to save the world. Not pushing and shoving. Robert was so ambitious."

"No—I think that's fine. Ambition is usually hell. Just to push around a bit—without the pushing and shoving: that's ideal."

"I know it sounds rather dull," she said. "Everyone has such terrible expectations."

"Nothing wrong with it. Except—" I thought of Owen Clark and the Baptist missionaries by the river. "Except, yes, it lacks a message —just pushing around. Lacks passion: Paul on the road to Damascus sort of thing. The blinding light department. There's still all that, I suppose."

We looked at each other a little sadly—two amateurs, not pushing and shoving, but lacking a light.

"Yes." She reached across and gripped my hand, a nervous, unfulfilled gesture: the same sort of involuntary, unfulfilled spasm she'd made with me when she kissed me that morning.

9

Quotidian Dreams

*L*ater that afternoon I took Eleanor round to see Vijay about the
rash on her arms. Vijay shared rather smart consulting rooms in a
downtown apartment building near the British Embassy, where five
minutes earlier he had opened the door and rolled his eyes at us both
very nervously, as if we'd come about an abortion. And now I sat on a
sunken chrome chair looking at my knees, and wondered. Today had
been a beginning for me of an almost conventional life in the city, where
you had sensible lunches, by appointment, and saw reasonably sensible
doctors afterward. Eleanor and I might go shopping later in the small
Belgian supermarket round the corner, where Africans lurked outside
the entrance and all the steaks and orange juice had been flown in direct
from Brussels or Johannesburg. We'd pack the cartons into the back
of a station wagon, returning to some bougainvillaea-shrouded villa in
the old Belgian residential quarter. . . .

Like a gift only just out of reach, the real, quotidian nature of the
city—for Europeans—began to offer itself to me: the sort of life one
might have led here as a permanency—with a wife, girlfriend, with a
woman at least. And for the first time I didn't feel the need to travel,
to escape from Kinshasa. Apart from the hopeless boats and the erratic
chances of getting a cargo flight up to the Kivu, I was having trouble
getting a visa for Rwanda. Its border with Zaïre seemed to be open and
closed on alternate days: open when the Rwanda Embassy in Kinshasa
was shut and vice versa. I'd been warned, too, of strip searches and
immense bribes at the frontier—and there was a vicious dog in the
compound at the Rwandan Embassy every time I went there. I was
beginning to have nightmares about Rwanda. How much safer, nicer,
I thought, to stay in Kinshasa; to pretend I was an inhabitant, a *Kinois*.
Eleanor seemed to offer me every good reason now—not for traveling,
as she wanted—but for staying put. With Eleanor I felt I could easily
come to like Kinshasa.

Whereas she, with me, dreamed of sharing the open road, I was looking in her for the domesticity I had lost at home. She was searching for adventure, the thrill of the African wild, pygmies, poisoned arrows, and mysterious beasts lurking in the distant rain forests; I was looking for afternoon tea and *Middlemarch* and crochet work. As the days passed I began to hope the big passenger boats would remain upstream—grounded, sunk, thoroughly abandoned. I needn't have worried—they did.

Each morning, first thing before breakfast, I would leave the Memling and walk down toward the port, looking for the big green and yellow funnels poking up above the rusting warehouses—and they were never there. Each morning I returned to the café terrace for *oeufs au jambon* and coffee with Harry. Each day made me feel more a *citoyen* of Kinshasa, where I began to take on the colorings of the place—the knowing walk, assured step, learning every nook and cranny, every turn in the central city; identifying each beggar too, outside the Post Office or the National Bank—by coming to recognize each separate deformity or frightful mutilation.

The awful shabbiness of the place, the despair and hurt of the gray city, which at first had so oppressed me, came to seem an appropriate setting for my new life. The grubby and unpromising can only suggest promise, I thought. At least they cannot disappoint. So I began to find a quality of hope in Kinshasa which I would not have looked for in some obviously lovely city, like Paris or Venice. Like Eleanor I came to see the best in the worst—the distinct possibility of finding something wonderful in the dust. Like Eleanor? No, because of her. For the time being we filled each other's needs. I offered her a firm towrope out into the churn and flood of life—and in her I found an anchor, a still center of attention and interest. We came to share our lives.

Eleanor would never come to my room on the top floor of the Memling. I imagine, since she didn't drink now, the memories were too painful there. The world of drink, that long drunk of hers in the weeks before she met me, together with all the mornings after—these experiences, for her, became objective, I suppose: the flaws, aberrations of another person.

Yet I wondered how real the change, how permanent the reform was? Just as a woman, facing labor again, will forget the earlier pain of childbirth—so a drunk, sharing the same psychological trick, may spend years off the bottle, forgetting the horrors, so allowing himself to take to it all the more vigorously one fine day—another miraculous alcoholic conception, another screaming birth in the drinks cupboard, leading to final defeat, a life of permanent shakes, without any forgetting.

I didn't know Eleanor that well, wasn't sure how much her sanity and sobriety really depended on me, or at least on my continued availability—or whether, like the tow rope on a glider, all she needed from me was lift-off into calmer airs, where she could then maintain her own course and equilibrium. After all, I thought, the hurts she had suffered or brought on herself were probably such that only a permanently intimate relationship could cure them. And I didn't think I could offer her that. Knowing this or sensing it—or coming to discover it—would she lapse? Was I to be the reason for one more such failure in her—harbinger of the longest drunk?

Of course, as she'd so rightly said, this was my problem—to see more flaws than hope in every experience offered, and thus to avoid events before I'd even started on them. So, as an alcoholic hides the bottle, I tried to forget my own secret badge of failure then. It was time, with Eleanor, to cure myself. If I could keep her off the drink, she could take me, lurking at the gateway, into life.

We met, often enough, in her room at the Amethyst. The little corridor-shaped space with its red lantern on the top floor became for me, as much for her, a home—a temporary home which we would soon travel from, for I brought all my African books and maps over, laying them out on one of the tin trunks, next to its neighbor where the chicken feathers and old mandrake roots from the witch doctors' stalls had been set out again. Here, on these makeshift altars, we played at Africa and African travel, opening the maps and plotting paths, summoning up all the mysteries of the dark continent, making dangerous treks through the rain forests, avoiding the poisoned arrow ambushes, without ever leaving the safety of the narrow room—the iron dormitory bed Eleanor lay on, the spindly chair I took beside the tin trunks, helmsman tending map and compass on these imaginary voyages.

"This road—from Kisangani northeast: it says it's a 'Route Améliorée,' " I said one afternoon looking at the big Michelin map. "An improved road as far as Batwasende. Then partially improved up to Isiro."

"Yes?" Eleanor said eagerly.

Getting to Kisangani, I knew, was only a distant possibility now, a thousand miles away on the great bend of the river. But that didn't matter. We had thoroughly imagined Kisangani, accounted for it: we were there already.

"There's a British Leyland man in Kisangani that Harry told me about: an Englishman—Regional Manager, for Land Rovers and trucks. Knows the whole area backward. Maybe we could hitch lifts with him, as he went his rounds. Harry said we probably could."

"Fine." We were getting a lift from the British Leyland man.

"Then there's Epulu Station," I went on. "Turn right about 200 kilometers after Batwasende. It's the only road right, can't miss it. Epulu is in the middle of the Ituri Forest, where the okapis are supposed to be—and the pygmies. Guide book says you can't photograph them, though."

"I don't want to. Just see them."

"You were keen on photographs, down in Matadi."

"That was to show Robert. I won't need to show you, if you're there."

"It says the okapi were all killed off during the troubles in the Sixties—and they were rare enough before that. Probably none left."

So we imagined the okapis. Part-zebra, part-antelope, giraffe-necked and donkey-eared, we made it an even more mythical beast, stalking it through the rain forest, the man from British Leyland with suitable initial transport, now with two pygmies as guides, cutting our way through the thick jungle with pangas, a carpet of foliage above us, the creeper and leaves so densely matted that we could only hear the animals overhead—monkeys, baboons, birds: colonies of unseen wildlife crashing about and chattering in another world, an aerial kingdom in the sun, where we were in darkness. Thus still unvisited, Africa became the continent of my childhood again. Enclosed in the small room in the Amethyst, I might have been back in my bedroom at home in Ireland, nearly forty years before, hearing the ivy rattle in the cold rain outside my window, where I imagined myself, beneath the sheets, tented in some warm jungle, the leaves caught in a tropical downpour.

We explored a pocket Africa then, a map shaped by our needs, cut by our imagination, a portable continent where visas and transport were unnecessary; where shanty towns and shoddy hotels were not marked; where sunstroke, mosquitoes, and black mambas never arose. Africa became a game. And we were children of the game.

"In Mount Hoyo," I said later that afternoon, reading from the guide book, "at the very top of the Kivu region, there are these strange grottoes. And an extraordinary waterfall, a cascade: the Venus Staircase."

Eleanor lay on the bed, hands clasped behind her curls, staring up at the ceiling. " 'In the grottoes,' " I read, " 'a thick layer of bat guano carpets the ground. The multiple galleries and mazes are a stupendous sight. The column stalagmites and stalactites could be the wondrous work of an architectural genius. Elsewhere, lines and inscriptions are visible on the ceilings, in the form of ancient script, animal paintings. Who is the Champollion of the tropics who will decipher these mysteries of the equator?' "

We became the new Champollions—crouching low, with flares, moving through the caverns of these Solomon's mines, searching for Gagool's bones, the only real mystery of equatorial Africa then. Over cups of tea from the dainty art-deco tea service we became Stanley and Livingstone as well. Though soon the good Doctor, left behind at the great lake, faded from the scene and we were traveling on alone with Stanley, among his troupe of Zanzibaris, attacked each day by the ferocious cannibals, going down the Lualaba to the sea.

" 'The first war canoe had two rows of upstanding paddles,' " I read from Stanley's journal. " 'Forty men on a side, their bodies bending and swaying in unison as with the swelling barbarous chorus they drive her down toward us. In the bow are ten prime young warriors, their heads gay with feathers of the parrot, crimson and gray: at the stern, eight men with long paddles, whose tops are decorated with ivory balls, guide the monster vessel; and dancing up and down from stem to stern are ten men who appear to be chiefs. . . . The crashing sound of large drums, a hundred blasts from ivory horns, and a chilling chant from two thousand throats do not tend to soothe our nerves or to increase our confidence. . . . Our blood is up now. It is a murderous world, and we feel for the first time we hate the filthy, murderous ghouls who inhabit it. . . .' "

Eleanor raised one of her long legs from the bed—straight up without bending it—as I finished. Then the other leg, as if she were sleepwalking stiffly and horizontally. "That's better," she said at last.

"What?"

"That sort of traveling—in the mind. Get so much further that way."

Suddenly she pushed herself up. "It's all so incredibly remote, that Stanley expedition: cannibals, a quite new world, first white man and all that."

"A hundred years ago, with your African interests, you'd probably have been part of it. Like Mary Kingsley: pushing through the rain forests. There's a bit here by her, from *Travels in West Africa,* about the great forests: '. . . a world which grows up gradually out of the gloom before your eyes. . . . As it is with the forest, so it is with the minds of the natives. Unless you live among the natives, you never get to know them: if you do this you gradually get a light into the true state of their mind-forest.' "

" 'Mind-forest'—that's wonderful. But we're not doing much of that, are we—living with the natives?"

"No. Maybe we should go down to the Cité more often. Meet some real Africans."

All the same it seemed unlikely that we would live among the contemporary natives. Their history in the simple, brutal confrontations of the past were more vivid—imagined future travels more congenial. We were just travelers, after all—not philanthropists, anthropologists, missionaries, Third World experts, charity workers. We were amateurs. So, when the roar of the Grand Marché died outside in the evening and the light turned suddenly from gray to dark, we returned to an Africa of the heart, letting the black flow in through the open window, our own red lantern dead. The dark seeped up over the print of Bruges Cathedral and soon smudged the poster of the Brussels World Fair. In the thick shadows now, where we could no longer see each other, we were entirely free, without any visual contradictions, to invent our own travels, for soon there was nothing to be seen in the room to remind us of our stationary plight. The real maps, the guidebooks, the compass were entirely obscured. It was then that the game could properly begin.

I would usually start it, with some factual comment, and Eleanor would continue it—a disembodied voice from the bed, a voice not like hers, though she didn't consciously change it: a lighter or much darker voice, excited, driven to these tones by the parts played, journeys invented, the tales she told.

"It said in the guide book—about the grottoes in Mount Hoyo— that they filmed *King Solomon's Gold* there. Never heard of it. It must have been *King Solomon's Mines*."

"I remember. There was Umbopa, a secret King, who went with them, back to his own kingdom—through two mountain peaks: Sheba's Breasts."

"And the map they found in the little leather bag, drawn in blood by the old Portuguese explorer hundreds of years before. His bones in the cave? Or was the body preserved in the eternal snows?"

"In the snows, eternally preserved," she said. "And there was a great white road, wasn't there—after the mountains: leading to a land of brave people, a place of sweet streams or something. 'But it grows dark,' someone said. 'It grows dark. Those who live to see—will see.' "

"Someone said?" I asked.

"Open sesame—three times."

"That's Arabia, not Africa."

"They knock on the vault with a stick topped by an ivory ball. The man in gray and red parrot feathers and a zebra skin. Tall, huge in the flare-lit shadows. . . ."

"Knock, knock—who's there?"

"Don't be stupid! You've ruined it."

"Sorry. What about the Queen of Sheba?"

"What about her?"

"Try her—instead of the parrot-feathered chap."

"You've spoiled the mood."

"What about going upriver in a boat then?" I said. "A little Victorian paddle steamer with an awning."

"Chug, chug, chug, chug—would the engine go like that?"

"Not really. It would have been a steam engine."

"I can do the poisoned arrows: Scch-fiishe! Scch-fiishe!"

"Not bad."

"You do Stanley—go on!"

"Little Taffy—I can't do the accent."

" 'The ghouls, " she said in a deep, passably Welsh voice. " 'They must be taught a lesson. Hand me my rifle, Ahmed.' I can't do the rifle shots."

I did them for her, clapping the open pages of a guidebook smartly together.

"I think I could do Mr. Kurtz," I said. "In one of his worst moods."

"Go on then!"

" 'Argh! Argh!—the horror, the horror!' "

" 'It grows dark. Those who live to see—will see!' "

It was quite dark now in the little bedroom: childhood dark and we were happy. "Well, where shall we have dinner tonight?" I said eventually, "the Pergola, with the cats? Or go Chinese at the Mandarin?" We made a continent of light between us then, not darkness.

The quotidian life of the city. . . . Of course, with us, it wasn't the real thing. It was the remnants of Belgian colonial institutions and pleasures which we became involved in—in private houses, restaurants, clubs: Le Cercle de Kinshasa, Le Cercle Hippique, the Olympia Casino by the port. We were neo-colonialists. And I hated it all.

We met Harry one lunchtime at the Memling bar. "I hate it, and I hate myself," I told him, "because without really knowing it, I'll just call this place a hellhole *when* I've cleared out—if I ever do."

"Well, it *is* a hellhole," Eleanor said, wide-eyed, amazed. "Do you want to lie about it? I don't understand you—wanting to apologize for the truth. Everybody seems to do that these days—in public, about Africa and other awful things: 'Oh no—it's all perfectly all right: a little corruption, a few bloodbaths. But just here and there. Just old tribal customs anyway.' No one will ever stand up and say, well, it *is* awful —and it's mostly their fault. All these guilty liberal ideas of ours as old colonialists, so that we have to be nice to the blacks and excuse all the awful things they do out here. Well, I'm perfectly nice to them in any case, that's no effort. But I'm *not* an old colonialist, so I'm not guilty, and I don't excuse them, and I still think the whole thing is awful— and this place *is* a hellhole."

"Maybe," I said. "But maybe we've not the right to say that, without living here, suffering it."

Harry smiled. "How long now—three weeks? A month? You'll both soon qualify."

Harry took us on to lunch at his Club, Le Cercle de Kinshasa, the most exclusive club in town, just beyond the Greek Orthodox Church on the Boulevard Trente Juin. There was a large golf course here, right in the middle of the city, tennis courts, swimming pools, a grand white entrance portico. Inside was a long bar, done in heavy browns and yellows throughout, so that, with the gray sky outside, the whole place had the air of a funeral parlor. The Club was nearly empty. A few morose whites sat on stools sipping Cokes or lagers. In the broad hall beyond, odd people came and went, without energy or interest, in track suits, running and tennis shorts, some of them pulling golf trolleys behind them like unwilling children.

"In the old days this place would have been full as a boot," Harry said. "No blacks—all white duck suits and Cabot Lodge tropicals and *'Bonjour Monsieur le Ministre, Bonjour Monsieur le Directeur.'* Now it's pretty moribund."

We sat at a table, sipping Cokes and lagers ourselves, looking up at the regulation photograph of President Mobutu in his leopard skin toque and twirly chief's staff above the bar.

"Surprised the place is still here at all," Eleanor said. "No Zaïreans, though, are there?"

"Oh yes. A few. But they don't come here much. The local professional class who would have come here—they're all in jail or exile now. Doctors, politicians, professors, architects—they're dead or in Brussels or Paris or Washington these days. Boots cleared them all out: possible rivals, you see. None of them here now. All those sort of jobs are done by the few hundred whites—Belgians and French, Germans, that Boots employs himself; a sort of private government, up on Mount N'Galiema. So-called "advisers"—of every sort: Belgian officers, doctors, engineers, money men. A whole corps of people, all paid double in hard currency—and white, too—so he can trust them."

"That's the real neo-colonialism, then? Boots as the front man?"

Harry nodded. "Yes. But you don't see them here. They're up living in the presidential domain, in a special compound. All their own facilities. It works," he added sagely, sadly.

"It would surely work a lot better, though, if all those intelligent exiles could have a hand in things," I ventured.

"Maybe. But maybe they'd be at each other's throats the moment they got back here. That's much more likely. Fine democratic words to begin with—but you'd soon be ducking the bullets. Power, you see: they all want *power* in Africa. Anyone who can sign their name. And no matter how many fine liberal courses they've taken at the Sorbonne or Harvard or the LSE, when they get home they'll do anything—but *anything*—to get it. And that includes knocking people like me, and especially reporters like you, *right* out of the way."

"Boots the lesser evil then?"

"If you'd been here in the Sixties you'd certainly say so."

"It's sad."

"Better than bloodbaths." Harry greeted a friend who had just come in. The man raised his hand lethargically—didn't come over, just went and sat by himself at the bar. As if commenting on this Harry said, "There's really only one thing to do here: hold your own small corner. Private lives."

The next afternoon Harry took us out to the Cercle Hippique beyond the Presidential Domain. Things were smart and run in an old-fashioned manner here: very pukka sahib. Rich, sophisticated, middle-aged women—bronzed, streaked blondes touching fifty in the fast lane—sat feet-up on the terrace sipping Perrier water and *jus d'orange,* looking out over the husbands and horses exercising in a small show ring. Beyond, behind the long rows of neat wooden stables, local grooms mucked out.

A huge, gleaming chestnut hunter called "The Hobbit" from South

Africa looked out over a half-door with a superior air while a bossy middle-aged Belgian woman, big-bottomed, in vast black riding boots, fussed over another great beast in the next stable—where a groom, a tiny dark figure, seemed to move about between the huge animal and human feet, scratching wood shavings and dung into a wheelbarrow. Everyone knew their place at the Cercle Hippique—and it was an old colonial station, the Club immune to change. Things worked here, too, among the remnants of Belgian families from the *ancien régime,* the new short-contract whites from Brussels, the Embassy and UN crowd: the horses had to be exercised, fed, mucked out—no question of that. The members didn't have to hold any corners here: the servants and grooms did that for them.

We went into the *sellerie* where the tack was all neatly laid out— dozens of bridles, saddles, and gleaming bits. The room smelled heavily of oiled leather, long rubbed and buffed, the waxy essence worked into the very heart of the tack. It was a distinct smell, but of Europe suddenly, not Africa. The damp-dry, sweet-and-sour, leprous smell of Africa disappeared entirely in the long room and I was back at home in the tangy, clear airs of some Irish stable, rescued in my mind at least, transported from prison to freedom. I stood there dreaming.

"You ride?" Harry asked Eleanor.

"Too much—as a child. In the Great Park."

"You want to? Maybe I can fix something up."

"I'd love to."

"It's a bit late now. Maybe tomorrow. I'll ask inside."

We went back to the clubhouse, the terrace and the long bar behind which there was another of the obligatory photographs of the President—but this time up on a horse and looking uneasy, as if he'd just been hoisted onto the beast by a crane.

"Don't ask me—yes, there are African members here too," Harry said as we looked around at the dozen or so whites out on the terrace and at the bar.

"They sort of hide in the wood, do they?" Eleanor asked.

"They don't come much."

"I suppose not. It can't be very 'authentic,' all this horse business. Not many horses in Zaïre, are there? In the stables—they mostly seem to come from South Africa."

The bossy Belgian woman with the big bottom came up then and Harry bought her a *jus d'orange* and asked her about the chance of a horse for Eleanor. The lady seemed doubtful.

"Peut-être. . . . Il y a un—"

Her sentence was suddenly broken by the most tremendous explosion from somewhere nearby, like an ammunition dump going up, which lasted several seconds and then reverberated round the clubhouse for seconds after that, rattling the windows, the roof, and the bottles on the bar shelves. Afterwards there was complete silence everywhere, together with a lot of chilled and startled-looking faces. Several men got up and went outside.

"The army camp next to the presidential domain," Harry said. "It's just over the road from here."

"But what was it?"

"A lot of high explosive—one way or the other." Harry grunted. "But no one will ever know—what or why or how. That's for sure."

The huge, secret, dangerous world of Africa lurked just beyond the lovely trees and well-tended lawns outside. Mystery and violence had suddenly echoed round this European oasis. It might well have been the start of a siege for the members of the Cercle Hippique, a return to the bloodbaths of the Sixties. The horses would be slaughtered first, heads and haunches severed with pangas. The grooms would turn traitor next and storm the clubhouse, riding crops turned on their masters. Whips would fly and then the sharp knives: white blood would flood and fizz like Perrier water, the big bottoms sliced like salami. The Belgian woman forgot all about the horse for Eleanor, her face suddenly fallen, anxious. Another country that she had never visited had suddenly run up its colors just beyond the clubhouse gates. Afterwards, before we left, the members took to stronger drink: large whisky sodas and me-dicinal nips of cognac. The Cercle Hippique, which had seemed so sure and firm a thing, hung like a flawed gem at the end of a thread attached to all the vast, irrational body of Africa.

"I told you," Harry said as we left, "the situation is hopeless here. But it could be worse, and the only way to survive is heads down—in your own small corner."

We went on with Harry afterward to his house in the old Belgian residential quarter by the river—back to what turned out to be a pretty palatial small corner.

10

Harry's Place

*H*arry lived on a side road just off the Avenue des Nations Unies, Embassy Mile, the narrow strip of asphalt that faced directly onto the river all the way down from the city proper to the Intercontinental Hotel. The American Embassy was almost next door, with the Greek, Swiss and British embassies only a stone's throw away. We passed their floodlit, high-walled compounds, picked out like tempting seraglios in the night, as we drove up the otherwise shrouded streets behind the river.

Harry's large bungalow, hidden behind a jungle of flamboyant and frangipani trees, was in darkness except for the bluish flames of a fire built next to the gateway, a great half-burnt log which sent sparks up into the night as a group of blanket-wrapped *gardiens* poked at it, sharing cigarettes, on their haunches—nights in the dry season for them a time of withering cold.

A semicircular drive led through the trees to and from a long covered terrace, with tall iron-webbed French windows and doorways beyond. Harry's *gardien* came with us and opened up the place. Inside was a huge living room, big as half a tennis court, running back the whole width of the bungalow, a dining area at one end, the rest given over to a succession of low, armless sofas and chairs set next to small occasional tables. The room was lit by half a dozen tactfully placed standard lamps, switched on by the *gardien* one by one as we went through it, so that successive gentle pools of light spread over the space, gradually illuminating African tapestries and wooden carvings on the wall, shelves of books, piles of recent magazines on the tables. The big room came to life in sections under the lights—floor and corners gradually exposed, displaying carved African statuettes, fetish figures, Congo masks, embroidered rugs where antelopes scampered across the forest weave and native *pirogues* stormed the rapids upriver. Spotlit thus, one after the other, these treasures came to light for us. After our small, separate hotel rooms here were half a dozen Aladdin's caves to be visited through a world of space. Eleanor and I just walked round for a minute, stretching our legs, happy in a house after a month of suitcase life, a house that you could walk through, from room to room. A long corridor ran off at one end to the kitchen, with a larder and laundry room beyond. Two other doors, midway down on either side of the living room, gave on to the bedrooms.

"My quarters," Harry said, opening one of them. There was a bedroom beyond and a big double bed; a dressing room and bathroom opposite. He walked back across the living room and opened the other door, showing us an identical set of rooms, where the double bed was even larger, with a fridge set opposite it which he opened, taking out some cold drinks.

"Hey," he said, walking back with fresh orange juice and Cokes. "It struck me, you know—if you people like to use that other suite, you'd both be very welcome. No problem with me. Colleague of mine was there, but he's back in the States on vacation now. And it's all been cleaned up by Joshua, my boy. No problem at all."

"Oh, we couldn't," we both said, almost simultaneously.

But we did. And that was the start of another life in Kinshasa— where the domestic and the intimate was added to the quotidian. Harry sent down his driver, Alain, with the big Cadillac and we moved our bags and boxes, tin trunks and the old scallop-horned gramophone in next morning. It was Alain, helping us in with all this luggage, who went first and put the lot in the same bedroom, piling it up by the big double bed: Alain who assumed that Eleanor and I were playing doubles, not singles.

"Of course we'll pay Harry," Eleanor said later, unpacking her things, her trouser collection, ranging them out on hangers in a big walnut *armoire*.

"It's difficult to get Harry to take any money. I've tried. . . ."

"We'll have to buy him something nice then." She turned back. "But just *look* at this place—all the space. Like being at home. So much *room!*"

There was a second big wardrobe by the fridge. I got my own clothes out, mostly soiled. They made a pile on the floor. "Harry said just to pay Joshua, for the laundry."

"We won't be here that long anyway, I suppose." She put away another pair of trousers—the sky-blue denim jeans.

"What a collection," I said.

"Yes!"

"You never wear skirts?"

"Not in Africa—obviously."

"Not to encourage them, you mean?"

"The mosquitoes, yes. I have *got* a dress—somewhere." She rooted around in the suitcase. "Formal occasions—if there are any." She took out a neatly folded frock, then frisked it in front of her, snapping it like a towel: a smart, loose-weave cotton dress. She held it up against her body.

"Very nice," I said. It was.

"Wonder if Joshua does dresses?"

We could hear Joshua padding about in flip-flaps along the kitchen corridor. Harry had gone downtown to his Academy that morning, but we'd met Joshua half an hour before. Harry's boy was an aged retainer, thin-faced and gangly, a real grandfather type with rolling bloodshot eyes; crinkly, tight-cropped, white-dusted hair and heavy moustache, a dark ruby-colored skin: a man of few words, liquid lips. "A wise one," Harry had told me privately before. "Used to work in the Belgian Governor's residence here. Likes his drink. That's why I keep most of it locked up in the big fridge—ration him a few beers every day. And maybe that's best in any case," he added, thinking of Eleanor, I suppose.

I took my books and maps and papers out and set them on a dressing table in front of a large mirror—Eleanor suddenly reflected in the glass behind me. She scratched her arms for a moment. Vijay's attentions had made them no better. She turned then, with the cotton dress and a pile of crumpled underwear and went into the bathroom. I heard the water run—washing her bits and pieces, I supposed. But she wasn't. She must have just put them to soak, for she reappeared a few minutes later wearing the cocktail dress. It fitted perfectly: the loose top a soft white against her brown neck and arms, the dress tucked in sharply at the waist, flowing out over her long bronzed legs. For the first time, out of trousers, Eleanor looked intensely feminine, almost as if she'd changed sex. "I thought you said it was only for formal wear?"

"This *is* formal—coming here."

She emptied the contents of her handbag over the bed. "My gold choker, I need that." But it wasn't in her handbag. She went back into the bathroom. I looked down at the pile—some old bills and letters, pills, the little makeup she used, a topless, empty lipstick case, eau de cologne spray, fat Mont Blanc fountain pen, checkbook, Barclaycard, passport, lace-edged flower-bordered hanky, some sugar lumps, a great bundle of 5- and 10-Zaïre notes: her life boiled down, sifted, like grains of gold in a panhandle—scattered nude on the bed before me. She came back with the choker round her neck.

"Now I'm complete! Lunch at the Intercontinental? It's just up the road."

"Harry's coming back here for lunch. Joshua's got it all ready, he told us."

"Joke," she said. I said nothing. "A joke?" she repeated plaintively. I smiled. We went back to our unpacking. She started to root about in her suitcase again, pulling out some papers, some old socks—then a flimsy nightdress. She let this fall on the pillow.

"Which side do you want?" she asked.

"I don't mind. But maybe I should sleep in Harry's dressing room or on one of the sofas."

Eleanor looked up, surprised. "If you want to."

"You said you didn't want to sleep with me."

" 'Not a wink m'lud.' But you're crazy. On a bed this size we don't have to. Siberia between us."

She took off her dress then, pulling it down over her breasts, stepping out of it. I found my own pajamas and put them neatly, some distance away, on the other pillow.

"There," she said, settling her own nightdress equally neatly, but moving it closer to the center of the bed. "All present and correct. 'In case of fire.' But I suppose you don't know that joke either."

She looked at me, head on one side—merry, statuesque, a lingerie ad straight out of *Elle*. We heard Joshua flip-flapping along the passage.

"You'd better get dressed." But she just stood there.

"You're not frightened—of women?"

"No. Just that he might walk in."

"Doubt it. Anyway, what if he does?"

"You don't want to encourage him—like the mosquitoes."

"But we're in the same room, supposed to be together, sleeping here. So what's wrong?"

"Nothing. At all." I rounded the bed and kissed her. She got dressed then and we went on unpacking—the detritus unearthed, organized, put away. This was what love was like, I thought: arrival in a new place, shared bed and baggage, emptying the luggage—the scattered lipstick, lotions and lace handkerchiefs; odd shoes and wrong socks. The bits and pieces of travel, which alone drives one to despair, were things held in common now, where they could be marshaled together. This was intimacy.

Domesticity came next. Harry returned for lunch and Joshua, in a white coat, served up lamb chops, with potatoes and tinned Smedleys garden peas, bottles of HP sauce and ketchup on the table, with neat green linen napkins, a silver cruet of Colman's mustard and glasses of water. It all seemed a bit like Thames valley in the Congo.

After lunch Harry listened to the BBC World Service news from London while we had coffee beneath a slowly twirling fan set high above us. I opened a week-old copy of *The Times,* scanning the headlines. While I was reading Eleanor leaned across and tickled the other side of the paper. I put it down. She pointed over to the doorway leading to the kitchen. A wary Siamese cat had just come into the room and was sitting on the threshold, looking at us while washing its whiskers.

"That's Mirabelle," Harry said. "Just eaten. She's got kittens somewhere in the back garden. Joshua hates her. But he's gone for his snooze—drops off every afternoon. She knows that, so she comes in for the scraps."

The afternoon was still and quiet: dry season siesta. There was no Grand Marché to disturb the calm here. The embassies were closed for the afternoon. Only the sound of cars swishing beneath the great forest of flamboyant trees over the road behind us every five minutes or so broke the peace. Here, in this old residential quarter, seemed an abiding city, last redoubt of the white tribes where there was HP sauce and Colman's mustard for lunch and fans gently stirred the airmail-thin paper of last week's *Times.* I went out to the kitchen to get a glass of water. "In the filter," Harry had said. And so it was, flowing from a small brass tap at the bottom of an Edwardian patent device, a tall clay silo with the legend "Puros Imperial Filter Company, Wandsworth, London, SW" stamped darkly on the outer glaze.

"Hey!—there's some barley sugar out there, sticks of it, or there should be—on top of the cupboard. Joshua lives on it, when he's not on the beer. Bring some in, if there's any left." There was. It came from Harrods. We munched the sugary sticks, sucking and quarrying the yellow twirls with our lips and teeth, the only noise in the heavy silence. I found a paperback among a pile of them on the little table beside me: yes, a copy of *Middlemarch.* Harry had gone native here—an English native, and we shared his adopted provenance. All I needed now was the afternoon tea and crochet work. And those things came later on, when Joshua woke from his slumbers in the laundry room and served us some Earl Grey Darjeeling, and Harry showed us the small needle-point tapestry he was working on, pulling it out from beneath the sofa as we held our dainty teacups up.

"Wonderful therapy," he said. "In the long evenings."

"Are those yours, too—round the walls?" Eleanor asked, looking at the other tapestries. Harry nodded. Eleanor held up the nearly completed embroidery on its waxed string matrix. It showed an old Congo paddle steamer, a run of dark wool making a lovely plume of smoke riding away behind the boat as it churned upriver.

"Beautiful," I said.

"I thought you might like it—the idea at least. If I could get it to float, you'd be home and dry for that trip up to Kisangani."

But we were home and dry anyway then in Harry's ordered house, in the midst of his calm domesticity. He put the tapestry away. Alain, in the peach-colored Cadillac, had just drawn up outside. "Back downtown," Harry said. He got up, went out, then turned at the doorway. "Hey—maybe we could go swimming tomorrow, take a picnic. There's a place, an island, down by the start of the rapids. And there's cricket on Sunday, I think. You might get a game. I'll check with Vijay. I'm seeing him anyhow."

I lay on the double bed while Eleanor pottered to and fro between the kitchen, living room, bedroom, and bathroom. She went out to the kitchen and began talking fourth-form French with Joshua: a confident, schoolgirl French, the words widely spaced, with amateur accents.

"Ah! vous êtes un pêcheur! Mais ici? Dans la ville? A Kinshasa—c'est possible?"

"Oui, Madame, très possible." Joshua's French was from the first form, and his voice, which was thick and slurred at the best of times, had now taken on an even more uncertain timbre. Harry said he kept his Primus bottles in the spin dryer. He must have had more than a few rounds already. *"J'vai' dan m' bicyc'ette,"* he intoned darkly. *"Cha' dimanse."* The washing machine began to grind then and I lost the rest of this Izaak Walton talk. Eleanor came into the bedroom.

"Joshua says he goes fishing here every Sunday on his bicycle."

"Yes. I heard. Sensible."

"We could go, too."

"Yes. We'd need bicycles though."

"What are your wife and children like?" Eleanor asked suddenly, her back toward me, rummaging in the wardrobe.

"All different."

"Naturally—idiot! I meant—"

"It'd take hours. They're fine."

She turned. "It's all right—you don't have to talk about them."

"I was hoping for a letter. I haven't heard anything for a month now. Of course, the posts are terrible here. I won't hear till I get to Nairobi I suppose," I said quickly. "I told her to write there."

"You must miss them."

"Yes."

The conversation died. We dropped the topic of my family. We relaxed—knowing that, among all the delays of Africa, there was plenty of time ahead of us to pursue such themes. Yes, with all our bits and pieces safely stowed in one bedroom now, we were starting to live together. There was no doubt about that. So my domestic difficulties, both our familial problems, all these would be best left behind as bad coin, discredited currency in the new country we hoped to travel through, as sensible friends, as new people.

Lovers always want to plumb each other's past—amazed, angry even, that a time could have existed for one partner in which the other had no existence—so trying to force themselves, like detectives, into that previous dimension where one of them was unaccountably absent. But we were not lovers and so had no need to look obsessively through such old emotional scrapbooks, longing to find our mark there. Or so I thought.

That evening, when Harry came back and Joshua had gone home (servants, under a presidential decree, were forbidden to sully themselves further by living with whites in this residential quarter) we had drinks on the terrace before I offered to make supper.

"You cook? We could go out." Harry was surprised.

"I love it. That's my therapy."

"There's some steak in the fridge, I think."

"Will Joshua mind?"

"Not if we clear up afterward—and don't touch his beer."

"Help?" Eleanor asked.

"No—that's okay."

"I'm no real good at it anyway."

"Nor me," Harry said to her. "You stay here—and tell me the story of your life."

I went away and started tinkering in the kitchen—got the steak out, pounded it a bit, found some garlic, Normandy butter, and a black pepper mill; organized a salad, opened a bottle of Beaujolais Harry had told me about—"It's in the bottom of the fridge—Joshua won't touch it that way: has to be well *chambré* for him. But I like it cool."

I liked being in the kitchen. This was what being in a house was all about, I thought: tinkering through it, like people messed about in boats—this was my pleasure and I had missed it. At home, living and working at home, I often did the cooking: bolognaises, stuffed peppers, sometimes even an elaborate leg of lamb *en croûte*.

I grilled the steaks, my hands working again at something sensible at last, smelling the burning meat, singed on the outside, moist red in the middle: mixing the tangy wine vinegar dressing, sampling a nip of the Beaujolais. This was what life was really all about—the domestic scene: the smell of garlic butter, the chilled fruit essence rising from the wine. And the long trip away to Africa, the weeks in hotel rooms, suddenly seemed worth it now by so forcibly reminding me of this. Fiddling in the kitchen, I was living again. I could even look forward to the washing up.

We ate on the terrace, behind the mosquito wire, in a pool of yellow light from a tall standard lamp, the *gardiens* out round the gate again by their fire poking blue sparks up into the night above the flamboyant trees.

"Did you get the story of her life?" I asked Harry. Eleanor sipped a glass of the Beaujolais.

"Oh yes, I got it all," Harry smiled. "My grandfather was in cotton —a broker in New Orleans. Eleanor was telling me about her father— a broker in the City. London days. Wish I was back there."

"I told Harry he must come and see us," Eleanor said. And for a second I thought she meant her and me before she went on, "out in Windsor."

"I will! Next vacation."

"Come down and see us as well," I said. "In Banbury."

Harry looked up from his steak. "I surely will. Be fine to meet your family." Eleanor gazed at me as well. I was the family man, the only one around, it seemed. I suppose Eleanor should have been in Harry's bed that night—and I should have been writing a long letter home.

As it was we slept, when we did, well covered, at a distance, a Siberia between us, chaste as ice. But we chattered on the way.

"Playing cricket—and I can play! What about that?" Eleanor said, sitting up against the pillows in her neat nightdress, running a hand through her curls. Harry had spoken to Vijay earlier that evening: a game had been fixed for Sunday afternoon up at the American school. There were always numbers to be made up on each team: I could play—and so could Eleanor, if she was really serious.

"All the way to the Congo," I said, winding my alarm, "to play cricket. . . ."

"But you said you liked it."

"Oh yes. Just it doesn't seem real. I should be interviewing some fat *Citoyen Commissaire*."

"Crazy. You're too serious anyway."

"I play most summer weekends at home—Adlestrop and Great Tew. Chestnut trees and real ale. It's the last thing I expected here. Though I once played cricket in Rome, behind the Vatican."

"Home. . . . You'd really prefer to be at home, wouldn't you?"

"When I'm not there. When I am, after a month or two, I want to be away. All living on top of each other. It's too small, the cottage. And I have to work there as well."

"Should be ideal: Cotswold cottage—and cricket."

"Well, sometimes it isn't."

"It's such a shame," she said.

"What?"

"Marriage."

"But you wanted it, all that, a week ago."

"But hearing you—"

"I've not said anything about marriage."

"Well, not hearing you then—just looking at you. You've got your month-of-Sundays face on now. Did you know? It's the same thing as hearing you."

We slept apart. The only problem was early in the morning when I woke and found her sleeping right beside me. Turning in the night she had gravitated toward me, the Siberia melted away between us then, so that I could feel her warmth inches away from me, smell the sweet mix of sleep and soap on her skin. That was difficult.

"You know," Eleanor said suddenly next morning, "when I woke last night—sometime in the middle of the night—you were right over my side of the bed, inches away, your arm on me. You'd better be careful. Maybe I should sleep on the sofa." She turned away, looking worried, preoccupied.

"I'm sorry. I'd no idea—"

"Joke." She swung round, looking at me sharply. "It was nice," she added.

The American school was closed for the summer vacation. But quite a little crowd turned up all the same to watch the cricket next day. Vijay was there, as one of the umpires, with a dozen other playing Indians, mostly from Kenya; a few of the commercial British in Kinshasa, three West Indians and some "colonials" from Zimbabwe and South Africa. And the Reverend Mustard—smartly kitted out in neatly creased gray flannels, white aertex shirt, long tennis shoes, pipe rampant, graying hair done to a turn—no flanneled fool at all. He seemed tremendously keen about the game ahead when we met him with Harry by the pavilion. This was a small windowless hut, where the crates of Primus were already being organised by two bar boys, some of the bottles dunked in buckets of ice, the rest carefully shrouded in damp cloths, though it wasn't hot, just gray and muggy.

"Will the pitch take spin then, Reverend?" Harry inquired mischievously.

"Swing, Harry, not spin. Matting wickets don't take anymore or less spin. But with this atmosphere," he looked up at the lowering clouds, "it should swing all right. Late swing."

The matting wicket, at the top of a long rise from the pavilion, ran across a sandy, coarse-grassed plateau, with a line of poplar-like trees and a main road beyond.

"You hit the ball down this leg side," Vijay advised me sharply, getting into a white waiter's coat. "And it's downhill all the way. Easy boundary. Make a lot of runs."

Two of the West Indians were getting ready to bat for the opposing team, who'd won the toss. We all trooped out to field. Eleanor—in a pair of cream-colored jeans, white silk shirt and plimsolls—looked suitably decorative. Her presence on our team, even though there had been several spare places, struck everyone else as decidedly odd. But since the whole game, in this odd place, had for me a complete Alice-in-Wonderland air in any case, I didn't find her fielding out at midwicket very strange at all.

Two of the Kenyan Indians on our side opened the bowling: quite fast, quite good. And the ball did swing in the muggy air. But the two West Indian batsmen were competent as well, stroking the ball firmly at once, soon nudging, cutting and driving it to all corners of the field. Though downhill to where I was fielding at deep square leg on the boundary by the pavilion was their favorite shot, so that, chasing the ball, I was soon in a muggy lather, strongly tempted by the cold beers already being lowered round the tiny pavilion just behind me. Harry, with his great bulk and immobility, made a suitable wicket keeper. Mustard fielded next to him in the slips, the two of them chattering between balls, Mustard explaining the nature of the "swing," moving his arms about strenuously, as if about to bowl.

"Who is that girl then?" One of the Indians behind me spoke to his neighbor.

"Friend of Harry's."

"American—a baseball girl?"

"Must be."

"What next? The bar boys, I suppose."

"Can't really play, though, can she?" the other Indian said. Eleanor, just then, had misfielded and her throw back to the wicket had been weak and womanly.

The two West Indians had made nearly sixty runs in just over half an hour before the Reverend Mustard came on to bowl. He measured out his run very conscientiously, five springy paces back from the wicket. Then he went back to the crease and rubbed his spinning fingers in the sandy block hole like a professional; then he adjusted his field for a second time, sending a man right out to long-on and bringing in Eleanor closer at midwicket. Then he bowled, left arm around. He was obviously quite a good bowler, straight line, teasing length, and he was certainly competitive, putting everything into it, running down the wicket, looking for a catch, appealing for LBW twice in his first five balls, from which the batsman scored nothing. The sixth ball was tossed up more, but well flighted. It must have dipped at the last moment—and spun a bit sharply—for the batsman, impatient now, and mistiming it, cracked it straight into Eleanor's hands, a sharp powerful shot which she clutched at, and then held miraculously as the ball drove into her stomach. The batsman, about to run, looked startled. Then he turned and made his way back to the pavilion.

"Those baseball players—maybe there's something in it," the Indian behind me said.

"Don't be crazy. Girls don't play baseball in the States."

"Must play some damn thing like it then. You don't take catches like that unless you've learned."

"Just luck. She got in the way."

And that may have been the truth. But it didn't matter. Mustard had gone over to congratulate Eleanor. And Harry had come out from behind the stumps, too. I was too far away to join in the celebrations. But just then, as a spectator almost, way out on the boundary, the whole business did strike me as very strange. A woman playing cricket in the Congo, and again, not just a woman, but Eleanor, with whom I shared a bed—a girl who ten days before had been drunk out of her mind pining for the unfaithful Robert. The girl who was so "bad" with people—dreamy, scatty, drinky, self-absorbed, unassured—was now something quite different: a confident, laughing person taking sharp catches at midwicket. That was the strange thing.

I had rather thought that Eleanor would take me into that sort of life, where I would make the sharp catches while she sat in the pavilion watching. Instead it was the other way round. I was the spectator while she strode out into the world, dealing with it nonchalantly, controlling destinies in the middle of the pitch. The thought crossed my mind then, like a slight ache: she might not be so dependent on me at all for her survival, her happiness, her "cure."

Mustard took several more wickets. But the other team got nearly 200 runs before they declared and we took a late and liquid lunch. Eleanor didn't figure in the game again until she batted—and that was with me, toward the end of the afternoon, when she came in number ten, while I was still there, having prodded about for a dozen runs, with thirty or so more needed to win in six overs—a distant prospect. I was no great hitter and Eleanor's approach to batting, I saw at once, was more suited to golf than cricket, where she swung at every ball, the bat held out at an angle away from her, like a number eight iron.

I successfully got her away from the bowling, looking for a single at the end of each over. Then I managed two boundaries in succession down the slope. Twenty to win in four overs: Eleanor, miraculously, nought not out.

"Easy does it," Vijay said when I found myself up his end. Eleanor had two last balls of an over to face on her own. She clonked the first one, a real golf drive, over a midwicket for four. Sheer fluke, I thought, as they'd brought their faster seam bowlers back on at that point, aiming to wrap things up quickly, giving Eleanor no quarter. But she hit the last ball in just the same fashion, a great agricultural shot, though slightly mistimed so that there were only two runs in it.

"Run—run!" she shouted at me as we crossed.

It was my turn to face in the next over, sweating, concentrating heavily, but happy. I was clean bowled second ball, a late swinging yorker. Harry came in as last man. Fourteen to win in slightly more than two overs. Harry's cricket was entirely in the baseball manner—bat held high, straight out from his hefty stomach, twirling it in the air. He swiped and missed the first two deliveries. But he connected with the next. It sailed right over the bowler's head and into the trees by the road: a tremendous six. And tremendous excitement by the pavilion.

"My word!" an Indian said.

Harry missed the last ball and it was Eleanor's turn to face next over. The first delivery hit her on the pad: loud appeals all round. But Vijay didn't move. The next ball bowled her, shattering the stumps. But before that we'd all heard Vijay's shout: "No ball!" Eleanor had another chance. She survived the over, even taking two runs off the last ball.

The two of them won the match. A few scampered singles, a miscued boundary from Eleanor, where the ball skied back over the wicket keeper, another baseball four from Harry and it was all over.

"I wouldn't have believed it! Harry's girl friend," another Indian shouted as they all came off the field. "Two damned Yanks—can you imagine!?"

The sweat was pouring off Eleanor's face as she came back. I'd never seen anyone so flushed or excited. Harry was gasping—the two of them surrounded by wild approval and applause now: a great victory and the cold Primus was ready and waiting. I stood on the outskirts with Mustard, who was clapping as firmly as anyone.

"Well done! And I thought she was just a hippy."

Eleanor toweled her face. I offered my own congratulations.

"A fluke," she said, fussed, still flushed, nervous in a way she had not been out at the wicket. She looked round her, the African night coming on quickly then—soft claret shades washing out the dull gray sky, big bats beginning to flip, an incongruous smell of linseed oil and grass cuttings in the usual sweet- and-sour African air.

"Isn't Africa wonderful!" she said at last.

Harry put his arm round her. "You'd better stay out here then. Need you for the cricket team. Get you a job in my academy. Speech and drama—you're plenty good at both."

"Yes," she beamed. "It's funny. I'm nervous now, shaking. But I

wasn't out there." She looked back over the darkening field in amazement. "I was acting, when I was batting. Forced myself—to act the
part. It's funny, I often manage things like that, when I act." She glanced
at me, as if seeking my approval for this gift.

"What part were you acting?" I asked casually.

"You!" she said, turning on me suddenly, almost shouting. "I was
acting you, when I saw you batting at the other end. You gave me the
cue, because you looked so *happy*—at last!"

There was silence. I tried to smile.

"Your month-of-Sundays face was all gone," Eleanor added more
quietly, wonder in her large blue eyes as if, in my cricket, I had escaped
her into some paradise where she would always be excluded.

"Ah yes, Joe takes Africa very seriously. He'll get over it," Harry said.
"But come on: it's Michel's party tonight. We better get ready. Black
tie, white tie, linen tropicals, ball gowns—whatever we can manage.
Nine sharp. He's got the little combo from the Intercontinental coming;
hundreds of people."

Harry toweled away some more sweat, then shook his head in amazement: a shuffly, pear-shaped figure, the irony in his smile running high.
"Tonight's the night," he added finally. "Great Gatsby, Congo style."

Upriver

*I*t was a tiny old river tug, nearly all engine, with a vast throbbing diesel set behind the raised foredeck where we sat on battered cane chairs under an awning in splendid isolation, while a crew of six lurked beneath us. One man tended the pistons, a second steered, peering out between our feet. The other four from the River Authority had just come for the ride, I'm sure—fascinated, goggle-eyed men who gazed up at us, incredulous, wondering what possible mischief this great white *bwana* and his woman were up to, sitting there above them, to no apparent purpose, me in my white linen tropicals that I'd worn to the party, Eleanor still in her cotton cocktail frock.

What mischief indeed? The two of us slumped, bleary-eyed, beneath the awning in our party clothes. We must have looked like players in some exotic drinks commercial gone very wrong. We'd not even been to bed. The Frenchman from Les Voies Fluviales had driven us straight from the party just after three that morning, down to the Port Authority dockyard where they were getting the tug ready for an inspection run upriver. It was only going out for the day, fifty miles or so, east through Stanley Pool and then on for another few miles up into the river proper. But, after the weeks of waiting, this excursion was better than nothing, and we'd jumped at the offer.

The Frenchman had been at the party. Harry introduced us. "There's a boat leaving very early tomorrow morning—I can get you on it," the man said convincingly. And here we were, finally on the river, my head throbbing with the engine's beat after too much sparkling wine—Eleanor equally quiet, though nursing only a lack of sleep. Once she'd heard we were due for travel and the river at last, she'd dropped her other liquid drug completely, stopped even sipping the wine, filled with genuine elation among the other falsely merry partygoers, drunk with just the thought of movement. I, on the other hand, believing this sudden plan would end in just one more disappointment, thought to drown my sorrows in advance. But no—we had actually escaped, forced our way from the wound of Kinshasa.

We chugged out of the dockyard, a small searchlight on the cabin roof illuminating the sleeping water villages, the rows of big, tarpaulin-covered cargo *pirogues,* then picking out the shadowed hulks of larger boats—half-submerged dredgers and sunken paddle steamers, which rose up about us now like an abandoned navy in the night. Half an hour later, out in the Pool itself, a gray, pearl-tinted dawn began to break over the wide water to the east—streaks of thin light along the horizon, forming a vague destination which soon became a faint haze of orange behind the clouds: a mark that we could aim for, which told us—the dark dissolving—that the waters moved, that we were moving. It was no great boat, to be sure: just an old tug that had nothing to do with my earlier luxurious dreams or plans. There was no scotch waiting below decks here, no dog kennels and no first-class restaurants. But at last we were going upriver, up the Congo, the "river that eats all rivers."

It was a crashingly boring journey. Once out on the Pool, getting away from Kinshasa, there was almost nothing to see, just the vast, flat expanse of drab-colored water all round us, with no horizon, for the early morning sky had changed and become opaque, and was exactly the same gray shade as the river itself. There were no margins, no dividing lines in this world. The water was as flat and undisturbed as the blanket of cloud tucked in everywhere above us.

Half an hour later, when the sun had risen secretly behind this cover, I was able to make out the right bank of the Pool a few hundred yards away—flat, marshy, reed-filled land, without any trees. Fishermen, moored overnight by the reeds, stood up in their shallow dugouts, seemingly standing on the water, roused by our engine; a few coffee-colored cows, stomach-deep in the stream, were already feeding among the water hyacinth, while the magpie-shaped birds on their backs, the *pique-boeufs,* browsed off them. Besides these little foggy cameos—nothing. None of the crew spoke French, except for the helmsman, whose gifts here ran alternately to *"oui"* and *"non,"* the responses given in strict rotation whatever the question asked. We were quite alone on the empty waterway, on this ridiculous voyage, going nowhere in our party finery.

Even Eleanor, after a spell confirming this sheer monotony, could find no more charm in the scene. "That fat *Commissaire* last night," she said at last, swapping present for past, "he should have been just your sort—for an interview. Did you get one?"

I sighed. "An interview? Harry gave me the big BBC buildup, so the man was on his guard from the word go."

Harry had introduced me to this sly *Commissaire,* a rubicund, dwarf-like creature, obscene pear-shaped head, with jowls and teeth that shook and rattled: an unamiable figure, with blocked-up heels to his tiny shoes, where the whole face and form had the rough, exaggerated shape of a cartoon, a nightmare dwarf, a Disney reject. We'd been cornered at the edge of a floodlit, jungly garden behind Michel's house. To one side, against a wall, ran a line of empty animal cages, something of a private zoo, I imagined, hoping the beasts hadn't escaped into the thick bushes, trees, and shrubs right behind us. On the opposite side of the garden the combo from the Intercontinental, "The Best," played sugary music for most of the evening, while people danced in fits and starts on a stone patio outside the huge living room: old tunes—waltzes, foxtrots, Latin-American stuff—interspersed with treacle-fed songs made the more sticky and soft in the deep bass amplifications of the group: "Ciao, Ciao Bambino" and other sweet-nothing numbers from twenty-five years before—the mid-Fifties perhaps, when the whole party might have taken place, in another age, colonial times in the Congo which the Belgians had never left. Local blacks were certainly thin on the ground: this *Commissaire* and perhaps half a dozen others, smart men in immaculate, shot-silk Kaunda suits and cravats, from the banks and ministries, sipping orange juice—laced with vodka, Harry told me afterward—some with their wives, standing a yard behind them, wearing elaborately chic *bubus,* the ultimate in mammy cloths, startlingly colored and folded tapestries that rarely moved, for this had been a formal party to begin with where everyone, vying for precedence, had seen themselves, not as guests, but as part of one long receiving line.

"An interview? There was no chance."

"You might have learned something all the same."

"Never. He had that wily, well-fed, oily look of real power in Africa—the sort that waits for you to make the mistakes, then cancels your visa and sends you packing next morning. The 'say nothing' look. I told him I loved Kinshasa—and even that was a mistake. Made him suspicious at once. He was suspicious of everyone—a real Robespierre."

I gazed out over the still water of the Pool. Now that the sun was well up behind the clouds the river started to release hints of its real character—forebodings, intimations. It was no longer dead flat, I saw. All sorts of secret movement creased the surface of the stream: minute eddies, ripples, dozens of plate-sized whirlpools. Something deep down—divisive currents, strange upsets—was continually agitating the dull gray mirror above, wrinkling it, creating elusive patterns, constantly, silently disturbing it. The river had seemed quite motionless in the early dawn light. Now you could see it was very much alive—but you couldn't tell why, for we were far from the shoreline, moving over great depths, and there was no wash from any other boat. The little silent, sucking, sluicing eddies—malign water sprites—had an unexplained existence here. If you concentrated your vision on these myriad disturbances for any length of time you became mesmerized, your eyes glued to the twisting hieroglyphics that had some message for you. What was it? You were tempted by them. Soon you would be sucked overboard trying to decipher them. Instead I closed my eyes and dozed. . . .

Eleanor stood under a huge, brilliantly lit chandelier in the center of the long hall, Harry and I just behind her, other guests pushing in after us. Music droned beyond us in the distant garden. The big, richly paneled house carried a great cargo of heavily scented people—lit up, a ship in the night, briefly moored next to the sad, dark squalor of the city. Eleanor turned her head. The light from the sparkling cut glass above seemed to blind her for a moment—isolating yet exciting her, like a limelight. "Well?" she said uncertainly, looking back at both of us.

"On! On!" Harry encouraged her before I could—Harry in formal dress: a white dinner jacket, scarlet cummerbund, and neat dark trousers, leaving a whiff of violets in the air behind him from some sweetly odorous dressing on his scalp that had smarmed down his few strands of dark hair. His eyes sparkled. A maître d'hôtel or a retired rear-admiral? Something in between. Though certainly there was a nautical air about him: a pilot come aboard to set things going aboard this stuffy cruise ship. He stepped forward smartly and took Eleanor by the arm. I was annoyed afterward that I hadn't taken Eleanor's arm myself. Harry didn't need leading into life.

The house was very grand. Near the top of Mount N'Galiema it looked over the dark river—a white stuccoed palace. Inside the furnishings and decor were heavy Brussels Second Empire with some violent contemporary contrasts in the shape of low, vastly cushioned, soft leather sofas and chromium-legged, oval-shaped tables cut entirely in mirror glass. Ancestral magnates—beneficiaries of King Leopold's Congo plunder—in lavish beards with steely eyes glowered from heavy gilt frames on the walls, while copies of the latest *Elle* and *Paris Match* lay prominently displayed in a crystal canterbury beneath them. But behind these vulgar furbelows, ancient and modern, lay a lovely old honey-colored paneling, a light Burmese teak perhaps, along with a splendid staircase in the same wood which ran up from the center of the hall.

We met Michel—most gracious host, his parents abroad somewhere—at the foot of this triumphal slope. Yes, he explained, the wood here had originally come from India. The house belonged then to the British Consul in the Congo, he went on. "You know—that Irish revolutionary and German spy."

"Yes—Roger Casement. But he couldn't have been here. His house was down in Boma, the old capital. Leopoldville wasn't the capital here until 1929."

"Yes, yes—this was his house. We have some newspaper cuttings about it."

It was hardly the time or place to contradict Michel. Casement had left the Congo for good after his famous report in 1904—long before such a palatial house as this could have been built up by the wilds of Stanley Pool.

" 'The ghost of Roger Casement is knocking at the door'. . ." I quoted Yeats's lines to Harry after we'd left Michel. "Not this door, though. I'm sure of that."

Harry shook his head, eyes heavenward. "Don't worry. I told you— the house moved: a transport of dreams. History is fiction in these parts. So is life. You invent it all as you go along. Relax."

We did. Sparkling wines were being served from a long table out on the patio. Tactful, dusky waiters cruised through the stuffed shirts, the Fifties ball gowns, the Kaunda silk suits and glittering mammy cloths, with laden trays: though the glasses were never more than half-full— an intimation, I felt, that nothing at the party was to go amiss, get out of hand. It was well past ten but guests were still arriving. Grander, more interesting guests perhaps? Or simply more bibulous ones—guests already halfway through a bottle beforehand, who would demand full measure now in the sparkling champagne flutes?

The Reverend Mustard strode forward down a receiving line—har-binger of change? I thought so. His eyes seemed a little glassy, his previous haunted entrances into the Memling bar something quite for-gotten: a studied, confident, almost jaunty arrival, dressed in a neat gray suit and wearing a dog collar for the first time; silvering hair meticulously coiffed, inclining his head gracefully here and there—for all the world a Home Counties vicar doing honors at a church bazaar. Given his tastes among the natives of the Cité, in the cassava and beer shops, I was surprised to see him here at all, among this remnant essence of the *ancien régime*. Though perhaps he felt at home—sharing with them, as he almost certainly did, such firm beliefs in native original sin.

Naxos, the Albanian dentist, was already there, a tiny, courtly figure in weathered dancing pumps and a rather threadbare dress suit, an unlikely costume of Edwardian vintage which must once have fitted him—or someone else, a considerably larger man. Finally Dr. Chillerjam made a late appearance, another small figure bobbing among the crowd of taller guests, darkly suited like a stockbroker's clerk running for Cannon Street down the City Drain. The three of them finally joined us out in the garden, beyond the patio. Our little band was complete.

"You're late, Vijay."

"Later the better, Harry—on these formal occasions. Not the done thing you know, in high society, to come anywhere near time."

" 'Punctuality is the courtesy of kings,' " Naxos said unctuously, looking severely at me, as if it was I who had been late. He turned to Eleanor. "I hear you had a great *succès* at 'cri-ket' today. I did not know that women played such a game in England."

"Oh yes—they do! In short white skirts and long white socks."

Naxos sipped his *méthode champenoise* and licked his lips. "I see," he said, flickering his old eyes appraisingly. "Do you play here—in such clothes?" Behind the gracious query lay a touch of salaciousness, I thought.

"Afraid not. Just jeans and a shirt."

Naxos tried to hide his disappointment. "How strange," he said. "How very strange." An elderly, big-boned Belgian woman approached him—one of the big-bottomed, horse-faced women from the *Cercle Hippique*.

"*Ah, Monsieu' Naxos! Comment allez-vous? Vous savez,*" she ran on, "*mes nouvelles dents—elles sont affeuses! V'aiment.*" She confirmed this point in her spluttering labials and unapproachable r's. She took Naxos by the arm, gripping him firmly as if, in return for his painful handiwork, she would now extract something equally painfully from him.

"Shall we dance?" Harry said to Eleanor. And they danced well, where their ease spoke of other confidences shared, growing between them as they moved.

* * *

I opened my eyes to the stream. The bank to our right had disappeared completely. We were right out in open water. There were no landmarks now at all: nothing to see—the whole world a void of cream-laid, ivory-gray river and cloud.

"What was it like—dancing with Harry?"

"Like anyone else—I suppose. Why?"

"He's rather taken to you."

"I suppose so." Eleanor looked away, looking out at nothing. "Do you think these people have *any* idea at all where we're going?" she said brightly.

"Does he really want you to stay out here—a job with his Academy?"

"Well, he asked me again. I can't of course."

"And you told him so?"

"Yes. What would I do out here, for goodness sake?"

"All rather sad."

"What?"

"These nice people. But all stuck here. Naxos, Vijay, Mustard. Nothing but dreams, fantasies."

"Any different from us—you and me? *Our* goings-on?" Eleanor turned to me sharply. "You know, we're really going to have to get out of here. Properly. Take a cargo plane, anything." She seemed genuinely worried now, gazing at me intently, her bronzed face starkly indented against the wispy white, gauze background.

"Yes."

"After last night."

"What last night?"

"What *you* said, not the others. Don't you remember? Or were you drunk, for once?"

Eleanor and I had danced together later on, much later, when I had drunk quite a lot.

"I don't really remember—all of what I said."

"How life was impossible for you at home."

"Oh dear, did I say that?"

"Chapter and verse."

"And what did you say?"

"That you'd better do something—to try and change it—one way or another. Just the sort of thing you told me, about drinking. That I could change that. Well, so can you—your problems. That's what I told you."

"How?"

"I don't know. 'Remains to be seen,' you said last night—in a heavy bank manager's voice." Having looked at me very carefully, Eleanor now looked away again, seemingly uninterested.

"Easier said than done."

"I've managed to stop drinking."

"Marriages are more difficult to stop."

"I wouldn't know." She gazed out over the empty view.

"But why do we have to get away from here—right now? How did that come up?"

She turned, amazed. "Don't you remember?"

"No."

"You said if you stayed with me here any longer—stuck here with nothing to do in Kinshasa, sleeping in the same bed together and so on—you said you'd fall in love with me."

"Oh dear."

"So we'd better get out of here—hadn't we? Before I fall in love with Harry—and you with me," she added tartly.

Suddenly we were in the fog, the plumes of grayish cotton wool congealing rapidly all around us, so that in a minute we couldn't see more than a few yards beyond the prow of the boat. I turned and looked down at the helmsman. "Do you have—*avez-vous un . . .*" I forgot the French for compass. I mimed the instrument.

"*Oui,*" the man said promptly.

But I wasn't sure. From where I was sitting I could see nothing of the sort on the small dashboard in front of him. "*Vous avez un truc— pour vous donner le nord, sud, l'est, l'ouest?*"

"*Non,*" the man spoke decisively. Then he shook his head, smiling, as if trying to reassure me. "*Non,*" he added again, breaking the strict rotation in his replies for the first time.

"The fellow's got no compass," I said to Eleanor.

"They must know the way—doing this trip for years."

"Some other big boat might run us right under. He doesn't even seem to have a hooter."

"A foghorn, you mean. But there aren't any other ships on the river anyway. We know that. Anyway, I rather like it—not knowing where we're going."

"I don't. I wish the hell I was off this damn river."

"Just when you're getting out onto it at last. That's you all over, isn't it? Stopping before you've started." She looked defiant now, wisps of fog curling round her head, a touch of the Rhine maiden. "You came all the way out here just to *get* up the bloody river!"

"Yes, I know. But I never said I was prepared to drown in the attempt."

"Get your feet wet? But you may have to. Isn't that real travel? Or are you really just an armchair traveler—or at best a window-seat one?" She was angry—just as I'd been about her drinking—knowing travel to be my failing.

"I just don't want to have to swim for it, that's all." My head was throbbing again. "There're crocs in this river, you know—"

"Yes. And hippos."

"I'm just—cautious. Reasonable precautions—"

"A hooter, a foghorn, a compass—"

"It seems the least in these conditions. I don't know why you think—"

"You'll be looking for lifeboats next, and an orchestra—'Nearer My God to Thee'—sinking with all hands."

"It's not *un*reasonable." The argument swelled.

" 'Nothing venture'—"

"Rubbish. You don't take unnecessary risks—"

"Can't foresee everything—"

"Boats like this should, though. Should be prepared."

"You're talking just like a scoutmaster." She looked at me severely. "You're so bloody nervous—you're making me nervous."

"I'm not good at traveling with other people. I told you—on the way down to the coast. I never do on these trips."

"You don't actually want me with you. That's it."

"No—"

"Why didn't you *say* so—instead of encouraging me?" She glared at me with a real, hurt anger. "Harry told me last night," she went on. Then she stopped.

"What?"

"That you were—" She changed tack again. "That you didn't really know where you were going."

"Well, that's true enough—right now. But he said something else— and you just stopped saying it."

"No—"

"I know what he said: he said I was no person to go across Africa with, because I was a married man, don't get involved and so on. That's it, isn't it? Well, you don't *have* to get involved. There's no pressure—at all!" I added briskly.

"No. He didn't say that. You're quite wrong," she said loudly. "Something quite different. He said. . . ."

"Yes?"

"I've forgotten."

"No, you haven't: as long as you didn't become 'involved' with me. Something like that—that's what he said."

"You're wrong again!" She was very firm. "He said you were too much of a homebody—if you want to know—to be a good traveler."

"He's something that way himself—with his needlepoint and lamb chops." I was angry with Harry for the first time, but only for a moment. What a fool I was, I thought a moment afterward: fighting him over a woman. I liked Harry as much as I liked Eleanor. "Anyway, why didn't you want to tell me that? Is it awfully wrong being a homebody?"

She seemed stumped at last. "I suppose," she said, "because it means your heart isn't really in all this." She looked out into the blanket of fog. "And I didn't want to tell you that."

"In case I decided to drop this whole trip and beat it back for toasted muffins in the Cotswolds?"

"Maybe."

"And you'd have no trip then: you'd have to go back to England too?"

"Perhaps."

I sighed. "I wish I could go back. But I took the money from the BBC—'Coast to Coast'—and I've got to finish it. So you needn't worry."

"But why *start* it all"—she turned on me vehemently—"if you hate this kind of traveling?"

"A change of scene," I said heavily. "Writers are supposed to need a 'change of scene.' " We both looked out into the thick fog. "I'd prefer the toasted muffins."

"Oh no, you wouldn't." Eleanor was suddenly very definite about something again.

"What then?"

"You just want both—the travel and the toasted muffins."

"Do I?"

"Yes—you want it both ways. You think that's my problem. But it's more yours."

* * *

Later on at the party, after we'd both had quite a lot to drink, I'd tried
to pull Mustard's leg a little. "You could always take that engine right
out of the old Citroën and put it in a boat," I told him. "You could
get upriver that way. Just put the bloody engine in one of those native
dugouts. Get up among the cannibals then all right. . . ."

"The engine's front-wheel drive—didn't you know that? No shaft
for any propeller."

"Turn the engine lengthways in the boat—make a shaft: a few uni-
versal joints. . . . Need to be lengthways in a narrow boat like that in
any case. Hadn't you thought of that?"

"I think you're being facetious."

"You said you were so anxious to get upriver. Your missionary work:
the Call. Don't you remember?"

"I'm not quite the fool you think me."

"I didn't think that. I was curious all the same: a one-man Church."

"You're working on your own out here, too. But I don't find that
curious." Mustard glared at me then. "You just want to see everyone
else as nuts, except yourself. We're all mad. But you're little Johnny,
the only boy in step. You have to see us that way, in order to see yourself
as sane, assured, unfrightened. Because that's your problem—you're
terrified of Africa. You don't go near the blacks out here, I notice. They
scare you. So you beat us instead—your white friends here—by making
us out to be dotty, fools, cranks, or whatever. At best, we're all good
'copy' for the BBC, or some book you'll put us in. That's how you see
us. What you don't see is your own fear."

"Fear?"

"Yes. You pretend it's boredom—or anger at all the things you can't
do here, or get here. But in fact you're frightened—and won't admit
it. You don't like Africa. But there again that's because you don't really
like yourself. You don't like the coward you are."

"You're more psychologist than priest."

"I just didn't want you to get away with the idea that I'm a fool.
Though I don't really care what you think of me. I know who I am.
And you don't. That's the only difference between us. A difference of
ignorance and fear. We're neither of us fools."

There wasn't anything more I could say. He was right about me. Or
at least, he was very nearly right. The little part where he was wrong

lay in the fact that I wasn't really ignorant of these problems in myself. I'd just carefully avoided defining them, as he had just done.

The fog was as thick as ever. Suddenly the helmsman cut the throttle. The engine coughed three or four times, then died. We slowed, drifting in complete silence. I turned and looked down at the man. His face was working, eyes narrowed, turning an ear straight ahead of us, listening. Another of the crew went forward and was standing at the bow doing the same thing.

"What's—*Qu'est-ce qu'il se passe?*" I asked. The helmsman said nothing. He put a hand to his mouth, then touched his ear. I turned my own ear ahead. There was no sound—a dense silence—not even the lap of water. We might have been on a mill pond.

Then I heard the churning rumble—muffled at first, but coming from somewhere straight ahead of us in the bank of fog: the sound of a large engine turning, big propeller screw flapping, pounding in and out of the water. The noise was coming straight toward us.

"Haven't you got a *foghorn*?" I yelled at the man, forgetting all French. I mimed the instrument—and the noise—like a mad huntsman. Again the man said nothing. Our tug was motionless, seemed glued to the water. We were a sitting duck: some huge ship must ram us in a few moments—its big engines reverberating strongly now, closing on us. I stood up, taking Eleanor by the arm, ready to dive overboard. But the helmsman motioned me to sit down. What was he so confident of?

There were raised voices then from somewhere high up in the fog ahead of us, Africans chattering, laughing. But we saw nothing of the ghost ship. Then the wash hit us—not the side, but the bow of the tug. The other boat must have passed us almost at right angles—twenty, thirty yards ahead. The helmsman started the engine. We moved forward again. In less than half a minute we were out of the fog bank and into clear air.

I turned to my left: a large cargo boat, a several-thousand-ton ship with its single screw high out of the water, with cars and trucks and a lot of passengers on its rear deck, was thumping away from us diagonally, skirting the fog bank. If we'd kept on our course a few minutes back, if we hadn't stopped, we'd have certainly run into it just as we left the fog.

"Jesus."

"But they heard it," Eleanor said. She had never been alarmed. "They heard it long before we did. They *knew* it was there. They navigate here, by ear." She touched her ear and smiled. "They don't need compasses—or foghorns."

"Well, why didn't *we* skirt the fogbank then? They're crazy." My heart pounded with anger. But of course, as Mustard would have confirmed, it was fear not anger, blind fear. I remembered what Harry had told me about the locals in Kinshasa: "They all have a code here, you know: a mysterious code. And unless you know it—you know nothing."

The helmsman had a code, all right. And I would never know it: I would never know anything of these men. Eleanor turned to the man. "Well done!" she said. *"Très bon. Très, très bon!"* She was becoming tiresome. No—more than that, I could have clipped her over the ear. The fourth-former in her was getting on my nerves. The rest of Africa like this? She turned to me, excited—companion in a dorm riot, as if commenting on a lucky escape from a housemistress: "We stopped just in time! Any nearer and we'd have hit that ship."

" 'Nearer My God to Thee.' Any nearer and we'd have been *dead,*" I shouted at her. "And we're not supposed to be dead. That's one thing we can't have both ways."

"All the same—it's a bit more like real travel," she said gently, upset by my anger.

"Yes. We're traveling—I'm sorry." And we were—into just the same dull gray view of cloud-and-river, both indistinguishable again now that we'd come out of the fog. We might have drowned for nothing, I thought, not even a view. "But there's nothing here," I said calmly, hating it all again. "We're not really going anywhere."

Even Eleanor had little to say on the way back that afternoon—overcome with the mood of bitter hopelessness and depression that surrounded us. The river had won; the river would never lose. Michel's party, by comparison with this excursion, had been almost a happy thing. But that was all over, too. Harry's little band envied and disliked us, I saw that then—and disliked themselves through us. Though no doubt they would find each other again, when we were gone, salvage their self-esteem from the wreck of our departure, gain their true shoreline, the nooks and crannies, the rock pools of Kinshasa which were their only habitat. In a few weeks' time, when the dry season came to an end, they would all meet again—at the Memling bar, the Pergola, the Restaurant du Zoo. When the gray clouds finally broke, with rain and brilliant sun, the chilled Muscadet would be set amongst them as usual, grilled *telapia* with butter—where later they would share a masonic fug of Harry's cheroots and chatter. Madame Yvette would recharge their cognac glasses; and then, surely, among them all, a boat going upriver would readily be imagined again—Mustard's missionary *pirogue* headed for the cannibals or Michel's big, refurbished paddle steamer filled with rich Americans. Without us, at any rate, these children of the country could dream without contradiction, happy in the city once more, savoring all its intimacies, the little changes in themselves, oblivious of Africa beyond where they would never venture: happy in the prison of their days.

BOOK TWO

BOOK TWO

CHAPTER

12

The Real Thing

We'd crossed half Africa that morning in the big cargo jet—high above and far away from the endless carpet of green rain forest beneath us. But now my heart was in my mouth as the much smaller Cessna dodged and spun between the two huge volcano cones in this mountainous, lake-filled Kivu region of eastern Zaïre, right in the heart of the continent. The pilot turned to Eleanor, then pointed up to the smoking summit on our left.

"That's Nyiragongo," Patrick shouted, taking us up from Bukavu—where we'd landed that morning—to Goma, the town at the northern end of the long lake. "It's erupting again, just started last week. Maybe we'll get high enough to look down into it." Then the plane lurched in a sudden thermal. I could see almost enough of this belching volcano already, I thought: a great mushroom of red-flecked cloud rising up into the lead-blue sky from this 12,000-foot mountain that rose over the lake. "Four years ago it really exploded," Patrick went on. "Burst a great hole out of the side of the crater, ran down the valley into Goma. Hundreds—maybe thousands—were just buried." At this information Eleanor turned from him to me in the back seat. Her eyes were glittering with excitement, I'm afraid to say.

The little plane lifted steeply in another sudden updraft, haphazardly, buoyant, unleashed, tossing about like a kite between the great peaks. Yet I wasn't frightened anymore. This was exhilarating, swooping about in the hot air above the lake, dancing round the craters, the tawny flat savannah land way beyond where the animals were, and much further north the pygmy tribes in the distant rain forests. Suddenly, after the weeks of gray in Kinshasa and by the coast, this was the real Africa at last—wild, hot, menacing, touched with coming adventure, a country straight from an old *Boys' Own Paper* or a reel of *Raiders of the Lost Ark*. Bouncing about in the thermals, it all lay beneath me—the Africa

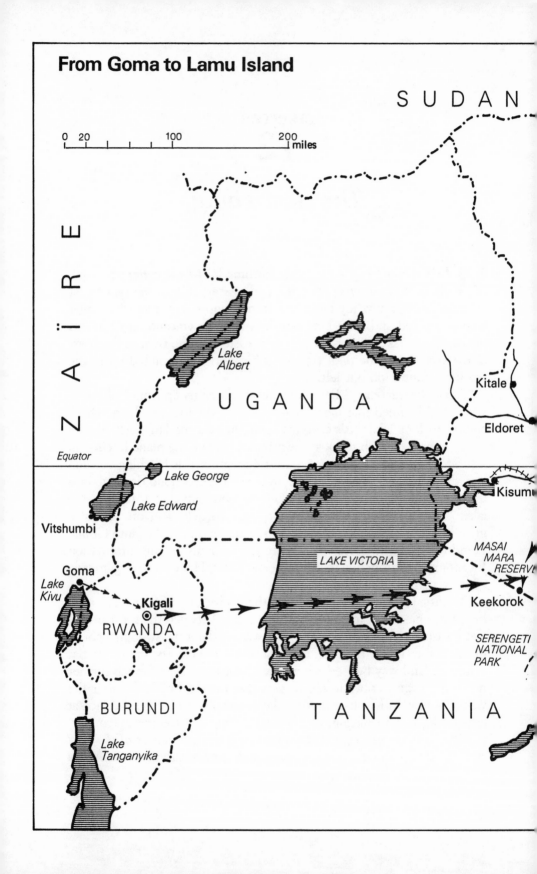

From Goma to Lamu Island

S U D A N

0 20   100   200 miles

Z A Ï R E

Lake Albert

U G A N D A

Kitale

Eldoret

Equator

Lake George

Lake Edward

Kisum

Vitshumbi

MASAI MARA RESERVI

LAKE VICTORIA

Goma

Lake Kivu

Kigali

RWANDA

Keekorok

SERENGETI NATIONAL PARK

BURUNDI

T A N Z A N I A

Lake Tanganyika

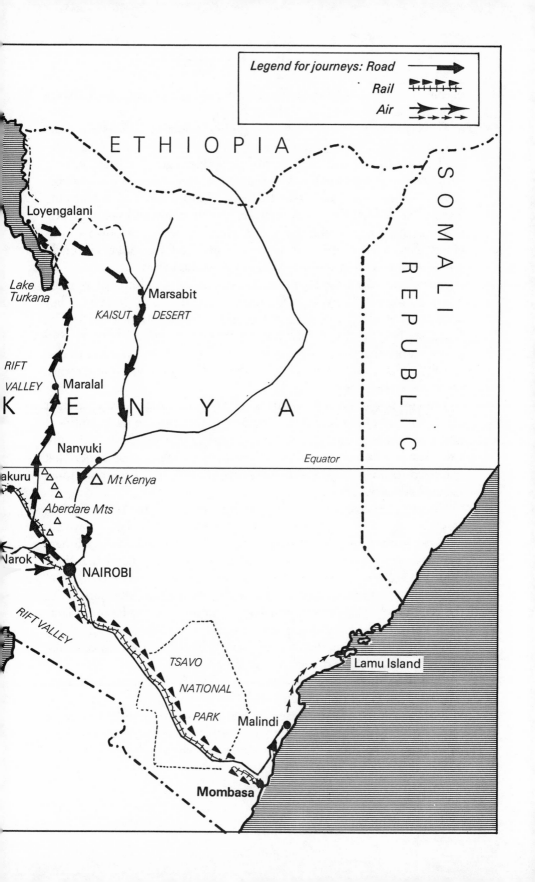

Legend for journeys: Road
Rail
Air

ETHIOPIA

SOMALI REPUBLIC

Loyengalani

Lake Turkana

Marsabit

KAISUT DESERT

RIFT VALLEY

Maralal

KENYA

Nanyuki

Equator

akuru

△ Mt Kenya

Aberdare Mts

Narok

NAIROBI

RIFT VALLEY

TSAVO

NATIONAL

PARK

Lamu Island

Malindi

Mombasa

of my childhood, Africa at my command, the way one had always expected, always secretly wanted it to be.

Midday: the volcanoes above us, gliding down over the stark blue, Italian-looking lake, dropping onto the runway just outside Goma . . . the heat on the tarmac, the first really blinding light of Africa, lapping like waves over my face, the first clean sweat already coursing down my chest . . . Kinshasa already a bad dream. We took our bags over to the Karibu Hotel bus, the pretty Zaïrean hostess ready and waiting. Yes, this was more like it: the real thing. Here we were, set down in this empty, fiery heart of the continent—just in time for a cold beer, lunch, a nap, and a swim in the hotel pool or the lake before sunset.

Then I saw the lone Japanese at the head of a column of porters, boxes on their heads, with two armed askaris taking up the rear. They were moving along the road just outside the airport perimeter. The Japanese, festooned with cameras—a tough, evil-faced young man in grimy leather shorts with days of stubble on his chin—looked at us and our little plane contemptuously before striding away into the distance toward the volcanoes.

The real thing? I'd just seen it then. This man, not me, was straight out of *Raiders of the Lost Ark*—journeying through the dark continent in the proper way, on foot, with native porters and tea chests and guns. I was just a cosseted tourist fallen to earth, the rough dream gone. That belonged to the mysterious oriental disappearing down the road to all the real adventure.

His was the journey I should like to have made across Africa, I knew, as we sat down to a splendid napkined lunch an hour later: traveling with tea chests and porters toward tents under the stars. Instead, here we were, once more, set down in an hotel: a luxury hotel this time, three miles out of Goma, perched on the edge of the lake. Apart from the hippy and mission accommodation I'd heard about, the Karibu was the only hotel in this whole vast region, along with the Rwindi Game Lodge which was part of the same excellent Tourhotel group, eighty miles north in the middle of the Virunga National Park. Spectacular tourist hotels, if there'd been any tourists.

"We could have stayed at a mission," I said. "Or crashed with the hippies. This place isn't cheap."

Eleanor frowned. She paused in her *pâté de campagne*. "I suppose so." But her guilt only lasted for a moment. "Except we're not hippies. And Harry changed us both more dollars on the parallel rate. We can afford it."

The circular restaurant with its great picture windows, lavish flower borders, a Hollywood swimming pool beyond that with reclining seats and parasols, then a long greensward sloping down to the lake—a bay of blue water without boats or any other sign of habitation along its shores: Italian blue and empty. There were only half a dozen other guests staying at the hotel, Belgians on holiday, some of them still straggling into lunch from the sixty or so white, Corbusier-style pebbledash cabins that ringed the central block. A couple came in with a child in tow just then, a bright blond seven-year-old with bangs. I suddenly realized I'd seen no white children for more than a month. Yes, I was living again, with the brilliant sun up here at 3000 feet cutting through the air like a knife, the first such sun in a month, a breeze raking the lake now and then, turning it from stark blue to aquamarine as it rippled over it, wind through watery corn. I watched the child, sitting near us now. "When do we go back home?" she asked her mother brightly. "In two weeks. In time for school," the woman said. "In time for work," her father added. Here was no little band of sad expatriates, locked in the country. These were tourists from Rwanda, I'd heard at the desk when we'd checked in—diplomats and international aid people with their families—who'd come over by road to this luxury hotel before going on up to see the game in the National Park: over for the weekend, for the border with Rwanda here was only three miles away along the lake shore to the east. Rwanda, where we both had visas for now— Rwanda and its capital Kigali, only 150 miles away, where there was a weekly SABENA flight direct to Nairobi and civilization. . . . For a second I had the lovely feeling that my journey was nearly over.

"Let's have some wine," I said, with happiness. "On the parallel rate." But then I thought of Harry. He and Alain had taken us out to the airport very early that morning in the gray, muggy dawn, shepherded us through the appalling customs and emigration holdups, despite the fact that our journey was only on a domestic flight and not leaving Zaïre.

"There you are," Harry had said, halfway through this stramash."Even they don't want you to go." Finally we were out on the apron. Our cargo flight—an old, privately owned 707—lay straight ahead of us. A hundred yards away a big khaki-camouflaged military transport, an American C131, was loading up with Belgian paratroopers.

Another jet, to our right, started up, an engine whining, then roaring. "Thank you, Harry—" I shouted. Eleanor bent her head up toward him. "Look after that old horn gramophone, won't you?" she yelled. "It's yours now." He nodded—a smile that wasn't really a smile. Harry had the gramophone and all the old French seventy-eights. Guetary's "Boucle blonde," the lilac-blue china tea service, along with the rest of the debris from the witch doctors' stalls, the mandrake roots and chicken feathers. Harry had all that now instead of us and I felt ashamed—deserting someone in the front line we were running away from. In a month we'd lived a chunk of real life in Kinshasa, I realized. We'd made a life between the three of us and with the little band. And now I was running from it—the gutted art-deco radios and broken bidets in the flea market: the red cloth making a lantern over the naked bulb in Eleanor's room in the Amethyst; the steel engravings of Bruges Cathedral, old Antwerp under snow, and the torn poster of the Brussels World Fair. I was deserting Harry's bungalow hidden in the frangipani trees as well, betraying the domestic life: Joshua padding about among his beer bottles in the laundry, Mirabelle cleaning her whiskers while the old man snoozed the afternoon away, the fan rustling a copy of last week's *Times*. What had seemed so hopeless and unpromising to begin with in Kinshasa we had transformed: Eleanor had changed me and Harry had altered both of us. A grace had come which we had all shaped together.

I'd wanted to tell Harry then, "We'll be back." But I knew we wouldn't. Instead I shouted at him: "Come and see us!—in England."

"What?" He cupped a hand round his ear. Another engine on the jet had started.

"At HOME!" I yelled.

"Yes, I'll still be here," he answered, misunderstanding. "Any time." At that moment neither of us wanted to leave Kinshasa. Harry, almost single-handedly, had transformed the terrible city into a loved place.

Now, eight hours later, in this irrelevant, isolated luxury by the lake, I missed the downtown squalor, the maimed beggars by the Post Office. And later, when I slept across the room from Eleanor, I dreamed of failure. And when I woke I thought what a long way I'd come to the heart of the continent to no real purpose.

It was Eleanor who woke me in the other bed. She was crying.

I said, "We're surely just being difficult—now that things are better."

"What's better?"

"The weather at least."

I'd seen Eleanor crying drunk—with the veracity that drink gives. Now her sober tears, since they were real, seemed forced, invented. I sat on the bed beside her. The eczema on her arms had never got better—the chalky, flaky scabs on her skin, above and below her elbows. Perhaps she'd been right about the drink: there was something there that cured this rash, if nothing else: a poison and a medicine—kill and cure together. I touched her arm, on one of the dry spots. The tears came like hiccups, in spasms, little convulsions, that she tried to hold back each time, biting her lip, closing her eyes, before the pain exploded once more.

"We *had* to leave Kinshasa. You said yourself, Eleanor. Come on. . . ."

"Yes." She drew her breath in sharply, then held it; the air still heaving up and down her throat, shaking her chest.

"You *said* so."

She nodded her head vehemently several times, eyes closed again.

"All right. So we can *do* something up here. That was always your point—*doing* things. The volcanoes, the pygmies, the game park. It's all here."

"Yes," she spluttered, finally letting go her breath.

"Well, then."

"I know it's all here. But somehow it isn't. Too perfect, too lucky, like you said."

She took a hanky and mopped her eyes. "Actually, I was sad—because I was thinking of someone I'd been cruel to years ago at the convent school I first went to." She stopped, bewildered.

"That's really why you were crying?" I asked.

"Yes. There was a fat unhappy girl, my age, nose always running, who was so homesick she was red in the face with crying secretly. And we were mean to her. I was mean to her, because I was as homesick as she was and didn't want to admit it. So I took it out on her. Louisa she was called. I remember her better now than most of my friends then. Louisa Watson. I wonder what happened to her." She started to blub again.

"You can't make the past right. There's no point getting into the vales-of-tears department over it."

"I can't—help it."

"You're just homesick yourself now. We've got to the middle of Africa. Can't see where we came from, can't see the other shore; too far to swim back, no knowing how far the other bank is. But it's all a matter of confidence."

"Is it?" she asked unhopefully.

There was a Gideon Bible on the bedside table between us. The room was as neat, anonymous as a pin. But there was something else wrong with it. I put the Bible away in the drawer, fidgeting. Yet it wasn't that. Of course—I knew what was wrong: we hadn't unpacked.

"Let's unpack," I said. Eleanor got up then and almost as soon as she opened her suitcase the tears went: the lace and silk, her pullovers and trousers eased her, a balm of Pringle sweaters and lingerie from Marks and Sparks.

I said, as we put our bits and pieces away, "That's really our problem—we should try to see Africa as more than just a succession of picture postcards—from airplanes, hotels, buses; or from Harry's house. We've been too comfy. Joshua, or a shower or a restaurant always just round the corner. Africa's a hard place. And we've done nothing of that. That's what we're going to do—see the game at Virunga, take a trip down the lake."

She turned to me, unrolling a pair of woolly socks, sniffing them. "You don't have to be frightened," I said. "In Kinshasa we were all together—Harry, other people, the city. Now there's just us. It looks more difficult. But it needn't be."

"It is. That's really why I was crying, I think."

"Crying before we've begun . . ." I said lightly. "You said that was one of my problems: never making the venture."

She turned to me abruptly. "But what venture do *I* make? It's not so much that I miss the people in Kinshasa. It's just that there's—just you and me now. No distractions. We can't pretend we're just friends anymore. City friends."

"Why not?"

"Because I'd be pretending, at least—that's why."

"I see." I put a clean shirt out. "But you wanted to come—you knew you'd be alone with me."

"Oh God, you're not that thick, Joe," she said impatiently, stamping her foot in frustration. Then she stamped it again, like an animal.

"I'm *not* that thick. I *do* see: you don't want me to end up as just another Robert in your life. Though since I'm married—I may be that way already for you. But you wanted to come. What am I to do? I *am* married."

"And you can't forget that—can you? Not for a moment."

"A moment? It'd have to be for another six weeks."

"You told me last week at the party, when you had all that drink—"

"Well, so you know my problems. Splendid—"

"Yes. So perhaps you don't have to be so . . ."

"Conscientious?"

She nodded. Now it was my turn to look away from her, embarrassed.

"And perhaps it'd be better if you weren't. You might be able to make things up at home that way."

"Position of strength?"

She nodded.

"Maybe. But how would I make things up with you then—in the end?"

"I don't. . . ."

"You don't see? But you do. You've a thing about fidelity. I could see it in all that Robert business. Once you start with someone—I bet you're as faithful as me. That's another problem of ours." My eyes were caught, mesmerized by the light fixture above my bed.

"Why don't you *look* at me—when you talk about these things?"

"Because I don't see any answer to them. I could look you in the face and pretend there was—that'd be easy."

"But there might be an answer, if you didn't run away from it. If you faced it—"

"*Faced* it? Faced leaving you—in six weeks' time. That's what I'd have to face. And so would you. No matter that I made things up at home afterward. And I mightn't. That's what I have to face. Not you *now*. But an end—in the end—if we start on it."

She was silent. "Do you want to go?" I asked. "You could get another cargo flight back to Kinshasa."

"All right," she said quickly. "I'd better do that." She turned at once and started to put her clothes back in her suitcase.

I watched her for half a minute, astonished—the sweaters and the tights and the rust cords, all stuffed down anyhow, anywhere. I stood there, unable to move, like a nightmare.

I stirred myself at last. "No."

"Yes." She reached round for her hairbrush. I held her wrist. She wrenched it away. I tried to close the top of her case, forcing it over her hands inside.

"Look at me!" I shouted. "*You* won't look at me now." I pulled her round toward me. Still she wouldn't look up, eyes firmly shut.

"*Look* at me. Just look—"

"No. No, no, no!"

She still had the hairbrush raised in her hand. The bristles pricked my chest when I forced her to me, the brush caught between us, her eyes still closed, trying to twist away from me. But finally she edged back an inch, letting the brush fall to the floor, so that we could hold each other properly, neither of us looking at the other, her head turned away against my shoulder then, my chin resting by her ear. We stayed that way for a minute. Then she went back to her suitcase and started to unpack it. Through the cabin window I could see the volcano casting a red-gray plume against the late afternoon blue.

How neatly we were blackmailing each other, I thought—denying emotions in ourselves, converting them into cruelties; testing, provoking the other, to see if there was really anything in the affair after all. And we hadn't found an answer to that, for all our scheming. We had simply confirmed our positions—wary, uncertain—still pressing for advantage in all sorts of ambushes, forays; still shamed by our retreats.

Eleanor took a shower—it was really too cold to swim now in this high air—and I went down to see the manager about plans. I was determined to keep my promise, to stretch myself up here in the Kivu, do something demanding, dramatic—tear a chapter out of that *Boys' Own Paper* serial or go bust in the attempt. Three hundred miles north of Goma, beyond the Virunga National Park, lay the pygmy tribes, still lurking in the almost impenetrable Ituri rain forests, still the territory of the tom-tom and poisoned arrow. I thought we might well further our adventurous careers in that direction. There were the very rare mountain gorillas, too, in the dense bamboo forests of Mount Kahuzi, a hundred miles to the south, on the ferry down Lake Kivu: machete country here, a two- or three-day hike to see them, clearing the jungle as you went. And there was the volcano.

There was plenty to do up here, mastering the wilds.

The manager, a latter-day *colon Belge,* said, "You can get to Rwindi Game Lodge in the National Park by road from here. But the road north from Rwindi"—he shrugged dismissively—"the 'Route de la Beauté' we used to call it in the old days—well, it's so bad now no one will take you, not even in four-wheel drive. And the road south from Goma, round the lake to Bukavu to see the mountain gorillas, is just the same: no go. They've let the roads go all to hell here. What can you expect?" he added superciliously. "Only way is to take a small plane."

"But what about the lake ferry? It says in the guide book. . . ."

"The ferry?" He laughed: a hard, dry laugh. "There's no fuel in the Kivu now. Ferry gave up months ago."

Apart from the game lodge, that left only the volcano, Nyiragongo.

You could see it everywhere from the hotel, a great spew of dull, steamy cloud lifting from the cone fifteen miles away.

"It's bigger than it looks from here," the man went on. He was bored already. Some Belgians, friends of his obviously, had just come into the lobby. "Never climbed it myself. But you take a guide at the bottom. There's some sort of cabin near the crater rim where you spend the night."

"Can't you do it in one day?"

"Maybe. But no one does. It's a 45-degree angle up most of the way. A three-thousand-meter climb from the bottom. And even"—he spread his arms in disgust—"even when you get to the top there's usually nothing to see. Clouds come in all round, the vapor. You never see down into the crater."

"Well, I don't mind. Nothing venture. . . ."

"I'm sorry?" He didn't follow my French.

"We'll do it in a day," I said. The man looked at me suspiciously. Then he looked up out of the doorway. We both looked up. The noise of the airplane didn't start in the distance. It was suddenly upon us. the vast coarse roar of turboprops coming in over the lake: then a crescendo as the great snail snout and black belly of the C131 military transport flew over the hotel just a few hundred feet above us. The manager, with his friends, went out onto the terrace beyond the lobby. I followed them. The plane made a dramatic turn, tipping right over on its side half a mile inland, then came back to us on another low level run. Strafed? Bombed? Were we about to take it, at last, in this irrelevant luxury hotel? But the manager and his friends smiled as the camouflaged transport crashed over us once more, tipping its wings this time, waving them against the pearl-blue evening light.

The manager looked at his watch. *"Sur l'heure—exacte!"* He was very happy. Going back inside he gave directions to the black desk clerk: the bar was to be made ready, drinks and ice gathered. The men would be here in less than half an hour. "I wonder—" I said to the manager, another question on my lips. But he turned away. I didn't exist.

Very soon afterward it was whisky-soda time at the Hotel Karibu. Half a dozen Belgian pilots and navigators and a few senior paratroop officers—including the Colonel of the regiment—all still in baggy flying suits or battle dress, were crushed around the bar. The hotel had suddenly come alight in the evening, cocktail hour for the warriors.

Eleanor had joined me, sipping a *maracudja* juice at a table near the crowd. "Probably the same plane, same people we saw at Kinshasa airport this morning," I told her. "There are two or three Belgian paratroop brigades stationed here permanently. They patrol the Shaba region, the copper belt in the south, then up along this eastern border: flying gunships, filled with Belgian toughs. Boots has a thing about communists or white mercenaries infiltrating the country over on this side. Reds or Rhodesians under the bed. Hence all those buddy boys up there. This must be one of their watering holes."

The men were into their second drink already, the manager an affable mine host in the midst of them. The talk was of Brussels—a party last weekend out at Uccle, a mistress taken for the weekend to Ostend.

"Do you see the Colonel?" Eleanor said. I looked at the man. He was short and wiry, in his fifties, a stubble of cropped white hair, not an inch of fat. Straight, and tough as a nail, with small, scheming, all-seeing eyes: he was in charge of the world. He took his drink away from the crowd just then, moving toward a table in the dining room where he picked up a menu. He looked at it, then brought it back.

"The *bouillabaisse*?" I heard him say to the manager. This was a special dish, I'd noticed at lunchtime, at 150 Zaïres.

"It's superb," the manager said. "Lake fish, came in yesterday. Or the *steack tartare*?"

"We'll have both," the Colonel said. "All around," he went on without consulting the company.

"Encore du whisky," the manager said.

"The ridiculous to the sublime?" Eleanor said. "That's what you thought, wasn't it, coming up here: the real Africa." She looked at me sadly. "It's really the other way round."

"I don't run the place."

"No. They do—up there at the bar. Just like that Belgian engineer we met at Matadi."

"There's nothing we can do about it."

"I wasn't thinking of *doing* anything about it."

"I saw all those scrawny old women bent double as well as you—on the way in from the airport this morning. And all the matchstick children. And I know this area, the Kivu, is the breadbasket of Zaïre. At this altitude fresh vegetables, everything grows here. That's what all the cargo planes that come up here are for: to take it all back to Kinshasa. Vegetables, meat, coffee—it all comes from here and—"

"Yes, and it looks like they're all starving here."

I sighed. "Yes. . . ."

"And you want the *real* Africa—the high adventure."

"That's what you wanted, too."

"Yes, yes." She threw the words away sardonically.

Eleanor's hair was damp again after her shower, the helmet of blond curls slightly subdued and dark-streaked with water. Her blue Pringle sweater was as blue as the afternoon had been—and her well-creased jeans a fainter, whiter shade in the same color: the color of the last of the sky above the lake now, the luminous pearl-blue tint that the altitude or the reflected water gave to the light here.

I looked at her now. It was always easier to look at Eleanor in company, when she was distracted, looking somewhere else: the long, straight nose, the reddish peach complexion, more colored now, after her tears perhaps, or after her hot bath. A familiar face as she gazed intently at the bar. Yet now there was something unfamiliar about it, I suddenly thought. What was it? Yes, her eyes were more deeply inset, set back in their sockets. Had that been the tears? She seemed older in any case. That was it. And I'd not noticed it before. Had age marked her in the four weeks since we'd met?

She turned, noticing my gaze. "What are you looking at me like that for?"

"You're getting older and wiser," I said, and I told her about her eyes.

"What—sunk in my skull? An old hag, suddenly?"

"No. Just a depth I hadn't seen before."

"And what does that mean?"

I shrugged. "I don't know. Knowledge? Secrets?" I smiled. "Or just tiredness?"

"*You* don't know. . . ." She was sarcastic.

"No."

"And yet you look at me like that!"

"Like what?"

"Just the way you look at me. You know. And I know. You won't say it. I won't say it. But we know."

"Yes," I admitted.

"Why is it," she said quizzically, impishly, head to one side. "Why is it you always look at me that way in public—in restaurants or bars —when I can't jump up and kiss you?"

We set off first thing next morning in the hotel minibus for the volcano, traveling into Goma, then through the outskirts on the other side toward the mountain. It was lava country here already, even in the suburbs. The shanty town itself had been built from cut blocks of lava and beyond this lay a whole rough sea of porous gray stone, with lines of great black boulders, like a tidewrack, marking the end of the lava run that had come here four years ago, burying the outlying villages. Now there was an open meat market on these ruined sites. A scrawny cow was being slaughtered with pangas just as we passed. It writhed on the shingly black stones, legs kicking, trying to stand up for the last time. This was rough country all right, adventurous country. This was the real thing. But I wasn't sure I liked it.

At the foot of the mountain I paid a $10 fee to the surly Park Ranger and after a lot of palaver and a not sufficient tip, I suspect, he gave us the smallest and youngest of the guides—a ragged, barefoot, consumptive-looking youth with a cast in one eye, equipped with nothing but a large panga. Looking up at the long stretch of thick rain forest and the steep slopes beyond that, neither he nor it seemed sufficient for the tasks ahead.

"You must be back here by five o'clock," the Ranger warned me. That gave us just over nine hours, up and down. And to begin with, for the first hour, walking across the sharp edges of an old lava bed, the going was easy enough. I had stout shoes on, Eleanor in substantial sneakers. How the barefoot guide managed I couldn't imagine. I asked him several times only to discover that he spoke no French whatsoever, only a few syllables in some arcane local dialect.

But once into the rain forest on the middle slopes things were very different. There was only the foot-wide, slippery, twisting, rising path to follow here, which often disappeared completely, so that we had to clamber over slimy, rotten tree trunks, struggle through snakes of hanging creeper and fantastically bearded branches, the little guide forging ahead through the moist gloom, cutting great swaths out of the dense undergrowth, grappling with the creeper, felling the arm-thick stalks of vast sprouting weeds—rampant, exotic vegetation that rose twelve feet in the air, showering us with tepid water when it collapsed. There was no sound. The jungle seemed dead beyond our cleared path—except, every so often, for the high-toned, continuous, eerie whine that came from the matted leaves above us: the noise of the Telegraph Bird as I came to call it, for the earsplitting noise it made was exactly that of a high wind singing through wires.

Steam rose from evil, marshy pools and faults in the volcanic rock now and then, clouding the gray gloom with a damp, sulphurous mist.

This certainly was *Boys' Own Paper* stuff, the impenetrable African rain forest—full of all the fears, nightmares, the dreams of childhood.

After an hour we left the tree belt, emerging on open, rocky slopes. But now, as the manager had warned me, the going was at forty-five degrees and I had to stop every few minutes, gasping, my legs withering with pain—Eleanor hardly any better off, as we pulled ourselves up, gripping the mossy lichens and glass-edged lava outcrop. The guide was never out of breath for a moment: this whole excursion was no more than a short stroll for him. Behind us rain clouds had come in and a great swirling fog had covered all the world beneath, moving up the slopes, edging toward us. The guide beckoned us on urgently. We had to move fast or lose ourselves in those thick, damp clouds. And that was agony, my legs seeming to burn now, a sweat of fear and effort blinding my eyes, images of horror jostling in my mind: our bare, picked bones found on this mountainside a month hence, *King Solomon's Mines* become fact. One mistake here, I felt, and I would be a part of, not an audience for, that boys' serial.

But the clouds blew away, sliding straight on over the shoulder of the mountain, disappearing as quickly and mysteriously as they had come. The fog had licked at our heels and now it had spared us.

"Was that what they call a 'near thing'—or the 'real thing'?" Eleanor asked, gasping, as we paused a moment, the guide rather a haughty little figure now some way above us. The air bellowed in and out of our chests.

"Both, I think."

"I don't know that I'm up to either."

We knelt on the mountainside, resting, leaning into the outcrop, knuckles on the lichened rock, keeping ourselves in a vertical plane against the sharp angle that ran away beneath us—two pilgrims, two penitents, not allowing ourselves the luxury of looking backward over the world, intent only on the Holy Grail ahead of us: the little tin cabin we could see now a few hundred feet above us and the dark crater rim five hundred feet beyond that.

We stopped for another ten minutes in the cabin and though we could still see nothing of the eruption, there was the acrid, nasty smell from the wispy gray plumes of smoke emerging from the cone: a mix of fourth-form chemistry and old socks on a bonfire. The last 500 feet to the summit seemed an almost sheer climb to me, so that when I finally got there, quite exhausted, blinded with sweat again, I nearly fell over the crater rim. The guide grabbed my leg and I slithered back.

I was astonished as much as terrified. I hadn't expected a drop, a fall, a vision—anything so sudden and sensational as this. I edged myself back very carefully to the top. The rim of the crater didn't slope away from me on the other side. It didn't fall vertically down into the vast chasm either: it sloped *inward* beneath me, so that in looking over the edge there was the absolute feeling of being suspended over the crater, with nothing but vast space beyond and beneath—a sheer, half mile-deep drop to an extraordinary molten lake at the bottom. And we were lucky with the weather. There were no clouds and little vapor in the huge gray cauldron. We could see right down to the spurting fountains of orange lava—which seemed to rise and fall in slow motion from this height, the liquid rock thundering up, jetting hundreds of feet in the air, with inky, spitting spirals of smoke above that.

The colors of the seething lake were a fantastic, changing mix: a shining silver white at the heart of the eruption, the fountains a ruddy orange flecked with blood, spreading to vermilion, then dark ocher, and finally a pink-tinted lead at the edges. I just gazed down at the whole stupendous vision, time lost to me, spellbound, looking on this seeming entrance to another childhood fable that had once brought Africa close to me—Jules Verne's *Journey to the Centre of the Earth*. And here it was, right in front of me, the real thing. No one could deny that. There was no doubt about it: we had been to the mountaintop. We said nothing for ten minutes. There was nothing to say, Eleanor leaning over, chin on the edge, beside me.

We had complained of Africa; we had failed to travel, either upriver or with native porters and tea chests to tents under the stars: we had had, instead, failure and depression and endless gray skies by the coast. Now, at last, we had won. Sated with the volcano, we looked behind us. The earlier rainclouds had moved away over the lake to our right. The great valley in front of us basked in hazy air, a filtered sun coming through ribs of mackerel cloud very high up. Across the valley, fifteen miles away, another, dormant volcano rose against the tawny, flat savannah land beyond; and above it a lead-blue arc of sky ran down to the horizon northward. Yet at 12,000 feet we seemed to be higher than all this, even the sky—the landscape, like the crater, a crucible beneath us. Motionless, it was not the fleeting sense of vision one has from an airplane—caught, moved along willy-nilly by its mechanics. Here we were in charge, Africa at our command, spread out beneath us, a vast tablecloth where we could feed at will.

The manager was surprised to see us back at the hotel that evening

—just nicely in time for a six o'clock hot bath. Now I felt I deserved all the luxuries of the little cabin. Eleanor soaked in the water, steam billowing from the bathroom door, while I lay out, bathed already, pink-skinned, warmly exhausted. She hummed a tune, talked to herself softly in the steam. Or was she talking to me? I was half-asleep.

"What did you say?"

"Did I say anything? Too tired to think even."

"I lost both legs somewhere up that mountain. But I think they're coming back now."

"I don't know about mine. Don't know if I'll ever find them again."

"But you're supposed to be fit and young."

"You climbed better than I did."

"It's all the walking I do at home—over the hills and far away."

"Walking, walking—you told me that was the great cure a few weeks ago, didn't you?"

"For a hangover—yes. But it's a cure anyway."

"I seem to have forgotten about hangovers."

"Like childbirth?" I said.

"What do you mean?"

"Else women might never go through it again—if they remembered the pain."

The water stirred in the bath. She got out. I could hear her drying herself. Then she came into the room with the big towel wrapped sharply round her breasts, falling sheer to her splendid knees.

"I didn't think you'd threaten me like that, with the drink business. I thought I was handling it all pretty well." She rubbed her midriff delicately—more scratching herself—for an instant. Then she looked at me, upset.

"I meant the past dies. And that's a good thing sometimes," I said.

"Because if it dies, if you forget it, you can start all over again—all the foolishness?"

"Or the beauty. It works both ways."

"Birth or drink?"

"Yes."

"Options?"

I nodded.

"Or us then," she said. "That's another option. We could start as well. If the past is dead."

"*Touché.*"

The ghosts of drink and marriage seemed to have disappeared above us both just then—the two of us quite free in the middle of Africa, the volcano mastered: Africa, where not one but both of us had at last been taken, lurking at the gateway, into life. Exhausted, suspended between past and future, we found virtue now, not fear, in being in the middle of an ocean, seeing neither shore. The places we had come from, our destinations, were both equally invisible. There was no panic for us in this total isolation from everything we had known or were to know. The only commitment we had was to each other. But we didn't make love.

It wasn't something one or other of us declined. We both declined it willingly, without words, happy enough already in the steamy cabin, relaxed with so much physical success on the mountain, sated with adventure—feeling that love itself could wait for thinner times.

CHAPTER

13

Flame and Fire

We flew in low, straight down the grass airstrip next to Rwindi Game Lodge, on a trial run to see that the ground was clear of animals. Patrick banked the Cessna round at the far end, leaning over steeply, and we saw a pride of lion in a dry gully just at the end of the strip—and another group lazing just a few hundred yards away. Coming back on the return run, a big warthog, tail in air, stormed into the undergrowth, moving down to a river that lay in a small valley in front of the lodge. The place seemed to be littered with game.

"The Belgians got Virunga together in 1926—the first game park in Africa," Patrick told us. "And still one of the best—especially now there are so few tourists out here. No one disturbs the animals, not even the natives—there's no farmland near Virunga. Just empty space between the mountains. This valley runs right up to a big lake fifty miles north, Lake Idi Amin. There's a small fishing village there, Vitshumbi. But nothing else. End of the world here."

Out of the plane, much lower down than Goma, the heat took us up in a great bright burning hand: shimmer heat, laced with wisps of baking breeze. The game lodge was a few hundred yards away—a central compound of old, single-story wooden buildings and two lines of modern, whitewashed, thatch-roofed cabins running away from it, down a street with incongruous lampposts. Rwindi was a tourist village set between great mountain ranges ten miles to either side of it—razorbacked peaks, a faint heather blue in the white light—with the savannah, the cropped grass and scrub, yellowy-green in places, burnt gold or tawny-brown in most others. But it was the light that struck you—burnished, crystal clear; a light without secrets, where every object, shaking in the heat waves, seemed to beckon one—dancing flame, fire, a land of burning bushes.

We checked in at the Lodge. The place was almost deserted. Patrick was taking back some Belgian tourists; he wasn't staying. Eleanor and

I shared another cabin, close to the small pool and dining room, more spartan accommodation this time, with half-burnt, wax-smeared candles on the bedside table, between the twin beds, and more candles in the bathroom. There was no Gideon Bible here—just a lot of dead beetles and mosquitoes caught in the window mesh and on the sill, and a camphor smell of some spray used to deter the bugs. The red tiles on the floor were all upset, askew, where the heat and the rain of the valley, the extremes of damp and dry, had pushed them up and down over the years, so that walking the room was an uneven, unexpected exercise: Proust's pavements of Venice come all the way to Africa. Though for me they brought back the squalid soap and mucus-encrusted red tiles on the floor of the shower room in my prep school in Dublin thirty-five years before. I told Eleanor of the memory.

"Yes. Those sort of things come back much more strongly here somehow. . . ."

"Filling the emptiness with something solid, I suppose."

I looked out of the small window, like the eyepiece of a telescope, that gave onto so much stark immensity. "Even unhappiness—that appalling little prep school—I can look on it with some affection out here. Peopling the spaces. The mad Major, drunk at four, scuttling down the laurel driveway for a chaser in the pub up Ranelagh road. He was the headmaster, too, with a splendid bosomy wife. The only man who ever taught us anything, though: geography. He'd been all over the world in the Army. Never used a book. Gave it to us all direct. 'This is Kenya,' he said to us once. 'I was stationed here'—and he pointed to somewhere north of Nairobi on the map. Then he told us all about his life out there, in Gil-Gil it was, some big army camp. Then about the local people, the Maasai, and the marvelous landscapes. That was another dream of Africa for me. He made it all live—so that I had to prove it one day."

"All sounds a bit too neat. . . ."

"It's true, though. There was the Major and my father before that. He was going to take us all out to Africa after the war: a job with the groundnuts scheme, up into life in some Happy Valley." And I told her about my father's cloudy, whisky-soda visions, with my godfather, in the chintzy service flat in Battersea in 1947.

"My father never wanted to go anywhere except the city—or tend the garden. Holidays were an appalling strain. We went to Mont St. Michel one Easter. Nearly killed him. That's why I've wanted to travel."

"What happened? Why did they divorce?"

"My mother took up with someone else. Rather simple."

"But with that kind of City, Thames valley, home counties background—I thought such people turned a blind eye, took a few large gins and rode things out?"

"Yes. But my father—he had what you call a 'thing' about fidelity."

"Rows?"

"Yes." Eleanor paused, remembering. "But more silences—which was worse. At breakfast: coldness over the cold kippers." She went into the bathroom, putting her things away there. "They couldn't talk about it. That was the worst thing."

"Did she marry the other man?"

"No. He was married already to a rather mousy little London woman—I don't think she knew about it. Mummy lives in London now. And they still go on with the same old sort of 'illicit' relationship. Wednesday evenings outside the Kensington Public Library: afternoon hotels in Paddington. It's all too sad. And squalid and demeaning," she added harshly. "Neither of them ever seemed capable of taking a decision over the whole business. Only my father—when he divorced her."

"Maybe it was rather a harsh decision?"

"Was it? Wasn't he just protecting himself? The pain of living with someone who wanted to live with someone else? My father was good at making unemotional decisions. That's what it was: a cold choice—not to go on being hurt. I understand that."

"And your mother—did you understand her side of it?"

Eleanor spoke sharply, emerging from the bathroom. "I did—and I didn't. I do—and I don't. It's not a question of having to *forgive* her for anything. It's just I could never see the intelligence in it. And she had that before. Some cog seemed to have dropped out of her mind in the whole affair: a blank space. I could never understand that."

"There's never any logic to these things."

"But that's the whole awfulness—that someone should so hurt themselves and other people for the *lack* of that. Not being able to order their lives."

"Yet you're frightened of the same thing?"

"Yes. I think I am. Of *course* I am. My drinking is all part of that. I couldn't—or wouldn't—get tied up properly with people. Because I'd seen my mother make such a terrible hash of all that. So I drank. That seemed a much safer commitment."

"Isn't that too neat—wanting everything cut and dried in emotions, tickety-boo, forever and ever amen?"

"Yes." She smiled wanly. "From what you told me about your domestic problems the other night—that's one more dreary thing we share: wanting everything 'tickety-boo.' That's just it."

The beer was warm for lunch. The fridges didn't work in the daytime. The lodge generator only came on for four hours after dark, the African manager told us afterward, taking coffee with us.

"No fuel," he added grimly. "Just enough for the beer run."

"The beer run?"

"Can't keep staff—let alone any tourists up here—without beer. More important than fuel. We go up for it once a week to Vitshumbi, the fishing village by the lake. The pickup's going this afternoon. You should take a lift. Only way you'll see the game park. Our own minibuses are out of action."

We left just after four. The heat was worse. Even the baking breeze had gone. Our driver had a vast bundle of 5- and 10-Zaïre notes hidden right up behind the dashboard. *"Les voleurs,"* he said darkly. He spoke reasonable French, a small man in a neon-colored Congo-Hawaii shirt, with a permanently put-upon, downcast expression: resigned to the worst, despite his good job here with the Lodge. The dust rose behind us, a thick, billowy fog that curled back on itself in great waves, as we swerved down the gully opposite the hotel and over a wooden bridge that spanned the small river.

"Fish?" I asked.

The driver nodded. "Tomorrow," he went on. "You will see His Excellency the Governor come to fish here. And last week the President himself was at Rwindi. He is a *great* fish man. Is best fish here in all Zaïre. Many, *many* fish."

"How do they fish?" I suspected nets or even explosives. But the driver flicked his wrist, miming the cast of a fly rod. Then he added, "Bread, worms. The President—he has learned it very well: he fishes in your country, in Scotland, every year. Very clever fishing man."

On the other side of the gully, the land flattened out completely ahead of us, thick scrub to either side of the track, with trees poking up here and there, so that the horizon disappeared, apart from the mountain peaks in the far distance. Even with all the windows open, bowling along at thirty miles an hour, the heat was terrific. The crates of empty beer bottles rattled in the back. We rattled with them, the three of us jolting about on the bench seat. The dust in our eyes, throats, and hair soon formed a liquid grime with the sweat that ran down our open shirt fronts, staining the cotton with dirty rivulets.

Often the driver swerved right off into the bush, avoiding great sandy depressions where the rains had completely eroded the track—where it had become nothing but a fifty-yard-wide strip of fine tilth, criss-crossed with deeply indented tyre marks, a quicksand for earlier trucks. In such places, making a wide arc, he would zigzag through the scrub, toppling over small trees with the bumper, swerving to avoid larger bushes or fallen trunks, land cruising now, hither and thither, like a boat searching for the right wind at sea: exhilarating but draining with the constant effort of keeping one's balance in the bench seat, where I was thrown against Eleanor or the door every five seconds, jolted upward to the cab roof every other five.

It was too hot, too difficult for any talk, spinning round the bush-burnt world like this. I closed my eyes, Eleanor's shoulder suddenly pinned against mine as we dipped into a pothole. I could feel her hot, damp skin through our soaking shirts.

I opened my eyes. Eleanor's shoulder was hard against mine just then. I put my arm across and squeezed it a moment. She looked round at me in surprise, a tired smile on her sweat-smudged face.

The bush thinned out after half an hour. And now we saw more warthogs and plains game: gazelle sprinting away beyond the truck's nose, delicate-legged, white rabbit tails bobbing as they leaped like dolphins, four feet in the air, swerving as they ran, the wide black nose of the Ford pickup like a whale rising and falling over the bumps and potholes.

An hour later, coming into the outskirts of Vitshumbi, a tall, thin elephant ambled across the village street right in front of us, another one nosing about over a rubbish dump a hundred yards away. An appalling smell of rotten fish lay everywhere on the air. Beyond the village we could just see the vast blue of the lake.

"Are they tame, those elephants?"

"No," the driver said. "They come in for the rubbish."

The village was just one long street running down to the bay—a collection of wooden or corrugated iron huts, planted down in exact lines: a few shops, a tin church, the fish market, the filling station and general store where we stopped. A huge Maribu stork strolled over toward the pickup, bigger than all the naked children that had crowded round us, attracted by this rare presence of two white people.

The driver went into the store. Eleanor and I walked past the empty fish market to the edge of the lake. It was the wrong time of day. The long, open boats, drawn up in rows, nets drying over the gunwales, were stalled here until nightfall or early dawn, the fishermen asleep somewhere. A group of children followed us everywhere, always keeping their distance, a precise few yards behind us, moving forward only when we moved, stopping in their tracks the moment we turned, like the children's game of Grandmother's Footsteps.

The shoreline was covered with the detritus of rotting fish, great knuckly backbones of Nile perch like human vertebrae, and slabs of discarded flesh, blackened, decomposing, moving to and fro in the small brackish waves. The smell was frightful. The children tittered, standing still in a group now as we looked at them. One of the older girls, almost naked with a matte gray skin, came forward hesitantly, hand outstretched, the palm supported by her other hand. I thought she was simply hoping for a gift. But she had something in her hand, I saw, a sort of shining medallion. It was a flattened and polished beer bottle top, a crown cap made into a medal, a little glinting sunburst in her white-gray palm. All the children gathered round us then, with lots of these polished crown caps—tossing, spinning them in the air, biting them with their teeth, offering them to us, pointing to my pipe, Eleanor's sunglasses. They were a currency for the children, playing at "Shop." They wanted to buy things from us. Instead we exchanged half a dozen of them for real money, a little collection of *makuta* coins we had on us. And they were disappointed. This real money seemed to mean very little to them. They still wanted my pipe and the sunglasses.

Our driver was sitting glumly in the pickup when we got back. There was no beer in the store. The truck from Goma that week had never set out, or had fallen off the road en route. The road was a killer, he went on, had been for some time. Vitshumbi was practically cut off from the world now. We showed him the polished crown caps. "That's become a real currency among a lot of the villagers," he told us. And I thought how Harry would have liked that—the people here, free of European influence and cut off from all their own hopeless African bureaucracy, were reverting to their ancient ways. An exchange of bottle tops for now, but soon they'd be using beads and trinkets again; then just pure barter—in a time when no white people would ever come to Vitshumbi, for the fuel would have dried up everywhere by then and they would brew their own beer. An arcadia on the lake shore by the end of the century? That had been Harry's vision. I wished I could have believed in it.

That evening the fuel at the Lodge must have given out, for the thump of the generator stopped after only two hours, so that immediately after dinner we made our way to the cabin in darkness, lighting the candles everywhere once we were inside. You couldn't see the stark and ugly furniture, and the harsh yellow paint on the walls had softened in the candlelight, replaced by cigars of gold which rose up above the still flames, the wax melting rapidly, dripping in black rivulets on the saucers, insects dying with a little spitting sound as they flew into the light.

Eleanor hovered in the shadows, trying to find something in her overnight bag on the far side of the room. We hadn't bothered unpacking here; most of our luggage was back in the hotel outside Goma. That sort of therapy wasn't available to us here. I put the crown caps out on the bedside table, along with my pipe and camera.

"I got a few photographs," I said. "But the heat was too much. And the jolting. I'd prefer to keep it all in my mind. Or write it up."

I got out one of the school exercise books I'd been keeping notes in since I'd arrived in Africa. They were only notes—nothing like a diary. I sat on the bed, close to the candle, and wrote about the children and their coins by the lake. The room, with the wax melting everywhere, smelled like Christmas years before, when there were real candles everywhere on the fir tree, set up in the study at the back of the house in Ireland; when some of the candles singed the fir sprigs above them and the air was filled with a crisp, sweet smell of wax and burnt pine: the smell of presents, the certainty of coming gifts piled up, boxed or wrapped beneath the tree.

Eleanor said, "It's Christmasy in here, isn't it?"—though I'd told her nothing of my thoughts.

"Yes. You had candles too, did you? I'd have thought it'd have been all electric in Windsor—little colored bulbs—in your time." I told her of my Christmases thirty-five years before in the wilds of Ireland, during the war, when there was very little electricity.

"No—we had candles. Our birthday ones, used again on the tree. My brother and me. Almost as old-fashioned a childhood as yours. . . ."

"Happy and cared for?"

"Yes."

"Which must have made the end all the worse."

"Yes."

"I'm still surprised—that they went through with it, divorcing, with all that family thing going for them."

"Yes."

"One could surely come to forget the other problem, with a family to care about."

She turned from her bag. I could hardly see her in the faint light. "I thought just that at the time. Until I realized what a hell life had become for them both. Christmases were no fun then. We always had as many relations and friends in as possible, or staying with us, to make things easier, to distract them and us. You see, it became a sort of running sore between them: a bloodletting." She turned away, speaking into the shadows. "He was weeding in the garden one summer—my father— getting up a lot of groundsel from the path. I was helping him—about six months before they separated. I was about fourteen, fifteen. He was stooped over the path ahead of me—a big, floppy, rather ungainly man on his knees, very busy with the weeds. 'You know I don't really get on with your mother anymore,' he said suddenly, his back toward me. I did know this. But I didn't know what to say then. My mind just dried up. 'Oh,' I said or something like that, as if he'd been talking about the weather. But I remember a great black hole opening up inside me, an awful, sort of world-collapsing feeling."

Eleanor was right over by the window now. We could hear the dogs howling—or was it a hyena?—way out beyond the staff quarters behind the Lodge. She opened the curtains. There was a huge moon over the mountains, almost full in a cloudless sky. Our room became brighter, the gold touched with a hint of cold silver.

"And?" I said.

"And nothing. I couldn't say anything."

"Your mother never spoke to you about it?"

"No. Not until almost the time she was leaving. Then she said simply they were going to live apart, that things would be easier, better that way. Later they divorced. Nothing ever came up in court—all very civilized. She took a flat in London—came down and saw us at half-term and in the holidays—and they came to see me at school, both of them together usually. All very civilized. And that annoyed me—all this sur-face politeness when I knew—well, that there was nothing really be-tween them, except thousands of little hates that I didn't know about. Irritation—that had been all that held them together."

"It's a frail boat, marriage. I'm surprised, after what you've told me, you were so keen to marry Robert. You were so set on it."

"Yes."

"Out of the frying pan, into the fire, surely?"

"Ah yes. . . ." I couldn't see if she was smiling in the shadows. But I thought she might have been. She came over and sat on the bed opposite me, shoulders slouched, head down, hands together between her knees.

"You see, I *wanted* the marriage thing. Because he was the only person I ever really got on with—never made me feel awkward, unsociable, ignorant, like I always had before with men. I wanted to sort of nail down all these new feelings by marrying him: wanted to frame them."

"Despite your parents—the fact that they'd probably wanted just the same thing when they married? Everyone does."

"Yes—despite my parents. I wanted to prove them wrong."

"Well, you were damn lucky you didn't marry him, since you can't have known him properly at all—if he just dropped you like that in the end."

"Yes—no." She looked pained now. "But why this postmortem anyway?" She slid off the bed suddenly and knelt on the floor, arms cradled on my knees, a cheek lying on her wrists, her face turned toward the candlelight. "I was going to marry him," she said vehemently, "because I'd have done *anything* to go on getting on with people, like I was getting on with him."

I fluffed her gold hair, running my hand through the springy curls. "You of all people," I said in genuine astonishment. "With so much: that you should feel like that—when you could have almost anyone you wanted, anytime. They'd come running. You could take your pick. This year, next year—"

"Sometime, never. I'd prefer to be a 'now' person." She looked up at me slyly.

"What about the 'then' person—when you and I become next year's people?"

"Cross that bridge later, can't we?"

The candle on the bedside table flickered. It was running low, guttering, the blackened wax spilling over the edge of the saucer. I got up gently to change it for a longer candle on the press by the door. I brought it back. " 'Here comes a candle to light you to bed'. . ."

" 'Here comes a chopper to chop off your head.' We played that game too, as children."

She stood up when I'd changed the candles, nearly strangling me with a kiss, her arms locked round my neck.

The next morning the Governor's fishing party arrived. The advance guard came at first light, waking us, rattling along in two military jeeps just outside our cabin. And when we got across to the dining room the big men with shoulder holsters and dark glasses, the Governor's aides and bodyguards, were already halfway through breakfast—pots of coffee and a bottle of scotch nearly empty on the long table looking out over the terrace. Outside dozens of raggedy local children were running amok in the bright African dawn, gathering up the Lodge's chairs and parasols and trying to cram them into the back of the two jeeps, an almost impossible task given the other larger urchins already installed there, clinging onto the seats for dear life, trying to guarantee themselves a place for the day's sport.

After our own coffee, when Eleanor had gone back to the cabin, I joined the men at the long table wondering if we might cadge a day's sport with them ourselves. But the toughest of the bodyguards gestured out of the window at the children. "Look," he said. "There'll hardly be room for us." He offered me a scotch instead. "The Governor likes to give the local children a treat when he comes up here. What can you do?" he went on, the picture of benign innocence. He was a very big man in a very smart beige Kaunda suit; a scarred face with flabby jowls hanging down like bags from his cheeks, that shuddered when he spoke.

We saw them all off later, the Governor arrived now in a smart Land Rover, leading the parade, the jeeps following, literally overflowing with children and half the Lodge's furniture. Then the manager ran out onto the terrace, holding up a blue and white picnic fridge box—waving and shouting at the disappearing cavalcade. One of the jeeps came back to pick up the box.

"What was it?" I asked. "Ice for the scotch?"

"No—more important than that. It was the fish."

I thought at first that this was just one more example of the farce of Africa—the happy farce, the adventure, all part of the real thing. But then I thought how I'd got this African adventure thing all wrong. Africa was really something else altogether these days—something more than volcanoes, mountain gorillas, pygmy tribes, a *Boys' Own Paper* serial. That was the white man's colonial country once, the hoped for tourist paradise now. That sort of Africa was the glint in the eye of the evil-looking Japanese or the same excited expectation among the blue rinse ladies, on package tours from Idaho. The real Africa was disappearing in front of me right then, in the crowded jeeps. Reality was the stalk-thin children fighting for a day's outing, craving a share of the Governor's Coke and crisps, stuffed in like chaff among the gross, whisky-slugging bodyguards. And they were the real thing too in Africa now: these vicious standard-bearers in the tribal power games, dark-glassed shock troops, Presidential fat cats, in Zaïre and elsewhere, propping up corrupt and brutal régimes all over the continent, ever since the white men had cleared out. Africa for the Africans now, of course. But only for some of them, a very few. The situation was different with independence. Indeed it was: it was worse. In that little airplane with Patrick, dodging the craters, and afterward climbing the volcano dreaming of *King Solomon's Mines*, I'd been indulging in all the lovely fictions of Africa, avoiding the reality at all costs, which was everywhere at hand, just waiting to strike. The following day, for example, on the lush valley road out of the National Park, when the drunken soldiers jumped the Lodge pickup—flourishing their automatic rifles, then firing them, the bullets spitting a neat line across the dust right in front of us. . . .

The Lodge driver was taking the pickup eighty miles down to Goma next morning—to try and get some beer and fuel—so we took a lift back with him. The road, or what was left of it, ran southeast out of the Park, and once beyond its boundaries, rising up the hairpin bends into the hills, we came into an African Switzerland, a land of bright green pasture valleys with steep terraces of vegetables, coffee and tea planted up the side of the breast-like hills, with thick forest above that, on the greater hills and mountains beyond. Dark kapok trees lined the road, neatly spaced out, French-style, every twenty yards or so, with eucalyptus and bamboo groves leaning over rushing streams as we bounced over great stones and gullies in the road, where the rains had long since eaten the tarmac away.

This, indeed, was the breadbasket of Zaïre. "Everything grows here," our driver said. "Just put it in the ground. Wheat, onions, beans, peas, potatoes, strawberries. Lots of strawberries." A group of women passed us just then with wicker baskets of the fruit on their heads. And as we neared the town of Rutshuru at the halfway stage there were people everywhere around us now, moving in long columns down either side of the road—everyone carrying something, on the way to the market. And the favored method of transport was to pile the sacks and baskets, head-high, on the footrests of little, low-slung, homemade scooters—

scooters where everything, including both wheels, was made of wood: wood-age inventions. There was food here all right—but the marketing infrastructure was prehistoric: a prosperous area, where the locals were as scrawny and downcast as any I'd seen in Zaïre.

I spoke to our driver. "All this produce is sent down to Goma," he said. "Then flown straight to Kinshasa. A dozen or so of the Big Men there—they own most of this land now: coffee and tea plantations, cattle, vegetables—it all goes to Kin, on the big planes, every day. It's a real cash economy in the Kivu these days," he went on. "They eat money here now."

The driver stopped every few miles, taking passengers on board, running his own little cash economy in the shape of a local bus service. There were hardly any other trucks or cars on the road and soon there were nearly a dozen lucky people hanging on to the supports behind us, tipping the pickup well backward on its rear wheels. It wouldn't be long until we had a puncture, I thought. It wasn't. We lurched suddenly, then pulled into the side of the road, beneath a bamboo grove. It took them almost an hour to change wheels—and unbind the rear brakes as well which had seized up. Eleanor and I sat on some stones by the bamboos. She drew the white wool cardigan she had on close about her, wrapping her arms firmly round her waist, shivering an instant. The sun was out but it was cool, almost sharp in the shade at this height. She looked exhausted.

"Beds in Africa," she said grimly, apropos of nothing.

"What?"

"It's useless, in those single beds we had in the cabin—last night. Barely sleep in them, let alone make love."

"There'll be better beds. In Kigali tomorrow. And certainly in Nairobi—when we get there. Double beds."

The soldiers jumped out of the bushes at us half an hour later—two of them, in tattered camouflaged battle dress, forage caps askew on their heads, swaying about, guns leveled, thirty yards ahead of us. Our brakes weren't much better and we didn't stop soon enough. One of them fired in the air while his companion aimed his rifle from the side of the road and the bullets whipped in a line across the nose of the pickup a few yards ahead of us. I'd never heard an army automatic rifle going off at close quarters. The noise was surprisingly innocent, like the "rat-tat-tat" of a child's toy. We slid to a halt. The driver was unmoved. He took 30 Zaïre out of his pocket and paid up at once. It seemed some kind of regular toll which he knew all about. The soldier took the money, then turned round, exposing a great tear in the backside of his army trousers. He spoke to us in some local tongue, laughing maniacally. "He wants the money for a new pair of trousers," our driver told us.

We got back to Goma late that afternoon—after another puncture and two more (bulletless) checkpoints. And when we arrived at the Hotel Karibu another flight load of Belgian air force men and paratroop officers were propping up the bar, guzzling scotch, Muzak playing in the background: "Under the Bridges of Paris."

"How was your trip?" The manager spared me a moment.

"All right. We only got shot up at one checkpoint."

"Yes. Pretty common up there. The Zaïrean Army never gets paid up in these remote regions. So they get their money by holding cars and trucks to ransom. It's a regular business. Nothing unusual here these days. Where they don't starve, the local people just have to pay up: it's their money or their lives."

He left me then to discuss the evening's menu with the officers. Coast prawns in fresh mayonnaise was the speciality of the day, followed by *steak au poivre maître d'hôtel*. "The prawns are superb," I heard him say. "Just came in this morning. King-size."

Early next morning we were woken by the sounds of dogs howling and people's voices, footsteps running down past our cabin toward the lake. Half an hour later, just as the sun was getting up, I was out on the cabin terrace, breathing the crisp air, when I saw them bringing the two men up from the perimeter fence: two Africans, their clothes in absolute tatters, both bleeding badly, one of them hardly able to walk, being dragged along, two Alsatian dogs on leads behind them.

"Les voleurs," the manager told me later after breakfast as we were checking out, waiting for the hotel minibus to take us to the airport.

"What were they stealing?"

He shrugged. "Anything. Everything. The usual thing." He went out onto the hotel terrace then and started shouting at the minibus driver. He was late. He went on shouting at him. On the way to the airport, over the sharp lava roads, the minibus lurched and slid into the ditch. Another puncture. The driver managed to reverse it out and I helped him change wheels, working desperately, as fast as I could, my hands soon covered in grease. Afterward, on the road again, Eleanor said, "I hate Africa, *hate* it."

I looked out the window at the belching volcano—a red-flecked vapor spume against the blue sky. It was rather splendid—and it was ours. "You loved Africa before," I said. "The whole idea of it—back in

Kinshasa. Now you just don't like—the real thing." And I shrugged my shoulders then. And Eleanor glared at me. "Go on—be fair," I said. "Nothing venture, nothing win, you were always saying."

"What have we won?"

"Another country. We'll be there in an hour. Rwanda's quite different. Kigali's quite a well-run place, they say. There's a decent hotel—the Milles Collines—and that SABENA flight to Nairobi at the end of the week."

"Take me a week to recover. . . . The horror of it all here."

"That's what Mr. Kurtz said about this country, the Congo."

"Who's he?"

"Doesn't matter. A man in a book—one of the African books you didn't read."

"Don't want to read it. I just want to stay in a decent bed for a week, head under the blankets. A double bed," she added weakly, looking out over the razed landscape on the way to the airport, the long gray lava flow, the tidewrack of great boulders and the open meat market where they were still slaughtering cattle, with pangas, as we passed.

14

Loving and Dying

"When the man says you've gotta go, you've gotta go," the laconic Texan pilot intoned, repeating this grim injunction just in front of us, as he began to set the Twin Otter down, flying in low over the bare brown hills on his final approach to Kigali airport.

"God," I thought, not caring one bit for this Humphrey Bogart commentary and its implications. After five hard weeks in Zaïre, the shoot-up at the checkpoint, and the mauled Africans outside our cabin at the Karibu earlier that morning, I was looking for a little rest and recreation in Rwanda, not some dumping on a hill a mile short of the airport. The plane dived sharply, nose down, and my stomach turned over—the guts upset enough already with repeated visits to the bathroom in the last twelve hours. I'd caught some Congo bug at last, although that wouldn't matter now at all if the Texan didn't level out soon.

In the event I needn't have worried. We were flying over the runway already, I saw, and when we landed nearly halfway down its length we seemed to go on taxiing forever toward the big airport buildings. Finally, out of the plane, I looked back on the longest, widest runway I'd ever seen—a vast great concrete strip disappearing into the hazy distance. But what was it for? That was the strange thing. There wasn't a single other plane on the apron—and no other travelers either when we got to the splendid, glass-boxed terminal building: no other passengers, baggage handlers, hostesses, ticket clerks; no officials of any kind. The place was deserted. It was as if some magic hand had set down this whole vast new airport overnight, while all the locals were asleep—as they still must be, I thought, quite unaware of its presence. The airport brooded there now in the sun, like a huge, dazzling space toy that some bleary-eyed African official would soon discover, out from the capital, getting the hell of a surprise in a few minutes.

In fact, some people had already been to this great new airport.

Outside, half a dozen smart cars with UN and other diplomatic number plates, Volvos and Mercedes, were well parked and locked—and beyond them a few local men hovered, one of whom told us that he drove the Mille Collines Hotel minibus. He didn't, of course. He was moonlighting with someone else's minibus. But we set off all the same, at a vastly inflated rate in every sense, for the capital, Kigali, ten miles away.

And now there was another surprise, for we were immediately out onto a spanking, equally new, four-lane highway, a splendid blacktop racing circuit that snaked up and down the dry, razed hills with round-abouts and bridges. Roads in Africa are rarely more than narrow quag-mires or sandpits, filled with dream-laden pedestrians and whole families camped out at every bend. But here was something on the smoothest, grandest, emptiest scale, a million-pounds-a-mile motorway with no other traffic on it bar the odd foot-slogging peasant, a scrawny beast in tow, both bent double with vast loads of dry sticks. Something was out of order here. The blueprints had got mixed up. Some brand-new autobahn or turnpike had been mislaid in Rwanda, like the airport, and set down in these wilds of central Africa, a place almost without cars.

The Mille Collines Hotel—sitting on top of one of Rwanda's thousand hills on the outskirts of the city—was as sumptuous a creation as the road and the airport had been: glass, marble, aluminum, a smooth blue pool at the back, a top-floor terrace restaurant; deep, club leather fur-niture and shops of all sorts in the lobby, airline offices, Telex machines humming. . . . By comparison with the airport and the motorway, though, there was one marked difference here: the hotel was full as a boot, bursting at the seams. They were white visitors mostly, not tourists, but businessmen, executives, pushing and shoving around the reception desk; eating, drinking, moving out to the pool, making endless self-important promenades up and down the lobby. The hotel was buzzing with wealth and wealthy people, a complete little First World city on its own. Were we really in Rwanda—perhaps the poorest and certainly the most crowded country in Africa? Nothing so far—in the airport, the magnificent approaches, in this grand hotel—smacked of Africa at all. There was a mistake somewhere, I thought again. I wondered what it was. But I didn't have much time to think about it then, after we'd checked in. My bowels were rolling. I was ill, shivering, filled with a churning nausea. I only just made it up to our bedroom, the bathroom there, in time.

"I have some special pills," I told Eleanor as I got between the sheets.

"Just some awful tummy bug. The pills are supposed to dry it up." I took them with a glass of water and Eleanor looked at me, alarmed.

"You certainly look—rather a fright. They'll have a doctor here anyway."

"Not as bad as that yet. See what the pills do."

To begin with, for the rest of the afternoon and early evening, they did nothing, and I was in and out of the bathroom every half-hour, a real both-ends sickness, the stomach empty now, my whole body retching, heaving on the emptiness, dipping in and out of fevered sleep between sprints. Our room, on the second floor, giving out over the hotel drive and forecourt, was the best I'd seen in Africa so far: a large double bed at last, everything in white, where the sun glittered through the white mesh curtains onto the white counterpane, the white cushions on the smart split-cane, Habitat-style chairs, the white walls with small Dufy reproductions of the south of France, red- and blue-washed Mediterranean seascapes, colored jewels in the chalk room. . . . Africa had disappeared completely here and if I'd not felt so ill I'd have been entirely happy with my release from the continent.

I woke much later on. It was dark in the white room and I thought I'd gone blind for a moment. There'd been a frightful dream, too: prep school days again, a common enough sleep torture with me over the years: wicked headmaster-and-matron department, the usual thing. Though on this occasion there'd been an added twist to the terror. I was being delivered by my relations to the awful school in Dublin—not at the beginning of term, but at the start of the holidays, all the other boys going home, the head, with matron, waiting for me, rubbing their hands, on the front steps.

Then I saw Eleanor, in the shadows, sitting in one of the white chairs. I wasn't able to speak for a moment, tongue-tied, sweating, the nightmare still with me. She came over and turned the bedside light on. "I'm worried," she said. "I've asked at reception. The hotel doctor's out in town somewhere. They can't reach him."

"Doesn't matter. It'll be all right. Just give it time for these pills to work." She straightened my pillows and I lay back again. It was time for a third pill. And another Veganin. And another glass of water. Sweat it out, that was the only thing, I thought.

"You're not supposed to take aspirin on an empty stomach," Eleanor said.

"Not supposed to die here either."

"What?"

"Sorry. I tend to make a meal of any illness. Not good at it. Just feel like death."

"I know the feeling—when I drank."

I'd forgotten about Eleanor's drinking. All that was another world, years before, in Kinshasa. Yes, it was perfectly clear now—I'd been living with Eleanor for years—literally. The fever seemed to stretch and twist my imagination as I drowsed in and out of sleep. I'd forgotten how or where I'd first met her, but I'd spent a long time with this woman in Africa, traveling around the continent, months in Kinshasa, months by the coast, weeks going up the Congo in some huge river steamer. Yes, someone was playing Cole Porter in the air-conditioned lounge outside our cabin, where I was laid low for some reason, sweating. I could hear "Night and Day" and the clink of ice in glasses, laughter in the air-conditioned dream next door: a dream I longed for but couldn't have, unable to move from the damp-hot bed of my own nightmare. It was Harry's laughter. Harry was in there, in the next cabin or at the bar. Or was it Vijay, drunk at last on Harvey Wallbangers and White Ladies? I must have slept and dreamed properly again then, because I was introducing Eleanor to someone at the mahogany cocktail bar on the lovely old river steamer—Eleanor beside me, smiling, in a smart beige safari suit and pith helmet, the jacket so deeply cut down at the front that part of each breast showed.

"Have you met my wife?" I said confidently in the dream. Then I woke again and looked about the room for my real wife, thinking, with certainty, that I was at home in our Cotswolds bedroom. But the bedroom round me now was empty. "Eleanor?" I called. There was a light on in the bathroom. She came through the doorway.

"Yes. All right?"

"I thought I was at home—and before that on Michel's river steamer. I was introducing you to someone. 'My wife,' I said. 'I'd like you to meet my wife.' "

"You've really got the marriage thing, haven't you? As bad as I had with Robert." She came and sat on the side of the bed.

"Yes. Like an illness," I said.

"You'll get better, though. Like I did. That's the only trouble—that we couldn't have had that illness together."

"Thank God we didn't. Why do we need anything as an illness between us?"

"No. All the same, it's not much fun—being introduced as your wife.

You must want everything made up there, at home, with her—badly want it. You dream about it." She looked away, hurt.

"I was dreaming about *you*, though." I reached out and touched her arm, the flaky patches still there on her wrist and below the elbow. "You had an astonishingly low cut safari jacket on, and a pith helmet. Sort of naughty nightclub act."

"Oh, good. If it makes you feel better." She went on looking away into the shadows of the white room. "As if that was all there might be between us," she added. "Naughty nightclub things."

"No. More than that. But all the other things are complicated."

"What?" She turned sharply. "It's complicated? Loving each other?"

"Yes."

"You're wrong," she said sharply. "Only if one expects too much."

"We will."

"Well, damn you all the same—for not trying, just dreaming about it." She was shouting now.

"Oh, I'll try," I said. "I told you, it's just an illness. But I want to get better."

She stared at me for several moments, down her long straight nose, a grave expression, before she reached out and touched my cheek delicately: then a look of happy astonishment before she got up and started to undress. Finally, a few minutes later, coming out of the bathroom, carrying her nightdress, she ran across the room and jumped onto her side of the big double bed, bouncing there several times, before throwing the nightdress overboard and joining me.

Was this the thin time on our journey which we'd saved each other for? This illness—and its cure by loving? We loved all right. Despite my fever, or perhaps because of it, we loved like famished people then. But the cure took longer.

I lay in bed most of next day, a limp rag, unable to eat. And I was worried. "How am I going to get out and about—get any material for these BBC talks on Rwanda?" I asked Eleanor as she sat by the bed later next morning.

"We've still got three more full days. The Nairobi flight doesn't leave until Friday night. I've confirmed the tickets. And I met a nice Scotsman at the SABENA desk too. A biologist or something, on some UN business here. I told him about you—seemed to know something about medicine. Will you see him?"

"I'm getting better."

"But you're not—really."

"Time, that's all." I pushed myself up, thinking to get out of bed. But the effort was too much.

"I'll bring him up. You'd like him anyway."

She brought Walter up after lunch. And he was a nice man—middle-aged, old-fashioned manse Scots, in a severe brown suit, thin hair running sideways over a thimble head: a small, academic, secretly intense man, I thought, with brown glittery eyes. But he wasn't a biologist and had nothing to do with medicine. He was a soil specialist, an agronomist, in and out of Africa for years on various UN and other government jobs, so that he knew all about African tummy bugs, first-hand, without any medicine.

He looked at me, then at the special pills I was taking.

"Same as I have. Red and white capsules. Dysentery—a mild go of it." He looked at me again. "Or rather more than mild in your case, I'd say. You have to be careful. Not to pick up anything else, while you're laid low with it. Stay put. And only two of these pills a day now, if you're not eating. You can overdose yourself with them. Dry toast, then maybe an omelette—when you feel like it."

"If I ever feel like it. . . ."

"He's worried he can't get out and around—for these BBC talks he's doing."

Walter smiled. "If you're leaving Friday night, you wouldn't have been able to get around much anyway. The roads run out here pretty soon, not like the airport road—that was a one-off. It's tough traveling everywhere else now. I know the country well. You'd only crock yourself up completely. Besides, there's not a lot to see in Rwanda these days. The view is mostly the same."

"What?"

"Grim."

He stood up. "I'm off to the Ministry of Agriculture. Spend most of my time there—not seeing people." He walked over to the bedroom window. Beyond the hotel forecourt, to the left, I could just see the long chain of heat-razed, dust-brown hills running away to the horizon. "That's where I should be—out there," Walter said. "Those 'Blue remembered hills.' . . . I knew this country in the old days, you see. It's sad." He turned quickly. "We'll meet again, I hope. Downstairs, when you're better. Meanwhile you look to be in good hands." He patted Eleanor's shoulder. "Wife will look after you."

Eleanor didn't object to this mistake after Walter had left. Instead she jumped on the bed again. Knees together on the white counterpane, hands beside her knees like a sprinter, she swayed to and fro gently as she looked at me, her face transformed, where the eyes were no longer sunken and she'd grown younger with me, not older, in the last twelve hours: a freshness, a new face where happiness had redrawn the whole picture, where pleasure, the certainty of love had remade body and mind. We had no need to prop each other up with the rituals of unpacking now—the emblems of lingerie, old socks, lace hand-kerchiefs: these trappings of our association had been replaced by the flesh and blood beneath. As she swayed gently back and forward on the bed, her blue eyes quite still, seeming to dream then, mesmerized by the movement, I thought, for the first time in years, "This is what love is like."

"What'll we do in Kenya?" Her eyes cleared suddenly and she lay down beside me, hands behind her head, looking up at the ceiling.

"Get to the other coast, the Indian Ocean—that's the aim. By train. The old Uganda Railway. There's a marvelous narrow-gauge track to Mombasa. Then to the island of Lamu, I think, up north on the coast. I never got to the coast when I was in Kenya fifteen years ago, working for the UN. But there should be plenty to do—"

"But *what*—exactly? Do tell me." She was eager, getting younger, more enthusiastic now by the moment: some splendid weekend treat at school coming up in her eyes as they roved the ceiling.

"There's Lake Turkana," I told her, as one tells a child a story, "five hundred miles north of Nairobi near the Sudanese border. The Jade Sea. I want to go there. And perhaps a game reserve, before they all disappear. And there's horse racing in Nairobi. I never got to see that last time. Point is, there are good roads and plenty of fuel in Kenya. We can actually move about the place. And telephones. And newspapers."

Life—a real traveler's life—opened up for us like a bright book in the white room. And instead of dreaming the impossible, as we had in Eleanor's red room in Kinshasa, we planned the entirely conceivable now. "And there's a "Turkana Bus" I've heard about, just a truck in fact, where you camp out every night for a week on the way up and back from the lake. We might take that."

"Yes. Your tents under the stars." She turned to me quickly. "Strange to think of Africa—happily."

"We're not there yet. I'm told this weekly SABENA flight to Nairobi is a real bum's rush. Comes absolutely packed from Dar es Salaam.

Only way for the Tanzanians to get into Kenya, now that the border's closed."

"Doesn't matter. We've got tickets. Just to be in a real world again —what fun that'll be. Telephones and newspapers. . . . It'll be funny to see each other, in the real world," she rushed on.

"Yes," I said, hiding the faint unease I suddenly felt at the prospect of this confrontation. For it struck me then that our relationship might best survive amidst difficulties, in the unreal, among the horrors of Africa. Pure pleasure—even the pleasure of just the ordinarily real— might erode and eventually kill what held us together. For once we moved into this reality of Kenya we would then be only one step, one country, away from the greater reality of our separate homes and lives in England.

"What difference will it make," I asked, "seeing each other in the 'real' world? Just taxis and newspapers and telephones?"

"I—don't know. Just make everything easier. A lot of ordinary things to *do* at last?"

But I knew the difference. Once in Nairobi, with all its mod cons, we would sooner or later have to face the life we might or might not pursue in England, in London, when we returned. Ambiguities, emotional decisions, covert arrangements, uncertain plans and promises: all this would have to be faced before we left Kenya. Every affair seeks a future, contains an urgent secret energy which one day must be sustained or explode. I could have played Professor Higgins and educated her in this. But I didn't, of course—looking at her, loving, afraid of loss.

Then she said quite simply, as if she'd read my thoughts, seen my fear, "I've never loved so much. Anyone." She shook her head. "No one. Ever. And the only difference in Kenya is we won't have to spend all our time just struggling for survival. We can be more ourselves. That's all. You look sad?"

"No. Just ill."

"But you're getting *better,* aren't you?" She smiled herself now, but a teasing, wilful smile; a dorm riot rising in her eyes. "Aren't you? *Aren't you?*" She shook my arm vigorously, unable to restrain herself.

"Yes. Yes—" Then a smother of kisses, trying unsuccessfully to control, suffocate her excitement.

"What did Walter mean," she asked later, "about those 'Blue remembered hills'?"

"It's from Housman's poem, 'A Shropshire Lad.' Didn't you do that at school?"

"No. Don't think so."

"It's famous."

"Why?"

"It's a fine poem, about his youth, a platonic affair that came to nothing: the past—long after he'd left it."

Of course, I thought then, love can have an equal impetus, taking one backward, and I remembered the white evening light on the sheep pasture, slanting sun and shadow on the small hills just above our cottage at home: the last evening before I'd left for Africa, when I'd walked up among the hills and come back through the cornfield, picking a full green ear as a promise of my return. "Home is the hero. . . . And the sailor home from the sea. . . ." That was another poem—not a memory, but lines with a future, a reality, an exact image which I would have to face myself with quite a different woman in a month or so.

I was better that evening. The pills had done their job and caulked me tight all round. I got up and went downstairs with Eleanor where we met Walter for a drink in one of the rich, club leather corners of the lobby. I sipped a tonic water with Eleanor while Walter had a beer—three mild, retiring people, surrounded by all the well-heeled, pushy executives, lowering stiff martinis before supper, whom I'd seen on my first day at the Mille Collines: frightful whites, for the most part, in synthetic tropical suits or lightweight business blue: flush-faced Germans, huge Americans, dapper French—but the majority from no identifiable country, anonymous men, entirely camouflaged by money. I could hear their voices, eavesdrop on their conversations. I could see them more clearly. And now I began to see what was wrong with Rwanda— how the mistakes had come about, in the great new airport, the vast highway, this luxury hotel—all these splendid artefacts laid like a very expensive jigsaw puzzle over the poverty of the country. Now the puzzle began to make sense.

Of course, the visitors here were Western business and salesmen, with as many Third World "experts" thrown in—bilateral and multilateral "aid" people, loan officers and officials from the UN and other government development agencies. I'd spent several years with the UN in this same business myself so I could spot these gentlemen fairly easily. Though far too well dressed and manicured, with tax-free jowls and bellies, they did their best, with a tired and elegant gravitas, to suggest a missionary air, one of concern and high purpose—and such hotels as the Mille Collines I knew, all over the Third World, were their churches.

The ordinary businessmen on the other hand, unrestrained by even the vaguest notions of charity, oozed a blunt confidence: men bent on all sorts of immediate and practical good works on behalf of the African poor, to their own special advantage. Valium, video games, naughty nighties, after-shave lotions, skin whiteners, grand cars, the latest (but quite inappropriate) agricultural equipment—there was no sophisticated Western product, from tractor to trinket, which you couldn't unload either on the unsuspecting locals in Africa or on the rich fat cats in government.

And where would most of the hard currency come from, to pay for all these unsuitable goodies? Why, from the aid men, of course, with their various development grants, dollar or Deutschmark checks to be drawn on UN agencies or on banks in Washington, Tokyo, Paris or Bonn. The aid men would pay for many of these high- or low-technology playthings—the men right there, all round me, in the lobby at that very moment, about to meet next morning with the Minister for Industry, Agriculture, Tourism or whatever. A hard currency grant or loan would be arranged—and another new and quite unnecessary motorway, airport or grand hotel would be put in train.

All the men in the lobby that evening certainly saw the flaw in these financial bargains—the fact that 99 percent of the local Africans involved were unlikely even to benefit from these generous arrangements. But what could you do about that? Very little. It wasn't your country. You'd made the effort, the gesture toward Third World development. It was better now to order up a vodka martini and think about that South African steak, the choice tenderloin, imported for dinner. . . .

Out of courtesy, obviously, I didn't voice these thoughts with Walter to begin with, since this was something of his world too, I assumed, with the various development agencies he worked for. So I was surprised when he took up cudgels on just the same theme, as if he'd read my thoughts. I suppose he'd noticed me looking round the lobby in some astonishment. He was certainly the canny Scotsman.

"Yes," he said. "They're quite a collection here, aren't they? Everyone in the aid-and-sales game in Africa ends up at the Mille Collines some time or other. Rwanda, in the last decade, has had more aid per hectare than any other country in Africa. But you'd be sorry to see what's been done with it. You're better off being ill, not seeing it, not talking about it on the BBC."

"What? What have they done with it?" I asked—though I thought I knew the answer already.

Walter shrugged his small shoulders. "It's the old sad story of aid-

and-trade in the Third World," he said. And then he went on to say almost exactly what I'd been thinking myself a few minutes before.

Afterward I nodded. "Yes," I said. "I worked more or less in the same line myself, fifteen years ago, traipsing round the barren places on behalf of the UN and the World Bank." I told him briefly of my career with these organizations.

"But why Rwanda?" I went on. "Why this intensity of Western aid and salesmanship in a place this size—tiny, insignificant politically, a sort of Liechtenstein of Africa."

"Just because of that—because it's a Liechtenstein, without any political importance. But with a military dictatorship and no Soviet alignments. So the West can play boss here, supervise the politics, run all the aid-and-trade games they want, without interference. It's a sort of miniature 'Scramble for Africa' in Rwanda. The Germans made the running a few years ago—equipment for a new radio station. Then the Belgians, who ran this place before, pulled up their socks, got in on the act again; then the French, the Americans, even the British. They have a lot of tea and coffee business here. Companies that used to work out of Uganda next door—some of them are over here now. It's safer, more profitable. You see, because it's such a tiny place, you can keep an eye on where your money goes here—and a better eye still on getting it back, with interest. Rwanda is like one big estate, just as it was under the Belgian Kings. But now there's half a dozen overseas managers involved, with the local bosses here employed as foremen. And it works, except for most of the ordinary people—seven million of them and rising desperately all the time. That's another matter: the farmers, peasants, food, the land. That's where I'm supposed to come in."

"Well—what's happening?"

But Walter stood up then. "Later," he said. "I'm expecting a Telex—if I can get near the machine. This hotel is HQ for Telexes in central Africa. Only place for hundreds of miles where you can get in touch with Europe."

Walter didn't join us again until we were halfway through supper on the rooftop terrace restaurant—and when he did we talked of other things, before I felt slightly queasy, though I'd only picked at an omelette and a dry bun. I went to bed early, immobile once more.

I said to Eleanor that evening, speaking of all these aid-and-salesmen, "Of course, I suppose these people are the modern Stanleys and Livingstones—or Stanley, at least: that beads and trinkets, eye-for-the-main-chance little Welshman. Not as brave as him—but rather like him, with their sales patter and samples, crossing the continent, up and down, east and west, in their first-class jets and hotels, flogging useless things to the locals to earn passage. And I thought I was going to cross Africa like Stanley did. Or at least on riverboats, lake steamers, trains. Instead it's just big jets all the time—and I'm no more than a verbal aid-and-sales man myself."

"Are you? I don't know." Eleanor was trying to comb out the tats and tangles in her hair by the mirror. "Damn!" The comb had stuck. "The wind that came this evening—my hair's full of dirt."

"Blowing off all those hills, I suppose. I wish I could get out to them."

"We're leaving tomorrow. Why not just get better—for Kenya? Give this place a miss in your talks." ·

"I've got to say something."

"Just say you were ill then. You were. Write about that and the hotel here. Write about *not* traveling for once. That might be quite original."

"Great. But those armchair travelers back home—they're hoping for pygmies, poisoned arrows, and tom-toms up the Congo; a ferry sinking with all hands on Lake Victoria or barging into wild animals on the footplate of a narrow-gauge steam engine. All that."

"Well, you'll either have to invent all that. Or tell the truth: that there's nothing left of all that out here apparently. No trains, no boats, no fuel. Only the big jets." She turned to me. "I'll have to wash my hair. And I've used the last of the shampoo."

"Use the soap. It's quite posh soap. Lux. We're getting near civilization."

She washed her hair in the bathroom, under the shower. Then she came and sat on the edge of the bed wrapped in a huge towel, another one curled round her head like a turban. The towels were thick and fluffy here, great white swards of cotton. She sat there, swathed from head to foot, seemingly twice her normal size, a Michelin woman, only the tennis-playing, girlish, Joan Hunter Dunn face available, the big blue eyes peeping out through a letterbox in the deep folds.

"There's nothing to be done," she said. "Just have to get across Africa any way we can. Or would it all have been easier on your own? Is that what you're getting at?"

"No—"

"You could have gone off on foot or something, without the trouble of me in tow. Tents under the stars, native bearers? Done something really wild and wonderful on your own?"

"No. I'm doing that already. With you."

"Yes," she said quietly. "But you can't broadcast that, can you?" she went on.

"No. But that doesn't matter. One has to live—as well as do little talks for the radio."

"Yes. . . ."

"And one forgets Africa then, as I've done, these past days with you—just getting odd garbled messages back from the front, in the lobby or the bar. We could be in the south of France—with that Dufy picture over there, all the white decor: going out for a *bouillabaisse* in half an hour."

"That'd be nice."

But we took these images and thoughts no further. The south of France, like England, belonged to a future we might not share, which at least we didn't have to talk about yet. We could only be sure of now. Loving now in the white room—Africa quite shut out, whatever disasters lurked in the hills beyond the window erased, unknown to us, as our future together was.

When she got into bed with me I said, " 'Ah, the deep deep peace of the double bed after the hurly-burly of the chaise longue.' . . . Mrs. Patrick Campbell."

"Who's she?"

"Splendid Edwardian actress. Mostly with Shaw. George Bernard. You've heard of him?" I pinched her gently.

"Yes." Then a few moments after I'd pinched her she said, "Ouch!" Then she said, "I don't remember anything on a chaise longue—with you."

"We had the hurly-burly though, that first night in the Memling in Kinshasa."

She didn't reply at once. But finally she said, coming closer, "Well, that's all over, too." So the past left us, as well as the future, long before we slept, living and loving only in the now.

We had lunch with Walter on our last day, high up on the rooftop restaurant, looking out over all the raw brown hills that ran away to the horizon. Walter waved his hand at them—over an elaborate salad.

"That's Rwanda's food supply," he said. "All those thousand hills. Trouble is, there isn't any food on them now. It won't grow."

"And you're out here—to help it grow?"

"It's really too late. You see the Belgians developed terraced cultivation here, steps with endless storm drains, conduits, around and down the side of the hills to take away the rains. But all that has been tramped down since they left, by the land-hungry farmers: flattened, ruined. So when the rains come the water just flows straight off the hills taking all the soil with it. And they've used all the scrub, the trees—whatever windbreaks there were—for firewood. Result? Total soil erosion, and no food. In five years' time? Famine. Complete famine here. Nothing less."

I could see the hills perfectly from this high vantage point, shimmering in the afternoon heat haze, bare, deserted, the blackened stumps of trees running up the razed valleys. The view reminded me of the Kingdom of the Elephants in the first *Babar* book, after the first Rhinoceros battle, where the whole landscape has been devastated by Rataxes and his evil cohorts.

Walter tapped his fingers gently on the table. "Africa since independence—well, it's become a shambles, I'm afraid, utter and complete. I remember the colonial times out here. It certainly wasn't good. But it was better than this in that few people ever actually starved. Everyone admits this now, including most Africans you talk to privately."

Walter had become almost roused. "Independence is fine," he said at last, waving his hand out over the bare hills. "But it hasn't fed them. They're free out there now," he added. "And they're dying."

All of us had stopped eating. I looked at Eleanor—as she looked at Walter. We said nothing. There wasn't much more to say. Then she turned and looked at me, a questioning look, as if I might have some answer to all this tragedy that lay beyond the rooftop restaurant—an explanation for our happiness among so much distress.

CHAPTER

15

Railways and Racing

"**B**ut can we afford to stay at the Norfolk? There isn't a parallel rate in Kenya, is there?"

"No. But they've said they'll give me a free room, in return for writing something nice about it. And that shouldn't be difficult. I stayed there before, when I first came to Kenya in the late Sixties with the UN. All paid for then, of course. International aid-and-trade. I was one of the commercial travelers."

"Grander than the Mille Collines?"

"Yes. Best hotel in East Africa. James Stewart stays there."

It was well after midnight; bright, cold, starlit. The smart new Toyota Corona taxi glided along the airport road, then out onto the smooth Mombasa highway. Even at this late hour there were other cars speeding to and fro, their bright quartz headlights dazzling us. We were in civilization—and the dazzle, for once, was a balm. There was fuel here, a genie with a lamp, a magic elixir, a potion spreading over the whole land which made everything possible: petrol—for late-night joy rides out of town, trips to the coast or to the open-air movie theater we were passing, its big dark screen a silhouette against the moonlit plainslands beyond. After six weeks' manic confusion we seemed to have come home. It was a curious feeling, as if we'd left Africa altogether and returned to Europe. A small, excited ache moved in the pit of my stomach—one of the nicest feelings there is. For we were not in Europe. This was still Africa, a new country still being offered up to us—the plainslands, the animals, the highlands: but with taxis, telephones, newspapers, and everyone speaking English as well.

I felt I might have been driving to the Ritz through the moonlight, where the animals, lion and elephant from the Nairobi City Park, would be nudging at the kitchen door for scraps: an irrational, ridiculous feeling. But I couldn't deny it—oncoming life, above all variety, a world of choice again, which had been entirely denied us in Zaïre and Rwanda.

209

Free will, which had quite atrophied in me, stirred again like an impending love affair: "Will we go there—or here? Will we meet in the Norfolk bar at midday—or that Italian place at eight?" Choice suddenly seemed better than sex.

"It's like the Ritz," Eleanor said, thought-reading again, after we'd walked up the red-carpeted ramp into the paneled lobby of the Norfolk and were checking in with the immaculately gray-suited African night clerk, who even at that hour wore a red rosebud in his lapel. The man, a tall Kikuyu in the Belafonte mode, was discreetly efficient, touched with a little hauteur and a deft style.

"Yes, Mr. Hone—of the BBC. We are expecting you." He glanced at a room plan. "A few days ago, I think."

"We were delayed—in Rwanda and Zaïre."

"Of course. It's not—uncommon." He raised his eyebrows a fraction—dismissive thoughts for the savage wastes everywhere outside the Norfolk—then glanced at Eleanor. But there was no embarrassment over names. We signed the register with our separate names and that was that.

"You must be tired. We hope you'll be comfortable. Our general manager will be here in the morning."

"I'm looking forward to meeting him. Is there any mail for me, by the way?"

The clerk shuffled through all the letters in a rack marked "H" behind him. "No. . . . I'm afraid. Nothing." I looked through the pile of letters myself then, offhandedly, but increasingly unhappy. There was nothing.

A porter took our bags through the hall to the back, along an open terrace by the dining room, out onto a pathway and then into a long, soft-carpeted corridor. The hotel had all been on one level as I remembered it, with a square of old verandahed, red-bricked cabins and bungalows set round a central garden. But now we were obviously in a new wing: wide, rich-grained hardwood doors, plated locks and handles, a faint smell of lavender polish. The porter opened a door halfway down. A large bedroom lay beyond; soft standard lamps lit a tactfully lavish scene—slightly masculine furniture: low hardwood tables, small, oatmeal-colored armchairs, a vast low bed, built-in dressing tables and chests of drawers, two telephones, a radio, a copy of that morning's *Nation* on the bedside table, a huge curtained picture window. On a table in the middle of the room was a wicker basket centered with a huge pineapple and surrounded by every other conceivable fruit, beside it a big box of Kenyan mint chocolates with a note—"Compliments of the Management." In one corner stood a wood-grained fridge with a selection of soft drinks, beers, miniature spirits, even a quarter-bottle of champagne.

"Well . . ." Eleanor said.

We were tired, stunned with fatigue—and by this vision of comfort.

"What *will* we do?" she went on.

"With what?"

She lifted a mango from the basket. "With everything." She turned, astonished. "Don't somehow deserve it all."

"No. But we do. We've just lost the knack. It'll come again."

"The only thing I miss is my old horn gramophone and all those French seventy-eights. That's all there isn't here."

And I thought—yes, we've made it into a world of mod cons with a vengeance, here in this splendid bedroom where there was no possibility of suffering. And already a nerve of guilt, fear touched my mind: a nostalgia for the pain and deprivations of Kinshasa, the horror there where things had been real—where nothing supported our relationship, where everything had to be worked for, created between us. Here in Nairobi, in this sumptuous room, our lives together would become prey to every distraction: all the business of the real world—meetings, arrangements, plans that would separate us; commitments on my part, now that there were telephones, Telexes, even telegrams, which would soon forcibly remind me that I had another life altogether: various commissions in Nairobi for the BBC; wife, family, home, a future quite apart from Eleanor—in London and the Cotswolds. I'd spent six weeks in the dark, black dark, quite cut off from all these things—dependent, to an extent I only now realized, on my life with Eleanor for survival and sanity. Now we had come out of the labyrinth, where she had been my silken thread, to where there were many other threads, all lines away from her, right in front of me. There had been no mail from home and that had disappointed me. But there was the telephone by the bed and a phone directory. I glanced inside it. You could dial London direct from Nairobi, I discovered: a new satellite link. Reaching my Cotswold number would be almost as easy. Now I could no longer avoid my dilemma: emotion discovered and prospered in one continent—quite different, older, deeper feelings, waiting to be taken up again in another.

We were late to breakfast next morning, and I was twenty minutes behind Eleanor, since she'd tactfully gone on ahead and left me on my own while I telephoned home, with no trouble at all. I got straight through. All was well there; mail was on the way. And I left it at that, listening to the family news without hinting at any of my own predicaments.

And Eleanor remained tactful—too much so—over her scrambled eggs, sausages, tomato, and bacon, where we were suddenly back in the vast-English-breakfast department: fresh fruit juices, porridge, cereals, eggs, melba toast, fresh butter, marmalade, strawberry jam, Kenyan coffee, Indian tea: a great house-style breakfast on crisp red tablecloths, where the choices you didn't take yourself from a vast circular groaning board in the middle were brought to you by splendid waiters like dusky Coronation attendants in scarlet and dazzling white.

"Letters are on the way," I said breaking the silence. Eleanor was studying her toast.

"Oh, good." She looked up brightly.

"It was funny—talking suddenly like that, all the way to the middle of England."

"Yes."

"Are you going to call your father?"

"I'll send him a letter, now that there are proper posts."

"But maybe you should call him, though. Tell him where you are, that you're all right."

The idea didn't seem to appeal. "It's expensive," she said, looking away. She hadn't looked at me once so far.

"You can have the call on me. You should—"

"All right, all right. Okay—don't get in a tizz. I will." She was petulant suddenly. The future was running out on us now that we'd arrived in Nairobi.

"I called the Nairobi BBC man as well," I said. "I'm going to meet him at his office this morning, after I've seen the general manager here. We could meet back here for lunch? Or walk downtown with me?"

My words lacked enthusiasm. I was preoccupied: people to see, things to be done, plans—plans that were not our joint plans for the first time in a month. I was preoccupied with home as well: the Cotswold summer—a high summer, my wife had told me, blazing August weather where friends of ours had been to lunch the previous weekend: a long outdoor Sunday, balmy heat, a table on the lawn, our cat picking at the cold chicken scraps: deck chairs and peace, books on the grass unread, the Frascati half-warm, walks in the afternoon.

I looked at Eleanor over my coffee—downcast, I suppose. And finally she returned the look, gazing at me. "You don't have to tell me what happened on the phone," she said. "But you don't have to look so glum either."

"There's nothing much to tell," I lied.

She smiled a little. "No. Just a whole other world—of yours. I can see that. But it makes you *sad*?"

"Yes."

"Homesick?"

"Partly, yes. Obviously."

"Obviously." She cracked a piece of melba toast.

"Aren't you?"

"What for? A bed-sitter alone in Gloucester Avenue?"

"Your house, your father's place—outside Windsor?"

"No, not really. He's there—I'll be seeing him soon enough. It doesn't make me *sad*, at least." There was silence.

"I'm sad for us as well," I said at last, embarking for the first time on what really worried me. "What are we going to do?"

"See Kenya, I thought."

I turned in my chair awkwardly, trying to cross my knees the other way, finally pushing the whole chair back.

"We're only crossing Africa, aren't we?" she went on. " 'Coast to Coast,' you said. Well, we've not got to the other coast yet. Another month at least, you thought."

She said all this so easily, so casually, so much the grown girl, that it seemed I couldn't mistake her meaning here. She and I were just part of a modern traveler's affair, companions more than lovers, on a color supplement voyage across Africa; an affair that would end neatly as soon as the trip did: easy come, easy go—or so her voice, even her general expression assured me. But her eyes didn't. They were as brooding as mine apparently were. Eyes looking toward winter, I thought.

I'd been reminded of winter already—looking up at the big mural, covering the whole of one end wall in the dining room—still there, just as I remembered it from fifteen years ago. It showed an idealized, prewar England of fifty, sixty years before: the local hunt meeting, well into their stirrup cups, outside a Ye Olde Inn, in some comfy, half-timbered market town in the shires. A genial, high-collared bobby observes the prehunt rituals—among the jolly farmers and tweedy women on the ground; the bibulous, scarlet-coated riders and their sidesaddled women on high: all was benign, reassuring, the little town embalmed in winter coziness, the painting so literal—in that snowy, coach-and-horses Christmas card manner—that one could very nearly hear the hounds yelping, the horses champing at the bit, both straining to be off out among the bare December oaks and elms that lie beyond the gabled roofs. . . . England, their England. . . .

My England. The little market town might well have been near us in the Cotswolds—Broadway or Chipping Campden or Chipping Norton. And suddenly I felt that here was my world, not Africa. This was the world I really wanted to travel and discover—my own homelands, a place which, even though I'd lived there for nearly fifteen years, I still hadn't found the heart of. A winter world, but a real world—where this African dazzle and all that had so far happened to me was just part of an excursion, an illicit day trip round the bay. My real topography was a remembered landscape as much as the troubled emotions that had grown out of it—and both were equally uncharted: the contours of land, maps of the heart. The mysteries lay elsewhere, 3000 miles away, not here. And I felt another ache then, a sharp twist in my stomach which wasn't exciting, which offered no future but simply a vision of homelessness: a horrifying sensation of loss.

The mural lay behind Eleanor as I gazed over her shoulder. She turned round to look at it with me. "An unlikely picture to have out here," she said, "in the middle of Africa."

"Last evidence of the Raj in Nairobi," I told her. "There's another one in the bar: the Mombasa train arriving in Edwardian times: lot of red-faced, sola-topied white highlanders waiting for their women off the train, as I remember."

"Well, that's more like it, isn't it?" she said brightly. "The Mombasa train—the little narrow-gauge railway you told me about? The one we're getting down to the coast?"

"Yes," I said. "That's right—the one we're getting." And we both managed a smile then—a truce, at least, in lieu of anything being resolved. How little had been resolved I only fully realized back in our bedroom, when Eleanor had gone out to look around the garden courtyard, and most of my big English breakfast came up in the bathroom lavatory. It wasn't the dysentery again; I was cured of that: it was a sickness of lies, evasions, self-disgust. What I needed was some fresh air, some exciting visions of the city. We walked downtown together twenty minutes later. But I was soon disappointed.

Nairobi is a soulless, glass-and-aluminum high-rise place these days— dark tower blocks hiding the sun, desecrating these lately wild African highlands: a city light-years away from the original rail-head camp it was only eighty years ago—and nearly the same distance from its subsequent incarnation as a home counties garden city between the wars, filled with Tudor-tropical villa residences and bougainvillaea-shrouded stone bungalows for the ruling classes, where the Indian bazaars, the Kikuyu and Somali quarters were different countries on the wrong side of the tracks.

But since independence twenty years ago, with Kenya taking on the accolade of being the only place that "works" in black Africa, Nairobi has become a vast concrete money box, an ugly haven for Western capital, where the big multinationals have deposited their cash and their staff, creating great concrete bunker headquarters from which they can make their trading forays into the less secure parts of the dark continent. A business city then and of course a massive tourist bridgehead, too—where both sets of these greedy, expectant folk that morning were crowding the downtown hotels and pavements, the cafés and boutiques, in their smart suits and false leopard-band hats, preparing their separate safaris: the first in search of commercial plunder, the second whimperingly anxious to disturb the rapidly declining stock of wild animals. And what I immediately asked myself then, in the crowded urban storm along the wide avenues, among so many whites beneath the ersatz skyscrapers, was, "Where is Africa here—and the Africans?"

The Kikuyu clerks and shop girls walked the streets in proud—or meek—imitation of their Western counterparts. They were like uncertain actors, black playing white, the men self-consciously dignified in just the same sort of neat, dark suits, with little briefcases and brollies—men who had passed from the colonial chit system to computer accounting without ever having known a life of their own in between. Yes, these mimic men would have taken over the old British suburban bungalows now, catching the early bus to their glass-boxed offices like any London commuter. With their own government and among their own people—their family, their country cousins—these were obviously good men, with a sure foot on the ladder which would soon make them Big Men.

There was only one obvious problem. We could see it clearly enough that first morning—the tattered poor here and there on the street corners, barefoot, match-thin boys scrambling for custom in the car parks, maimed or leprous shoeshiners trying to make a pitch near their more successful, well-established rivals round the corner from the New Stanley Hotel. And these were just the tip of an iceberg, I knew—the flotsam froth percolating downtown here, from a hundred thousand others of their kind lurking in the shanty towns on the outskirts of the city. People without land, and with no chance of a downtown office or a red rose in their lapel: a whole dispossessed race without land at home, without a stake in their own tribal world but who would never handle a smart computer for a multinational on Kenyatta Avenue: the usual sad story of post-independent African overpopulation, land famine and consequent migration to the cities, where only a few can ever successfully thrive in an urban manner, while the rest—all the landless, rural Johnnies—are inevitably headed for the cardboard and corrugated iron shanty towns.

All the same, walking downtown that morning, the beggars seemed insignificant, fleas on a very robust body politic; there was a formidably successful air about the city. It looked, demonstrably, as if it "worked." Yes, there were telephones and telegrams here and the world's newspapers inset among blatant girlie magazines at every newsstand; Mercedes taxis belted along the avenues to the busy main railway station round the corner; cars were everywhere; the city was a racetrack. The Indian shops still did their usual canny business in everything under the sun and the smart, *haute couture* safari outfitters, with names like "Sir Henry" and "Sundowner Style," were booming. We looked inside one. Germans and Americans were kitting themselves out, disguising their pot bellies and round shoulders, and promoting their preposterous illusions, in well-cut and padded beige safari suits—getting the false hair on their chests, falling over themselves in their eagerness to play Hemingway up-country. Big groups of other cheaper package tourists made a fevered, rapacious show everywhere else, congregating outside innumerable tourist agencies and "international" hotels: battalions in a permanent big push, constantly embarking in their zebra-striped animal assault wagons. Downtown was Tourist City and little else.

At lunchtime, when I got back to the Norfolk and met Eleanor in the terrace bar, we found ourselves surrounded by the new young set of British Kenyans—groups of smart-aleck, short contract boys in shorts and jeans together with their mindless sweater girls, all dripping with Tusker lagers, yelping loudly in grating suburban accents about the "Yew Kay," about planned car rallies into the bush, and how they would "bomb the coast" in their souped-up Minis next weekend. A poster over the bar advertised Shaw's *Candida* at the Donovan Maule Theatre. "Glittering Nights" were on offer at the International Casino and the last meeting of the season was coming up at N'gong racecourse that Sunday. Nairobi worked all right, in business and pleasure—and it was all infinitely depressing, a place without heart, without history. Twelve hours before, coming in on the airport road, I had longed for it all: a sense of civilization, the Ritz. Now it was like being stuck on the Kingston bypass in some roadhouse among a lot of appalling juveniles.

"How did it go?" Eleanor asked. "Your 'appointments' ?" Her great eyes flickered in some amusement.

"Fine. All very helpful."

"Is that all?"

"Well, a lot of talk. This and that. . . ."

"But what are we going to 'do' here? What are *you* going to do?"

"Anything but the political scene. Our BBC correspondent here does that."

"Doesn't look as if there's anything to do in Nairobi—except get out of the place in one of those zebra-striped minibuses and take a lot of snaps of the animals. And as for this terrace bar. . . ." She looked round at all the young swillers.

"I thought you might like it here. Remind you of home, summer Sunday in some Windsor inn."

"You're being snide."

"Sorry."

"You're not like you at all, are you, today?"

"No."

"Sort of meanness—and not saying anything sensible."

"I just feel I haven't got going—and don't really know where to go either."

"Two drinks below par: you need to cheer up."

"We'll find something to do," I said half-heartedly.

"Lunch? Or maybe you're not hungry. There was a smell of something sick in the bathroom this morning when I got in from the garden. Were you sick?" she added tartly.

"Yes. That great breakfast."

"You should have told me. I might have helped. . . ." She looked at me, concerned. We shared everything else, her expression suggested, why not this? "The dysentery again?"

"No. Just the huge breakfast," I lied once more. I was being private. I was slipping away from her. "I'm sorry." I picked up a collection of tourist brochures I'd gathered up that morning. "Who wants to admit being sick at ten in the morning—if they don't have to? You were out in the garden." I thumbed through the glossy, tourist literature, endless mini-tours in endless minibuses. "Let's try and not get involved in any of this," I said. "But get out of Nairobi all the same. There must be something else besides photo-safaris. All this concrete dumped down last week—absolutely no history in the place, except the murals here."

We looked at the second big mural over the Delamere verandah bar: the Mombasa train arriving seventy years before among the sunstruck white highlanders, the original settlers. That was still in place. But for the rest of Nairobi—there was no hint anywhere of what had made the city, what its traditions were, African, Indian or British. It was simply a well-oiled tourist trap now, with a lot of vastly ugly buildings, travel agencies, international banks, and hotels. In Zaïre the grass and the jungle had grown over everything again; here in Nairobi the past had been buried in concrete: that was the depressing thing—and it wasn't just physical, it was mental. If you weren't a package tourist you were alone in this city with no guidelines to the past or future, no sense of any earlier civilization, tribal or European. Without a camera and a zebra-striped minibus you were dispossessed, déraciné here as much as any of the beggars and shantytown dwellers. There was nothing to possess you in Nairobi—except the porno magazines, the high-heeled tarts, and the equally voracious transients from Rio, Idaho, and Tokyo.

"Look," Eleanor said, handing me a brochure I'd not seen. It advertised the Nairobi Railways Museum downtown, off Haile Selassie Avenue.

"Ah," I said, finding a lifeline again, thrown to me by this woman, leading me to her, saving me from myself and all the despairs of the morning. "That's a good idea."

She put her head on one side, smiling in the old quizzical way. "Yes. Play 'Railway Children.' "

An hour later, after lunch, we were running for our lives across the race track of Haile Selassie Avenue when I suddenly saw the smokestack of a great black steam engine stalled in a marshy back lot beyond the lines of fuming traffic. Across the avenue, behind some tin shacks and an open sewer, we soon saw half a dozen other vast old steam engines with cowcatchers and coal tenders, parked alongside a number of small wooden maroon-and-cream passenger carriages. We'd found the Kenya Railways Museum—and with it a key to some real continuity in the country, the past living appropriately with the present, for as I'd seen outside the main station that morning, it's the Kenyans, not the tourists or the remnants of the old British Raj who use the railways these days.

Beyond the stranded engines lay a long, prewar stone building with steps up on the outside, as if into an old station waiting room. Inside, the big space was deserted except for one old gray-haired Kikuyu, a real station-master type sitting by the door at a table organized just like the booking office of some rural branch line in England sixty years ago, complete with an ancient telephone and ticket punch. He issued us with passenger tickets in the traditional form, cigarette card-sized, heavily printed on stout cardboard—and then he clipped it with his punch: a resounding "snip" that pierced the heavy silence.

All about us, crammed in dozens of glass cabinets and covering every foot of wall space, was a marvelous, quirky collection of old railway bits and pieces, taken from every stage in the development of the Uganda Railway, which the British started in 1896, to open up the interior—running, as it still does, from the Indian ocean at Mombasa up to Lake Victoria and beyond. "The Lunatic Express"—but in fact a miracle of engineering, 600 miles over the deserts, plainslands, up into the highlands, down the Rift Valley and into the swampy central lake area: a narrow-gauge snake that defied everything. And here were examples of all the vital artefacts. Nothing was missing. You could have reconstructed an early station, complete with rolling stock and half a mile of the original track, without any trouble at all. There were detailed engineering and contour maps and sepia-tinted photographs of turbaned Indian station wallahs, leisurely Edwardians on safari and Teddy Roosevelt in a hurry; American calendar clocks, clear line tablets, dâk boxes, meticulously modeled engines and lovely green-and-gold cast iron engine crests and nameplates rescued from defunct rail companies all over East Africa: the Tanga line, up through German East Africa, taken over by the British after the First World War; the Tanga-Dar es Salaam Light Rail Company; the Dar-Tabora-Mwanza line; lines that had crisscrossed this whole eastern region fifty years ago—part of the dream of travel I'd had before coming out here months ago, when I thought I could cross the whole continent without getting off a lake steamer or a narrow-gauge railway.

And I dreamed again of that kind of journey when I gazed at the equipment taken complete from a 1930s dining car on the main Mombasa-Nairobi line: wood galley stove, cumbersome prewar commercial hotel cutlery, heavy wine glasses, brass mustard pots, Bombay cane chairs, and the actual five-course luncheon menu, featuring "Windsor Soup," "Baked Lake Fish—Au Gratin," "Braised Veal Chops" and "Cream Trifle," dated December nineteenth, 1935, and priced at three shillings inclusive. The whole display was so real you could have stepped into it there and then, ordered up a hangover Pale Ale, and taken an instant trip to Happy Valley. The world of the Railway Museum smacked of colonialism, no doubt. But it was a real world. It possessed you.

The world of N'gong racecourse brought the same thoughts when we got out there the following afternoon for the last meeting of the season that Sunday. There were few, if any, tourists or international money-grubbers among the crowds strolling in the sunshine around this sensationally beautiful park five miles south of the city. Ringed with tall, glitter-green trees, the white rails tracing brilliant lines against the shamrock sward, one might at first sight—like the mural in the Norfolk dining room—have been in an England of fifty years ago. The paddock and the reserved stand—apart from several large groups of Wabenzi, the Mercedes men, richest among the Kenyan tribes—were filled with the remnants, the very last of the old white highlanders come to town, or out from their Nairobi bungalows for a final spree before the rains: elderly hawk-eyed *grande dames* in bulky tweeds; younger women, Happy Valley reincarnate, in Gucci scarves; others more formal, nearly at Ascot in flowery dresses and floppy hats—all with their cavalry twill and trilby escorts, ramrod men, thinly moustached, choked by Guards ties. The bars beneath the stand meanwhile were awash with a much rougher white element, among them, I noticed, the Norfolk terrace cowboys, out in beery force—the local Brits, still braying about the "Yew Kay" and bombing the coast.

But outside, in the betting tent and behind the paddock, this very English picture suddenly took on a different color: the bookies were all Indian and the stable boys all black. Looking around, I thought how this careful class and color structure simply reinforced the prewar feeling of the racecourse: here, it seemed, was an exact reproduction of former British times, at home and overseas, a world where everyone had known their place.

The small horses thundered round the curves. The sun sank into the trees, dipping into the N'gong hills. Hints of velvet twilight leaked into the air, this colonial ethos lovingly preserved at N'gong racecourse, the vision riding clear above the smell of saddle leather, the rich tangy dung, the hop-filled beer. Perhaps the whole thing was indefensible. But then, I thought, it must be the black Kenyans themselves—the ones outside the shantytowns at least—who defended all this, by allowing it, by involving themselves in it. And why not? For all its political wrongness, the crass arrogance of the whole colonial setup in Kenya, there was more vibrant life even in its legacy here than in any of the glass and concrete monstrosities which the new colonialists had built downtown. The Kenyans at N'gong—black, brown, and white—reflected a knowledge, an involvement in the life of their country which few of the new money men had, or wanted, and which none of the tourists would ever gain on their frenetic safaris. There had been a real past in the Railway Museum and a real present out here among the racehorses—though I supposed the Kenyan future lurked somewhere down in the shanty-towns, already stirring itself; men with a famished envy and violence for land and food which might one day be theirs—food from the grand tourist hotels and tillage out here where this lovely green pasture would be cut up into pocket handkerchief plots, the trees felled with pangas that had already cut down all the rich—white, brown, and black.

We were watching the last race, standing by the rails near the winning post, two horses neck and neck disputing the lead into the last furlong, when an elderly lady came up beside us. I was aware of her, as of some bizarre force, before I even looked at her properly.

"Quickly!" she shouted. "Come on—put a leg into it. Quick—QUICK!" A demented, husky, horsey voice: prewar county tones straight out of the hunting mural in the Norfolk dining room, except that there was more sophisticated class here. This voice had dined at the Ritz and gone to the 400 Club, I thought, as often as it had cut through the dull ice of hunt breakfasts. I half-turned to her. She was tall and long-faced—wide, high cheekbones, narrow chin—slightly stooped, a weathered outdoor type with deeply age-creased, mottled skin; a scraggy toss of white curled hair—but well dressed in a contemporary county manner; sleeveless beige parka over a check Viyella shirt, smartly cut tweed skirt, a red silk scarf knotted loosely round the throat; fine big eyes—vivid dark and fresh—surviving the impending wreck of her body. She had been an obvious beauty once, with all her elongated delicacy of line; a *grande dame* now, but bearing the title lightly, as only a partial, inexact reflection of her true capacities, which lay in a regal grasp and informality well beyond the confines of class or age. Indeed, such was her air of being above it all, with that husky voice and reed-towering height, there was something inhuman, even witchlike about her. Beside her, black pawn beneath white queen, was a small nondescript African carrying a tartan rug and shooting stick. As the race finished the woman pushed forward right up to the rails, jumping about like a child. She must have been in her seventies but she displayed a tremendous vigor, as if springs had been released all over her body.

"Wonderful!" she shouted at the end, her fancied horse having clearly won. "Wonderful—oh, sausages-and-mash!" She clenched her hands, waving them in the air like a football player after a goal. "Wasn't it fantastic?" She turned to us. "Storybook finish—quite utterly. . . ."

She dragged this last word out in what would have been an affected manner had she not so thoroughly possessed the affectation. She rushed on—knowledgeable comments on the race and its ending—the words coming in a storm of confident intimacies, a personal argot, as if she'd known us both for years. "Celebrations," she said at last. "Drinks at the very, very soonest."

She lit a cigarette. "I'm Petal Cunningham," she said, still gasping for breath. The little African offered her the shooting stick.

"No, no. I'm going back to the stand, Jomo—while you pick up the winnings. Will you?" These last words, added as an afterthought, did nothing to soften the imperious tones of the order.

16

Happy Valley

*P*etal had friends in the stand: a young, bland English couple who seemed to know her only slightly—and to be much in awe of what little they did know of her. Introduced to us they looked at her nervously, warily, as if she were a cat which had just brought something frightful in from the dump. In fact it was clear from the beginning what Petal was up to. She wanted more congenial, amusing company and had spotted this potential in Eleanor and me. She produced a silver flask, man-sized, from a floppy-smart leather shoulder bag and we swigged some warm brandy. The English couple, pleading the early hour, declined. And very shortly afterward they continued their excuses and apologies—an impatient babysitter and much else—as a prelude to leaving us entirely. Petal let them go without demur.

"Friends—of friends, of *old* friends out here," she said, as we left the stand, moving toward the car park. "Nice. But not the same sort of people. A little down in the mouth somehow—young people these days."

Jomo had joined us now, clutching a wad of Kenyan shillings.

"Well, you'll be paid today," Petal told the man, who smiled slightly at this news, a token beam that vanished rapidly.

"No. You *will!*"

"Yes, Ma'am," Jomo said, and the grin was offered up again but with no more confidence.

"That's better," Petal said, ignoring the man suddenly. Eleanor and I had started to talk about a taxi. "But of course not. Jomo has the car."

We moved off in a large black hired Mercedes, Jomo crouched forward over the wheel, driving very circumspectly. "Only driver I trust out here," Petal said as we took a funereal pace into the city. "I knew his uncle, and his grandfather, before the war—up near Gil Gil."

"You lived there?"

223

"A farm, a lovely bungalow. I've come out to see the last of it all," she said. But there was no regret in her voice—rather the opposite: a touch of venom, even cruelty. "I'm staying at the Hilton," she told us, when we'd talked some more about our separate and various reasons for being in Kenya. "Couldn't get a room at the Norfolk. Why don't you have dinner with me tonight?"

"Of course not. Come up to the Norfolk, with us—"

"My dears," she said, putting a hand on Eleanor's arm. "It's *my* party. But we'll have it at the Norfolk. My room is splendid at the Hilton, right at the top, see way over the horrid city out onto the plainslands. *De haut en bas.* But the restaurant is a bit *bas.*" She turned and looked out at the straggling Africans on the roadside, the rutted lanes that led here and there into the miserable shanty villages. She was suddenly quiet and when she turned back her eyes were glazed, with a faraway expression—tears even—as if she'd been sympathizing with, contemplating their plight deeply. But then she said very briskly, "Seven-thirty. But not the Delamere bar. It's too common. Meet in the dining room —there's a little apéritif corner there. And remember—my party." She dropped us at the Norfolk. Two hours later she was sipping Tio Pepe with us in the apéritif corner.

She looked round at the smartly renovated red-and-brown decor. "You won't believe it, but ages ago my first husband was manager here. Nothing grand like this—much more country inn style: the dining room was across the hall, billiard room beyond. But the Arabs or someone blew the whole place up a few years ago."

She wore a dark-meshed cocktail dress—several flimsy layers of the fine silk-like material which rustled faintly like cigarette paper when she moved. Sitting down, you could see how long her legs were, the shin bone running in a perfect line from knee to ankle. The flesh had sunk away but all the right foundations were still there and you saw what legs they must have been. She smoked; then lit another one. She coughed. She chain-smoked.

"They gave him five shillings a day to feed all the guests here. But eggs were sixpence a hundred, big chickens sixpence each and the best steak ninepence a pound. So it wasn't too difficult." She looked at the grand menu. A single dinner was now about 150 shillings. She laughed at the discovery. "Sausages-and-mash. . . ." she said again, talking to herself in her rough *sotto voce.* Then she looked up. "The food was plainer here than in the Muthaiga Club. But better. And a better place to stay, really—certainly if you wanted to stay sober. I just remember the old lady who owned the place. *Very* fierce. Didn't put up with any hanky-panky."

"The old Happy Valley crowd?" I asked.

"Yes. I suppose so. Though I always thought that was something of an illusion, got up by the papers. Least, it was hardly a valley full—just a small group of Royal drunks out here with their women—and other people's women. The de Janzès, the Traffords, and Joss Errol, of course."

"They shot him—the man they shot?"

"They? There wasn't more than one: Broughton, the husband, shot him—and got off scot-free. Though that was no more than justice, perhaps. Joss was a frightful cad. I knew most of them slightly. But they were a tight little group, in every sense: a drinking-and-sleeping school. Not my style really. I mean—" She looked at me carefully, her big hooded eyes full of irony. "I mean they weren't the sort of people I ever wanted to drink or sleep with. You could do that out here without being a Happy Valley wallah, or living in the bar of the Muthaiga— and with *much* more congenial people. They were the dregs socially, I thought. Drank away any sense of intelligence they ever had—and didn't know it. Bee's knees, they thought—because their chums told them so. But they were all so *boring*, you really can't imagine. Nothing so boring as *one* drunk for an evening. And here were dozens of them, sloshed for months on *end*." She lit another cigarette. "Another Tio Pepe, I think. And I've asked for champagne."

I remembered the brandy flask at the racecourse. Eleanor was drinking tomato juice. Petal must have sensed some awkwardness in the sudden silence. She leaned over to Eleanor, smiling, as if embarking on some conspiracy.

"My dear," she said softly, "you're not teetotal, are you?"

"No. But—"

"Good. I thought for just a moment—but you're so much not the sort. *So* much so." She drew back, looking at Eleanor fondly. "Beautiful," she said, again more to herself than us. Then she turned to me. "Are you married?"

"No." I was lost for words. But then I remembered the old joke. "We live in Nairobi."

She nodded several times, lips slightly pursed, an opponent savoring an interesting move in chess. "I knew you'd both be good company." She launched into her second Tio Pepe.

"I left at the end of the Sixties," she said. We'd embarked on the champagne over the fish *pâté* now. "Jimmy died then, my nice second husband. Nothing to stay for really. Sold up. Not that the going was good then. But I didn't mind the little money we got for Edgewood and the farm—sold to some Kikuyu bigwig. And not that I minded their independence out here one bit. I was all for that. What I didn't care for was the corruption and the cruelty that came with it. Not so much to us whites, but the Indians, the Goans. Of course, it was tit for tat in a way. The Asians had cleaned up here over the years—not a high-minded lot, commercially, to say the least. But still it was all a very abrupt, brutal business against the *small* Asians, which I couldn't forgive them for—waiters, cooks and people, who were nearly all Goan in the old days. And the small shopkeepers. They got a terrible push, first to go. . . ."

She left half her *pâté* and lit a cigarette. "But they couldn't get rid of the bigger Indians so easily—the larger shops, garages, all those import-export businesses they had. So what did they do? They threatened them—Chicago-style. And the Asians responded by bribing them to keep away. And that's where the corruption started. Before independence no African here would have taken any 'incentive.' Just wasn't on. Now there are none who won't. Well, that changed everything. Wasn't for me. That wasn't independence—just a license to extort. And I didn't want any of that—quite apart from Jimmy's dying. One thing I can't bear—any sort of blackmail."

Petal lived alone now, in Cascais, an exile in Lisbon's Atlantic suburb resort, with her family—a son and daughter—living in England.

"I go to London once or twice a year: can't say I like it. I suppose I've never really liked anywhere but here. But here it's changed even more. Even seven years ago, when I was last out, you could still recognize something of the old town here. Nothing now. Nothing. And up-country—well, it may suit the tourists. But I'm not a tourist. All this" —she gestured round the dining room, arms and eyes reaching way out beyond the confines of the room—"this was really my life."

We ate steaks of sea bream up from Mombasa, and drank more champagne. I was fascinated by the old lady. Eleanor, refuting the earlier charge of teetotalism, drinking with us both glass for glass.

"And your old friends?" I asked. "Are there many of them left out here now?"

"*Old* friends?" She laughed, then coughed frightfully. "That's about it," she said finally. "*Very* old. Dead! No, there are one or two. Stayers on. But more or less housebound." She mentioned several people in Nairobi—a couple on the coast at Malindi, a man out in Karen. But

then she said with more enthusiasm, "And there's Willy—still up beyond Gil Gil, lived near us at Edgewood. Still king of his castle, though
all his land's gone. Taken from him, just the house left, which he won't
get out of, surrounded by little *shambas* now. They took his good land,
some minister—compulsory purchase. And squatters moved in on the
rest of it around the house, bit by bit. And then bit by bit they started
killing off his livestock, pulling down the fences, nearer and nearer to
his front door. But he won't leave—always was a bit of a war horse.
Writes me splendid 'over my dead body' sort of letters. I'm going to
see him tomorrow. Like to come?" I said yes. And we drank some more
champagne.

By the time Petal left that night Eleanor was tipsy. Later in our room
she became quite drunk, continuing the earlier champagne with the
quarter-bottle in our bedroom fridge, before going on to the cognac
miniatures. I'd shared these drinks with her at first, celebrating, as I
thought, a good day, a lucky meeting, a civilized spree, an interesting
future with Petal on the morrow. I should have seen the signs, the other
quite different reasons for Eleanor's sudden intemperance.

"Apart from that drunk you were on—that party in Kinshasa," she
said, slurping about in the bathroom, "you've never *really* told me, have
you, about your problems at home?"

"No."

"You don't have to, of course—"

"Then why keep bringing it up?"

She emerged in her nightdress, scratching her arms which had started
to flake again. She'd been quite free of this eczema since our days in the
Mille Collines Hotel in Rwanda. "What's home got to do with
anything—now? Here?"

"Just—interest." She hesitated, seeing my firm look. She was bleary-
eyed already, puffy-faced for the first time in a month. Then suddenly
aggressive: "I'm not sure I want to go up and see this Willy person
tomorrow anyway. What does she want *us* with her for—seeing her old
friends? Something phony. . . ." She looked toward the drinks fridge.
Then she moved toward it.

"We've had enough," I said pleasantly.

She opened the door, drew out another miniature, unscrewed the
top, drank half of it by the neck in one gulp—and then I got the message.

"What's wrong? I thought all that was over. What's upset you? Petal?"

"You're only going up-country with her for business—as you are
with me. 'Copy' as you call it."

"Not at all. I like her. And she asked you as well. She likes us. It's company."

Eleanor didn't say anything, drinking the rest of the miniature. Her face was set in a withdrawn scowl: the frustrated, ill-tempered child had emerged in her once more—and I recognized all the bad old days again, when we'd first met in Kinshasa. And I felt no nostalgia now for anything of our life in that city—nothing I'd shared, good or bad, with this sullen, truculent girl: reverting to type, I thought—an incurable juvenile sot.

Rwanda had been different. But the passion there seemed a flash in the pan now. And now I was back in limbo—it was as simple as that, with no emotion to offer. All that was locked away again, frustrated, questioning, operating in sad forays deep into the past—where it could do absolutely no good at all. Yet still I fought a rearguard action, lying to Eleanor, when I knew the truth.

"Why?" I asked her as she staggered about the room. "Why take to the drink again?"

"Oh, you have another life. Nothing to do with me—wives, families."

At least she saw the truth of the matter, in vino veritas. "Only one," I said.

"Doesn't matter. Same thing. You can call home. . . ." She sighed, a drink-filled sadness clutching, overpowering her.

"I told you to call your father, on me—"

"As if that was the point. Are you mad or something? Games. Since you called home from here you've been playing games. You're not *you* at all. I can't see *you* anymore. You're back at home now, not here, in your garden mowing the lawn or something. You're not here with me anymore anyway."

I sat down on the edge of the bed, looking away from her. "So what am I to do about it? Never have started anything with you?"

"I should never have started it."

"Shouldn't have started drinking again. That's the only real problem."

"If that satisfies you—fine. Always find an excuse."

"Like you—to drink. Easier still. I'm the excuse now. But I never said anything other than to come across Africa with me. And you said—yesterday morning at breakfast—that's all you expected. Now you're behaving as if I'd betrayed you."

She looked at me carefully then, her puffy eyes wide open in anger. "*Betrayed* me?" she said, startled. "That's what *you* think—guilty party, from your own mouth. *I* don't think that. Nothing half so grand as 'betrayed'—unless yourself. No, you just took fright—after the first ditch. Got over that all right. We both did. But now you've run away. Always was your problem, wasn't it? I told you, in Kinshasa: frightened off—before you've properly begun anything. A coward," she added finally before taking out another miniature.

She went on drinking, fiddling in the fridge, walking about the half-lit room, long after I'd gone to bed. Next morning I left her, sleeping deeply, with a note on her bedside table: "Gone to Happy Valley. Back this evening. Be happy too. (Try a prairie oyster. . . .)" The tone was lighthearted. I was still trying to have things both ways, still the coward.

"Little tiff—or just a little hangover?" Petal asked when I'd vaguely explained why Eleanor wasn't with us. I must have looked as glum as the weather. The bright, high skies were gone and it was drizzling, a damp-gray day as we left Nairobi, up the main highway to Nakuru, Jomo doing his undertaker act at the wheel while the two of us stretched out in the back seat.

"A little tiff," I said. "And she has the little hangover."

Petal lit a cigarette and lowered the window a fraction. A sweet mix of warm-wet vegetation and hot tar swirled into the car. One side of the dual carriageway was being repaired here. Folds of low cloud were stitched right down, hiding the horizon. There was little to see beyond the Indian stone bungalows dotted along the wayside. And further out the crowded African *shambas,* hacked out everywhere on the wooded hills, disappeared altogether in the rain-mist capping the escarpment. On the road huge trucks and mad taxi drivers sped past us, tires sizzling in the rain. If you didn't look at anything too closely one might have been driving out of Birmingham or any other dreary, rain-drenched British city.

"This was the only road when I first came out here. Nairobi–Nakuru. After that you were stuck everywhere."

"Oh," I said. I was still thinking of Eleanor. Petal resumed her earlier theme then. Like Eleanor, she seemed to be able to read my thoughts.

"I'm sorry," she said. "Tiffs," she went on vaguely. "And then hangovers—hand in hand. Always a problem here. People used to say it was the altitude in the white highlands—and the light—that drove people to mischief. Not certain I believe that. Look at it now. And when it rains up here, it rains, often for weeks."

We looked out on the sodden countryside, the weeping sky crowding over the larger hills. We were halfway up the great escarpment.

"It wasn't anything I said last night?" Petal asked.

"No. An old problem." I didn't enlarge on it.

"All the same, I must admit it, there is something—there *was* a mood in these highlands that made you lightheaded—in those days—when the landscape up here was pretty well empty. You looked across it— up to the Aberdares or over the Rift—and you thought: I can do *anything* here, God-like, and won't be punished. Of course it was a white settler look; it's all *mine,* you thought—as it usually was. There were some really vast farms up here then. And if it wasn't yours, well then, the land over the hill belonged to Johnny or David, or someone else you knew. Friends. And it was all that feeling of *possession* that gave you a thrill out here then. Childish thrill, but that's what it was like—huge nursery paradise, divided up among a few other children, where you could do anything you wanted, parents back in stuffy old England. That was the point. You could live all your fantasies here— go on living them, even if rinderpest got the cattle and half a dozen different bugs and molds got the corn or coffee—even when the drink really got you. Tiffs and little hangovers!—that was the least of it. But you see what I mean?"

She turned with an unhappy smile. "It wasn't that a lot of us didn't work hard out here; a lot of us *slaved.* But mentally we looked on it all as a Never-never-land—Peter Pans. Didn't want to grow up. That's the point. And the land up here confirmed all this. Oh, it did—sunset and all the animals and so on—even if you'd heard you were broke that morning. Didn't matter. Not one bit. David and Johnny came round that evening and you had a party. And next morning, in the sun with the hundred-mile views all still there, the place was just as breathtaking. And you could always borrow another five thousand next week in Nairobi. You didn't *have* to grow up, you see."

"Yes," I said. "I do see that." And I did. Children of the country, I thought.

After we turned off the main road at Gil Gil, traveling north beside a little branch railway line, we moved into open pastureland, a broad rich country, the Aberdare Mountains hidden in cloud to our right, rain-rippled cornfields, rolling away like English downlands on the other side to the edge of the Rift. Further on we drove into a thickly wooded valley which opened out after a few miles into what seemed the remnants of some vast estate on either side, an English parkland with the road running straight beneath great arched branches and between rotten post-and-rail fences, where great single trees—oaks, beeches—had been planted out Capability Brown-fashion years before and had now almost reached maturity—a startling English vision carved out here a few miles from the equator by an extinct white tribe.

"There," Petal said, a few minutes into this majestic woodland, lovely even in the rain. "There's the gate. 'Edgewood'—and it still does. Always did, even before we cleared a lot of the bush and planted it out properly. The farm, the real land, is behind the house, you see, and we opened up the front as a sort of lawn with trees and a polo field. So you couldn't see the house from the road. And the man who owns it now"—she named a minister in Nairobi—"well, he's kept it that way, so the local small farmers and squatters can't see the good land behind. Give them notions. . . ."

The estate was well fenced now, six feet of barbed wire behind the decaying post-and-rail. We came to the concrete pillars of the gateway. "Have to pick up a man here," Petal said. "Fixed it in Nairobi."

An African, carrying an umbrella and a night stick, emerged from a small hut behind the barbed wire when we tooted: young, well dressed, not a laborer, just a sentry. He unlocked the gates and got into the front seat next to Jomo before we moved off along a winding drive between the dripping trees, a thin drizzle that had lasted all morning.

"You remember this, don't you, Jomo?" Petal was alert now, sitting forward, looking everywhere, eyes roving round her old domain—sharp eyes, not sentimental at all, as if she was looking for some expected, present life in this dank overgrown parkland: a troupe of old friends coming through the trees to greet her, the thwack of a ball from the polo field, now a flat expanse of scrubby pasture away to our right.

"Used it as a little air strip, too," Petal said. "Up and down from Nairobi. Willy had a plane—Willy that we're going to see later: Arbour Hill Farm—it's only five miles down the road. He and Henry, my first husband, played a lot—at everything. Polo, flying, and Willy kept his plane here. Got down to Nairobi in half an hour. Dinner at the Muthaiga or the Norfolk, back up here next afternoon, plane full of goodies."

She looked about her pleasantly now, smiling, content. I was surprised. In her shoes, I'd not have wanted to come back here with such memories, to this dark, overgrown wilderness of an estate where she had been happy—or back to the house somewhere beyond, epicenter of that happiness, which she had described as a ruin. I'd like to have asked her why she'd come back but it wasn't the moment. "It must have been an extraordinary life," I said instead.

"It was *quite* something," she admitted slowly, pulling deeply on her cigarette. "And I suppose you wonder why I've come back to it all, to the ghost of it, the ruin." She didn't look at me, smoke curling up into her tossed-white hair.

"It did strike me. . . ."

"Well, I came to see Willy, really. And since the house here was nearby, why not?"

"Painful enough though?"

"I'm wondering. . . . I don't *feel* any pain. Yet." Then she turned to me. "That's one reason I asked you to come. On my own I might feel the pain."

"Of course. I'm glad to."

"On the other hand," she said brightly. "*Why* pain? So much an expected response. It was *part* of me—all this. Came into my bones. But I've still got my bones. So it's still part of me. The reality of it all has gone. But not me, not my thoughts about it. They're both still here."

"That's exactly what might make it still painful."

"Only if I was out here to haunt the place, laying ghosts. And I'm not. I regret nothing I did here. Or very little," she added. "No ghost to lay. Actually, in a strange way, it makes me feel rather buoyant, coming back up here. I've survived it all."

The deeply rutted avenue came out of the trees. On a rise a quarter-mile ahead I saw what looked like a great clump, a long mound of bushes and creeper, no stone visible anywhere from this distance. It was the house, the long bungalow—"Edgewood," which had been entirely obscured, undergrowth become overgrowth.

"Just *look* at what the bougainvillaea has done," Petal said in happy surprise.

We took coffee from a thermos flask some distance away—the car couldn't make it up to the house itself, for the drive ran out here completely, some hundred yards away from it. Later we walked up to it, just the two of us with an umbrella, Jomo and the sentry left gossiping in the car. There had been trees all around the house but apart from a small stand of fir to one side, arm-thick saplings, there was nothing left standing, just a few stumps, one or two branches deeply embedded in the scrubby soil—a whole lichen-covered trunk lying across the remains of a lawn, and some wildly overgrown herbaceous borders.

"He cut the trees down, of course. Our friend in Nairobi. Get money for them."

"You've not been back since you left?"

"No. Last time I didn't bother. But I'm seventy-five now—won't have another chance."

We moved right up to the great mass of dripping creeper that covered the long bungalow. And now, here and there, we could see the stone of an end wall, a jutting eave, a patch of gray tile. The roof, in fact, had fallen in, we saw when we got round to the back, where the climbing blanket of vegetation was less overwhelming. Here there were the remains of a yard, with ruined stone outbuildings some distance away, and a big stone urn on a pedestal which we discovered, tucked in, just visible by what had been a back door.

"We had four of those, for flowers, along the front verandah. I wonder where the rest are? Thought they'd gone at the auction." She bent down and started to poke about among the creeper roots, the wet thick mass of bougainvillaea and hibiscus. She cleared out the top of the urn, put a hand down inside, drew out a lot of old leaves and soil. Then she delved deeper, more urgently, as if she was looking for something she knew to be down at the bottom. But there was nothing and her hands were filthy now. I gave her my handkerchief.

"It's funny," she said, perplexed. "We always kept the keys there, house keys, car keys and things. The urn was just next to the door." She rubbed her hands, the ocher soil smearing the entire hanky.

I pushed my way through the creeper then, seeing if I could get in by the back door. But I was stuck and drenched in the matted gloom after a minute.

"Be careful," Petal said. "There won't be anything in there anyway." I pushed and thrashed about again, moving forward very gradually, opening out the thick strands. But I could see almost nothing. It was hopeless. Then my foot hit rock or stone. I put my hand down, felt a circular rim filled with earth and leaf mold: it was another of the urns. I could feel the same serrated edge. I rooted about in it, just as Petal had done, scooping the debris out. There was nothing else to do. I could get no further. Near the bottom my fingers touched something solid, just a stick. No, it was metal. I pulled it out. It was a key. I could feel the circular hasp, the long shaft, the deep metal fingers.

"Front-door key," Petal said, without surprise, when I emerged with it from the creeper. "I *knew* we'd left it in one of the urns. Never used it, you see, of course, because there was always someone here." She held the badly rusted key out in the drizzle, rubbing at it, letting the rain flake away the thin wafers of metal. "Or is it our key?" she said eventually, considering it carefully, undecided. "Don't remember it this long or big. Willy has a huge baronial door to his house. I wonder if it might not be his?"

A curious expression—half-happiness, half-despair—spread over her face as she turned away from me and looked up into the mists shrouding the Aberdares. Happy Valley: the key to it had been returned, I thought. Or had I found a key leading to some quite different country?

Willy's house was closer to the road. But here the remains of the old woodland drive were no more than a village lane now, the trees felled, running between small squatters' huts, *shambas,* patches of decrepit, rain-bent maize: a long rural slum leading almost to the front verandah of a two-storied, rough stone house, a formidable building, where the tiny, metal-framed windows gave an added air of impregnability. It was like a castle, a fortress—towering over, surrounded on three sides by the encroaching *shambas* of the landless peasantry, groups of bare-bottomed children paddling about in the rain, brought up sharp by the passage of the big car, staring at us, huge-eyed, motionless, expression-less, these glistening-dark infants. Like Edgewood, the house faced west-ward. Though on this far side there were no woods or *shambas:* another barbed wire fence fifty yards away gave out onto a long slope of cornland leading down to the invisible edge of the Rift: the good land.

"Perhaps—you'd prefer to see Willy on your own?"

"No, no. He'd like the extra company. Never sees anyone. I told you—he's practically barricaded himself in here."

He had. A chicken wire palisade covered all the open verandah, with a makeshift entrance in the same material which we climbed through. And the hall door was huge—a great double door in hardwood with raised metal studs, Arab fashion, set out in rectangular designs; a large keyhole, now filled in. The key I'd found would certainly have fitted it. A dog barked inside when we knocked: another joined it in angry counterpoint. Rain leaked in a steady stream through the verandah roof above. Bolts were shifted, things went thump, a chain rattled. One half of the door opened.

"Petal!"

"Willy!"

I really felt they didn't need my company. So my excuses were all the more heartfelt when I met the small, white-haired, dark-tanned man.

"Not at all, of course not. Delighted. Come along in."

He was small, pugnacious, wiry, Scots—everything I'd expected: old flannels, tweed jacket, thinly knotted regimental tie, neat laced brown shoes, well groomed. A fire smoldered in a vast stone grate at one side of a large, stone-flagged drawing room-hall: Arab-patterned carpet in front of the fire, great metal-spoked wheel supporting the slow blaze; zebra skins, crossed assegais, fine trophies—antelope, leopard, a black-maned lion—high on the walls; shelves of tall quarto sporting books and novels in one corner; English hunting prints, an elephant's-foot wastepaper basket, a card table where the legs were made from four crossed oryx horns; another table by the French windows on the far side covered with papers, magazines, whisky decanter, glasses; a divan bed against the far wall with medicines, pipes, books on a bedside table—huge cushions beyond for the two big Alsatian dogs. A large, cozy den where Willy had come to live, retreating into this one main room in the house—an armed retreat, I saw, when I turned and noticed the big sporting rifle and a shotgun standing in a rack by the door.

"Sit yourselves down. Sit down. . . ." I didn't. I moved away, glancing at things about the room, while Petal and Willy continued their greetings. Yes, everything here was as I'd expected, as though I'd seen all the details of this crammed colonial space in a dream. The only thing I didn't expect was the framed single photograph of Petal, among a group of others, on one of the upper bookshelves—fifty years before perhaps, in a leather flying helmet, smiling sweetly. I could see it was her—the height for one thing, towering over the rear fuselage of a small plane. And there was the same long face, high cheekbones, the same haughty foundation beneath the posed smile. It was Petal alone, where all the other photographs were made up of groups. And now I wondered more than ever why she had brought me here.

Willy made tea for us on a little camping boil-up: tea and dry biscuits. "More like whisky weather," he humphed, listening to the rain. "But we'll get to that later." Petal sat on rather a grubby, high-backed armchair with a faded patchwork quilt spread over it: obviously his chair next to the fire, a place of normally lonely honor for him.

"Don't you have any boys at all now then?" Petal asked.

"Wouldn't let them into the house. *None* of them. You see how it is—they're right up to the door already."

"Yes. . . ."

"Have to carry me out—no other way: dead body." He laughed, a dry, spry cackle. "One of the boys from the village over the road—not the squatters—he comes in once or twice a week. Does a little laundry, cooking, shopping. That's all. Besides, my needs are few. I've got my books, the wireless, the papers up from Nairobi and out from London.

What more do I need? Body and soul together, as long as I can keep the blighters outside from storming the place. . . . So you saw Bob and Mary. How were they? The old cockleshells. I'd like to go down and see them. But if once I leave this place—they'd be in the door like a flash."

They gossiped over mutual friends, dead and alive. We sipped our tea. Willy poked the fire into a small blaze. The rain increased, whipping in gusts against the French windows. Petal and Willy chatted very amiably about this and that—sitting, for all the world, like an old, comfortably married couple on either side of the great fireplace. And though there was absolutely no strain in their conversation, no sign that they were in the least tongue-tied by my presence, I felt more *de trop* than ever. It was the way they sometimes looked at each other that gave me the feeling—an extraordinary full and easy expression, a famished regard where everything that really mattered passed to and fro between them via their eyes.

"Ah, Willy . . ." Petal sighed, when later we'd been offered large cut-glass tumblers of scotch. "You make me feel so much I should never have left here. If you've been able to stick it out."

"No, no, dear girl." He was vehement. "Quite right to go. What would you have done out here on your own, once Jimmy went? I'd probably have gone myself but for Violet. She wanted to stay on. And on. Till last year, when she finally went: crossed Jordan, the dear good woman."

He drank his scotch. There was silence. Only the logs hissed and one of the dogs stirred in its slumber by the fire.

"I'm glad about the key." Willy turned to me. "Clever of you to find it."

"Just luck."

Willy looked at Petal. "Of course it's the key to the old door over there," he said. "Had it made up in Lamu—some marvelous carpenter and ironwork chaps there in the old days. But I can't think how it got into the urn over at Edgewood." He looked perplexed.

"Some tomfoolery—in the old days," Petal said. "After a party or something. You dropped it in the wrong urn. Or I did." She looked at him for a moment, a wry conspiracy in her hooded eyes.

" 'spect you're right. Some tomfoolery. . . ." He smiled back at her quickly. "Plenty of that," he added. The two of them seemed to cast their minds back on all the tomfoolery, silent now, a long silence, the years rolling back. The dog woke and scratched itself vigorously.

"*Will* you stay here forever?" Petal finally asked.

"What else, dear girl? Oh yes—be buried here. With Violet. What else?" he said happily. Then he added, frowning, thinking along some other line that I couldn't follow at that point, "Can't waste time with regrets—the might-have-beens. Have to get on with it. On, on!" He poured more whisky all round. "No, no. I'll end up with Violet—out there in the old garden. Happy safaris through the great beyond. How could I not? How could I ever leave her?" he said, looking at Petal now. " 'spect she needs me more than ever. Never was much good on her own, the old girl. Must be bloody lonely up there."

He glanced upward, then at Petal again. "So you see how it is? How it's got to be." He nodded his head for emphasis. "I have to stay with her."

Petal said nothing, her face quite blank, the eyes dead coals, nodding her head with him. The two of them sat there looking at each other, nodding in agreement against the firelight, the room almost dark now, the day gone, the rain still falling heavily all over Happy Valley.

"I suppose you see now why I wanted someone to come with me," Petal said as we drove back to Nairobi.

"I think so."

"In the circumstances, I don't think I could have faced dear Willy on my own."

When I got back to the Norfolk that evening I found Eleanor in the Delamere bar whooping it up with the juvenile Brits over cold Tuskers: Eleanor in her red pirate pants, flushed, cocky, abrasive—just as I'd first met her in Kinshasa weeks before; Eleanor after a whole day, it seemed, sampling every hair on the dog.

"Look who's here!" she called out.

I had one beer with her and her awful friends, then went and had dinner by myself. Hours later she turned up in the bedroom—pushy, drunk, bedraggled, wet—for they'd all been out in the rain for a bibulous meal downtown: an exact repeat, as she staggered in the bedroom doorway, of her moist arrival at the Memling, except that this time she still had clothes on. I was in bed reading.

"Nothing so boring as one drunk for an evening," I said. "This makes two drunks, for two evenings."

"Ha, ha." Her best home counties voice. Then she hiccupped. "You told me to have a prairie oyster this morning. Your fault."

"I didn't tell you to lace it with vodka or whatever—and booze on it for the rest of the day."

"Oh, yes! Wodka. *Wodka*," she added. "Must get it right." She went into the bathroom, taps ran. "Did you have a lovely time, with that old flower?"

"Yes. Interesting."

"So did I."

"Those frightful people."

"You're just a snob."

"Yes. Certainly."

Then she got sick—a long sickness, retching. Then there was silence. Then she came back into the room—sorry for herself, speechless, shaking, ashen-faced, all the sassy punch gone from her. I gave her some Veganin and water and put her to bed.

"At least we've both been sick now," she said when she'd settled down at last, a little happier, as if this notion in some way excused, explained her long drunk. And perhaps it did in a way. I'd been sick that morning as part of my cowardice. So now had she. If I was finding difficulties in loving two women, she was quite unable to stomach my problems here. With more courage she would have left me that morning when she woke up, and gone off with her new friends: with more courage or less love. And, of course, had I possessed such sterling, loveless qualities myself I would have done just the same thing—got out of her life that day without more ado. But in these matters we were both cowards, sisters under the skin.

CHAPTER

17

The Mara Flight

N ext morning Eleanor, as usual, had sobered up miraculously and
at breakfast we said nothing of her twenty-four-hour skite. By
lunchtime, over mineral water, we were friends again, and that afternoon, the weather having cleared into brilliant high skies, we went down
to the Hilton and took tea with Petal in her room, almost at the top of
the thirty-story hotel.

Later when I picked up a pair of binoculars by the window, casually
focusing them on what I thought would be the suburbs of the city, I
saw instead an old silver DC3 rising into the blue from a country runway
that seemed just at the end of the street.

"That's Wilson—the original airport," Petal said. "Even now Nairobi
is much smaller than one thinks, stuck down on the streets beneath all
these phony skyscrapers. In the old days, with field glasses, you could
see the animals in Nairobi Park from the top of most buildings here.
Not now. Fewer animals, more poaching, more skyscrapers, more
tourists."

"Where's the best place to see the animals then?"

"Maasai Mara," Petal said at once. "Game reserve, 200 miles southwest of here, on the Tanzanian border. We always went there hunting
in the old days: best lion in East Africa. And I was there ten days ago,
for a last look. Still pretty unbelievable—the package tourists haven't
got into it, costs too much. It's really a continuation of the Serengeti.
You can take a plane from Wilson, right there, just down the road. Or
a car, do it in about a day. You'd be just in time for the wildebeest
migration. That's quite breathtaking—sausages-and-mash. They start to
cross over the border about now, hundreds of thousands of them, going
north looking for the fresher grass. Never seen anything like it."

"You take a truck out after them, do you?"

"No," Petal said firmly. "You take a balloon out *over* them. They run one every morning from Keekorok Lodge now. That's how I did it—utterly extraordinary."

"Costly," I ventured.

Petal nodded. "Worth every penny, though. Worth a week's safari pushing about on the ground. Once you've done it—well, I couldn't believe it: really the only way to see game. And Maasai Mara is the last place for that out here anyway. All the other parks are overrun—with tourists, of course, not animals."

I took the glasses up again. The DC3 was rising high now, a silver flash in the sun above the N'gong hills, moving southwest toward an armada of little puffy clouds that ran across the sky, all suspended in a perfect line, at exactly the same height, like dazzling meringues seen from beneath on a transparent oven tray.

"That must be the Mara flight now." Petal looked out the window with me, and Eleanor joined us. "The one I got. Leaves every afternoon—and there's nothing else in that direction—just Maasailand, and beyond that the last really wild plainslands left in Kenya, like it all was a hundred years ago before we came out here, shot most of the animals and put the rest in parks. Out there in Mara it's like it was," she added abruptly, turning away suddenly with a couldn't-care-less look, lighting a cigarette. I recognized the form of Petal's emotion now, for things she really felt about in Africa: it emerged in a clipped short-hand, the voice of a bored and irascible telephone operator conveying the words of a marvelous sonnet. Only in such dull telegraphese could Petal accept the content of the message.

I hadn't really wanted to see the animals this time in Kenya, be part of any frenzied safari groups in zebra-striped minibuses. But something moved quickly in my stomach as I watched the silver DC3—a sharp twinge of adrenaline, that magic moment in travel when a plan not even dreamed of a minute before suddenly comes to you fully formed—kicking you, beckoning irresistibly. Suddenly I had to be out there in the sky, among those puffball clouds, on the way to Mara and a hot-air balloon, no matter what the cost. We'd made plans already to move off due north, to Lake Turkana, the Jade Sea, 500 miles in the other direction on the Sudanese border. But that could wait. Yes, if we moved fast enough we might just be able to make that same flight tomorrow afternoon. Africa as it was a hundred years ago, suspended above it, like Jules Verne in his Victorian balloon? If this was true, if this was pos-sible, it would be worth every penny: a once in a lifetime adventure—Africa of the heart, the Africa of my childhood almost within my grasp.

I had to snatch it, it was now or never and hang the cost. I told Petal, I told Eleanor. They both nodded. "I'd come with you, come again," Petal said. "But enough is enough—and I have to see Jimmy's grave. Besides," she went on casually, without looking at either of us, "there's nothing like Mara for sorting oneself out. We all went down there for that in the old days. Little tiffs, hangovers, even deaths—whatever awful things—we all made off for a few weeks' safari in Mara. That was the greatest cure of all out here."

Twenty-four hours later Eleanor and I were in the same silver DC3, the great wings bumping over the N'gong hills, pushing up into just the same little blobs of cotton wool, about to launch ourselves out over the vast brown depths of the Rift Valley. "Sausages and mash," Eleanor said quietly, looking down on the stupendous view. The passengers with us were straight out of an updated *Grand Hotel*-type movie. A fashion-plated, real blonde in tight designer cords and an almost diaphanous silk shirt sat right behind us; on the other side of the aisle was a cultured American genealogist from Maine. Right in front a chic Parisian family, parents and two teenage children, commented on the sensational view in the purest, money-laden tones of the *seizième*. The others in the plane were similarly varied, individual and well heeled. This was no cheap package tour certainly. The costs of staying at Keekorok Lodge, if you included the balloon flight, worked out at more than £100 a day, where you stayed right in the center of the Reserve or at one of the two luxury tented camps beneath the edge of the escarpment. The manager at the Norfolk Hotel had fixed the trip for us. "Trouble is there are no rooms at the Lodge right now," he'd told me. "But I've fixed you both up to stay with the balloon pilot and his wife for a night or two, so you'll be all right."

And we were. The plane shivered and bounced continuously in the hot thermals over the desert. A sudden delicate rumor of *eau de cologne* and the rustle of a sick bag came through the air of the cabin. These very rich, slightly out of bounds on this escapade, were being mildly punished for their temerity—gazing nervously down at the blazing desert wastes far below us—red-brown, endless, empty except for a few Maasai *manyattas,* circular *bomas,* portable thorn bush camps, which from this height appeared simply as mysterious human patterns on the floor of the red valley, archaeological remains of some long lost tribe.

But twenty minutes later the tawny slopes of the western escarpment rose up on the other side of the great valley, then yellow-streaked hills, and ten minutes after that the desert was all gone as we swooped down over a very different world, making our final approach, skimming in just above a line of lush green river trees, startling an ostrich that gangled away like mad before the engines roared again and we powered in to Keekorok airstrip.

As soon as my feet sank into the springy yellow meadow grass I knew I'd come somewhere special: grass, I thought, nothing but gently undulating grass—twenty or thirty miles of it disappearing away toward the thin purple hills far away on the horizon—not the clapped-out, eroded soils and gloomy rain forest that I'd seen everywhere else on this African journey. Here was real land at last, untouched, singing in the wind beneath a huge sky in the blade-keen light. The equator was just a hundred miles to the north, but at over 5000 feet, high up on this great plateau, the air was only warm, not hot, air that had never seen a city or a smokestack, that cooled you in little eddies as you looked into the great distances through the light that was clear and blue as old Mediterranean water. And now I knew the truth of Karen Blixen's words, from her classic memoirs *Out of Africa:* "Up here in this high air you breathed easily, drawing in a vital assurance and lightness of heart. In the highlands you woke up in the morning and thought: Here I am, where I ought to be."

We stood together on the grass airstrip. The plane left again at once, engines roaring as it turned at the end of the grass strip and hammered away, up like a heavy bird, toward the north. The French woman said, *"Alors. . . ."* Even she was speechless, the warm wind flicking at her silk Gucci scarf. Eleanor touched my arm, unconsciously I felt, the two of us, with the little group of other passengers, standing there, amazed swimmers about to dip into a limitless green-gold sea.

Dudley Chignall, the balloon pilot, came to meet us in his new Toyota jeep—a small, fair-haired, delicate-featured man, whose eyes saw everything and whose mouth said only what needed to be said: young, with a milky tan, in shorts, but already with that sunswept, wind-weathered face, the narrowed eyelids, the easy gait; the marks, colors, that frown against the dazzle, that every white frame must take on here in time: toasted, enriched, relaxed, by the limelight intensity of these high plainslands. He'd made a life here floating over this rippling sea, a young oldtimer already. We left straight away for his little bungalow where he and his wife Vicki lived on the very edge of the Keekorok settlement— where at the end of their small back garden there was nothing but a bamboo fence between them and all the rest of empty Africa beyond, the vast, rolling plain running away forever.

"Buffalo and zebra—and sometimes lion—they come right up to us here all the time," Vicki told us, looking out over her gardenias and geraniums. "And we have an elephant that leans in over the fence too often as well—trying to get at the flowers or the washing. And if you go down to the Lodge after dark, keep to the lighted path. Else there's a chance of unexpected meetings."

"Ending up as, not at, dinner?"

"Well, not quite—I hope."

It was late afternoon now, the silver-ringed sun beginning to dip into the violet light over Lake Victoria a hundred miles to the west. "The sunsets here are unbelievable," Vicki said. "Reflections from all that water, I suppose—with the clouds above it. You'd think the sun might go down the same way once in a while out here. But it never does, each night's different. You'd go mad trying to paint it. But come on before the light goes. We'll go out in the wagon, see what's to be seen down by the river."

I offered a present of gin I'd brought from Nairobi and Dudley took it away to the kitchen where we heard the clunk of ice, the chatter of a blender. "Sundowners—I expect," Vicki said. And a few minutes later Dudley was back with a pair of binoculars and a big thermos flask, and then we were out in the Toyota, moving off into the creamy yellow evening light. And I had that sixth sense then, a kick in the stomach again, when you know some pure pleasure is about to offer itself up, when I knew I'd have to pinch myself in half an hour to know it was all true.

Moving southwest out of the settlement we left the dirt track almost at once, speeding through the long grass, swerving round thorn bushes, missing hidden logs and tree stumps by inches at the last moment: real land cruising, using land just like water, like the sea this great space was, avoiding the reefs. Soon we came to a twisting line of shaggy, green-topped trees, where the ground fell abruptly, and suddenly we were hanging over the steep, forty-five-degree angle of a sandbank above the river, before tobogganing down it, bumping through the shallow water and climbing straight up the far side like an airplane coming out of a dive. The leaves of the trees above us exploded as we passed and a lot of small, stork-like birds—all bedded down for the night which we'd woken—flapped away, crying, long-legged, long-beaked heraldic devices against the pearl-blue sky.

Finally we stopped half a mile beyond the river, facing the sunset, and Dudley got out the thermos flask cocktail. I raised my glass to the dwindling sun, the horizon now a violent, sweeping mass of colors. But so far there were no animals—or none that I'd seen. Then Dudley pointed ahead. What was it? A lot of dark, motionless shapes—I could see these all right; they were just thorn bushes, rotten branches. But no, they moved minutely now and then—and then I smelled something heavy and rancid on the air, a mix of old goat's cheese and socks, and then I saw them. It was a large herd of wildebeest, grazing quietly, barely more than a hundred yards from us, these black, high-shouldered, tousle-headed animals that I simply hadn't noticed against the darkening plains.

"The beesties," Dudley said. "They're beginning to move again. They might really get going tomorrow, cross the river here, so we should get a good look at them from the balloon."

There comes a moment, like the acceptance of a drug, when Africa finally "takes," when after weeks of incomprehension or distaste, stumbling across the continent, you finally discover its special quality, what all the old-timers like Petal loved—and you can still love—about it. A mix of extraordinary space, air, light, potent sundowners perhaps and animals moving like silent armies through the dusk—all that. But there's something more to this sudden revelation: it's when intellect, worry, fate all die in you—and all your senses correspondingly sharpen: when you become at once more human and more animal, too, living miraculously in the best of both worlds. Like a drug it's a sort of "high," an elation you know you could come to crave, so that you'd want to stay here forever, just as Willy did. Africa "took" for me at last that evening by the river. For Eleanor, too.

We were sun-stunned and exhausted and hardly spoke about it at supper. But later, in the Chignalls' spare bedroom-cum-workshop, sharing a small divan, she said, "Why did we take so long to get here?"

"Yes. But so much the better, after all the horrors."

"Now I've seen this, I hate the rest of Africa."

"As bad as that?"

"Of course. Unless one wants to fib and pretend and be all Oxfam liberal about it. The rest *is* a horror."

"The rest is where they live. This is a Maasai reserve, with the game park in the middle, miles from anywhere. Totally untypical."

"Suits me fine."

"And you were so keen on all the *real* Africa before. All those bits and pieces in Kinshasa: the masks, the witch doctor's business, old chicken claws, roots, magic potions. What happened to all that?"

"I hadn't seen all this. That's the dark side. This is the light. You're suddenly yourself here, not having to know all that, knowing who *you* are. That's the knowledge."

"Almost what Karen Blixen said: 'Here I am: where I ought to be.' "

"Yes, well I *have* read her, you old bookworm."

I looked over at the dark shape, humped up, womb-curled, under the bedclothes. It was cold at night here, next to the window, where you could lift the curtain three feet away and look out at a world of stars.

"Good," I said. "You've found yourself. You didn't really want to discover the other things—the 200 different Congo river dialects and masks. You wanted—you."

"Sounds neat. Don't suppose it's that simple. But I've found something." She paused, then turned suddenly, stretching out on her back. "I feel older, that's what it is. Getting out of the plane, and this evening by the river seeing all those animals—I felt older and it didn't matter. It was just like a gift. Older." She repeated the word, a jewel in her mind. "And loving it, which is strange, because I've always had this thing—of wanting to stay young. As a child, even, I can remember saying to myself: 'I never want not to be other than this way.' "

She stirred slightly, uncrossed her legs, then lifted the curtain. You could actually see the night outside beyond the bamboo fence: it wasn't real darkness. But there wasn't a moon. It was just starlit.

"Well, you've 'found yourself,' " I humphed. "Think I'm too old for that. I think I found all there really was long ago. And it wasn't very nice."

"Not even here?"

"Well, yes. It's wonderful. Literally. But I'm not going to go on living here. Am I? It's back to the real—tomorrow. And the real me."

"You're being glum again."

"Sorry."

"Do try not to be so *gloomy*." She spelled the words out, with the accents of a nanny: roles reversed once more.

But then she said, "It's *me*."

"Me too."

She let the curtain drop, lay down, then turned round, putting her arms out.

"Never get older than this," she said. "Not either of us."

* * *

A hot air balloon ideally travels in the cool, calm airs of dawn. So we were up at six with Dudley and Vicki and down to the takeoff strip half an hour later, where the big wicker basket was on its side and there was the sound like a jet engine coming from it as the huge flames, both gas burners full on, spouted into the vast nylon canopy. Dudley took over, crouching inside the wicker basket now and manning the burners like a machine gunner, the balloon gradually inflating, then slowly rising into the vertical, where it finally stood up against the brilliant dawn: a pear upside down, striped in vivid red and orange, ten stories high.

With the three other passengers from the Lodge we stood there mesmerized. But there was no time for dreams or faint hearts now. The basket, held by half a dozen sliding, dangling Africans, was straining upward. Dudley, already inside, had his hands on the brass control knobs above him—and then, tumbling in with him, we were lifting off, imperceptibly at first, still earthbound, but suddenly free, moving straight up into the air, but so smoothly that there was no sense of the gathering distances beneath. I'd expected the feeling to be like going up in a lift. It wasn't. Once airborne, we were entirely part of space, quite unrestricted, not part of any mechanical contrivance. That was the essence of the thrill—especially when the roar of the burners died suddenly at 500 feet and we started to float westward in dead silence—that we'd come to live, glide through, another medium, as only birds and insects normally do. That was the thing—as it had been the previous night by the river watching the animals: we were no longer ourselves. Beneath us, as we rose, the tawny yellow-gold plains gradually lengthened, unrolled in front of us, displaying their real size now, and their intimacies, where you could see all the secrets of the land hidden from the ground—the shade from the low sun behind us exactly outlining the contours of the small hills, uncovering the hidden twists of the animal trails like a railway layout, tracing the gunmetal shine of the Mara river away to our right, explaining all its hidden snake turns as it ran down from the escarpment.

And there were the animals now, of every sort, displayed below us as if we were all players leaning over a Noah's Ark game: the striped white flanks of leaping gazelle, pairs of topi standing head to tail on anthills, canny lookouts gazing in opposite directions, a herd of elephant like overloaded trucks out of control crashing through thick scrub by the river, and a group of boot-black buffalo beyond them, that rushed for cover when the shadow of the great balloon passed over them—nervous, dangerous-looking animals now that yet, like all the others, never looked up at us, unaware of where the threat of noise and shadow came from. But most of all there were the wildebeest and their outlying runners of zebra, on the move this morning as Dudley had thought, really vast black herds of them, 100,000 strong, massing along the southern horizon and ambling forward in the dawn, seeking the fresher grass, Indian file on the trails, in dozens of long lines—trails that met other trails, so that the animals merged in dusty, turbulent traffic jams before spreading out again. From a height they moved like thick rivulets of treacle down a window pane. But then, the burners off, the balloon dropped, gliding down in the morning breeze right over them—a hundred, fifty feet above them, so that the rancid, cowey smell was everywhere in the air again and I thought we must crash into the herds, before Dudley gave another long blast on the gas and we sailed away above the animals at the last moment—the tousle-manned, big-shouldered, crooked-horned, small-assed beasts galloping madly, swerving and charging, spurred on by the noise, dancing and kicking like bucking broncos, over the Tanzanian border, prancing in their holiday excitement, some with all four feet off the ground, these comics of the plains.

"Designed by committee," Dudley said, watching them stream away. "But the buffalo are quite different. No joke at all. See that one there? That male—gone in behind the bushes, right next to the river? There, turning outward now, back to the water. If you stumbled on him—and that's exactly what you would do, walking along the banks—well, you'd meet the charge at about zero feet. Almost no chance. Most dangerous of the big five. The others will try to avoid you. The buff, in that position, is just looking for trouble."

"But he doesn't see us up here," I said.

"No. But he knows something is up. Good smell, hearing, sight, and can turn on a sixpence. One of them got in amongst a walking safari here some time ago, by the river down there. Havoc. Gored and tossed one woman, tried to shake another down from a tree. The warden grabbed his tail and the ranger got a shot at him. But he galloped off. It was flying doctor stuff afterward."

The balloon was coming down then, while Dudley was talking, sinking toward the dark shape hiding in the bushes by the water. "I wonder. . ." I said nervously, looking up at the silent gas jets. Dudley gave the brass knob another pull.

The sun had risen as we rose again, up into a sky where the night-blue of dawn was beginning to whiten out, dissolving into the light blues of morning, the sky seeming to expand above us, a great milk-streaked arc running away into the universe. And the early chill was beginning to fall from the air as well—brightness, a frail zephyr warmth replacing it, pushing us imperceptibly westward: higher up now, then higher still, to a thousand feet when Dudley cut the burners and one was barely conscious of any movement across the earth far below. In the absolute silence I could hear Eleanor breathing beside me. An Egyptian vulture, a great white-headed bird with finger feathers at the end of each wing, sailed slowly past beneath us, floating on an early thermal, moving away to the east, where we seemed suspended, quite stationary. That was the strange thing—to be up here, above the birds—they quite unaware of us—yet sharing the same medium, free as they were. I couldn't get over the feeling—this mysterious buoyancy given me, inexplicable, yet without any sense of vertigo, an overwhelming confidence where you had left your human frame and mind behind and had entered every other natural dimension: air and space, animal and bird, sunlight, sky and landscape which was all yours, gliding through this vast aerial ballroom which was home to you now, inexplicably home, where you had returned after every exile.

The balloon was sinking again, dropping toward a thick tree-covered ridge, a shoulder that rose from the plateau with a huge shadow beyond, so that the hill was spotlit by the rising sun in brilliant greens and golds set against a background of night. "We saw a leopard with her cubs a week ago here, hiding out on the top somewhere," Dudley said, and we all craned round to look. The balloon was sinking fast, in a long sloping glide, straight toward the treetops. Again, I couldn't see how we could miss them, crouching over the edge of the basket, trance-like, waiting for the crash. But there was no crash. I'd misjudged the distances—not long enough a gliding bird, as Dudley was. The top branches rubbed gently along the bottom of the basket. I reached out and touched a leaf—and suddenly we were over the top of the ridge, looking down into the valley again, leaping over it, the ground falling sheer away for hundreds of feet, and then—with this unexpected mix, this roller-coaster conjunction of earth and space—there was the heart-thump in the stomach, that belly-left-behind feeling, as we swung away from the trees, launched into air again, gravity-free, the stuff of dreams, gliding above woods, where you will: the classic dream of repression, they say, of lost sex. But here I felt what nonsense this was—how such night thoughts, earthbound, were but a longing to slough off mortality and reenter the thoughtless kingdoms which we sprang from. Animal or bird—the balloon brought us home to them. There was no question: we were all of us allowed to play God for two hours that morning. And when finally we fell to earth, sitting on the padded gas canisters over a champagne breakfast—the chilled bottle corks exploding, the only gun-shots in this vast, spectacular Eden all round us—I had to pinch myself, to know it was all really true. Champagne, cold chicken, mango chutney, brown bread, fresh rolls and orange juice, coffee, cold beer if you needed it—basking in the middle of Eden. This was Africa of the beautiful people, of course—the rich, silk-shirted blonde in the designer jeans, the money-cultured genealogist from Maine, the chic family from the *seizième:* Africa on a "high," without cares in the world. This had nothing to do with the real, contemporary Africa at all. Yet for all that it offered another reality: valid history—a look into the past of the continent, this empty world where everything was just as it had been a hundred or a thousand years before. Money was the key to this paradise now certainly. Here it was only the rich who could go through the eye of the needle. Though even here the Kingdom was eroding.

"Only last week," Dudley said, "they found two rhinoceroses, dead, with machine gun holes spattered all over them, minus the horns. There are probably only half a dozen left in the whole Park now, with fifty or sixty a few years ago. The Arabs will pay up to $20,000 for a good specimen, a dagger handle."

Later in two trucks that had followed our flight from Keekorok, we went down to the banks of the Mara river and watched the crocs lazing in the sun, malevolently beady-eyed, before sloping off like card sharpers into the water. Beyond them, in a wide pool, hippos wallowed and snuffled, big-snouted, toothy burblers, tiny baby eyes set out in orbs from punch-bag faces in car-sized bodies: the glistening black skins erupting slowly like islands in the stream—first a water spout, then a nasal promontory following in line ahead, with liquid eyes emerging for hills, then the great backbone rising over a parish of flesh, the island complete for a minute, before the whole cumbersome geography disappeared like Atlantis beneath the waves. Afterward there was a long game run, back among the beesties, standing up in the balloon's wicker basket in the back of the truck, running right in among the herds, swerving round them, as they swerved in ever bigger circles round us, so that it became giddy-making, the truck a spinning carousel, the dust rising now, the sharply acrid cheesey smell churning in the air. It was wild-westish, with these thousands of dark-maned beasts drumming, thundering over the earth, colossal rhythms where the world danced.

Back at the Lodge we had coffee and biscuits on the sun-filled terrace and exchanged names and addresses. We'd never really write to each other or meet again. But that didn't matter. We were friends for life after what we'd shared—would share that journey, and something of each other, in thought, wherever we were. And if we did happen to meet, on a street corner in Paris or in Maine, we would immediately shine for each other, in the secret we'd been part of, like miraculous survivors of a wreck, where here the miracle would be reversed, in the knowledge that we had seen Eden together and lived to tell the tale.

The silver DC3 flashed against the blue walls of the escarpment that afternoon, dropped in over the river trees, the fuselage shimmering in the heat as it ran along the strip before it sat down on its tail and turned toward us.

On the flight back Eleanor said, "You know how a week seems a month sometimes, when you're away and pack it full of things."

"Yes."

"A year," she said, looking out the window at the blazing red floor of the Rift Valley again. "How a day becomes a year." Her face was tanned now, sunswept, wind-flushed, her body sated—as if indeed we had spent a year in Mara—and all the dry, flaky patches on her arms had disappeared.

The next day, back in Nairobi, I called Petal at the Hilton. Her voice was more abrupt, caustic, dismissive than ever. Willy had died—a heart attack, in the big stone house beyond Gil Gil. The message came down the line in the tones of some unbelievably rude operator—cruel, furious words, the anger of love.

"I am sorry—" I said.

I was cut short, frozen out. "Oh, much the best thing in the circumstances," she said contemptuously. "Wouldn't have survived much longer on his own up there anyway." She didn't want to think of Willy in a kindly way anymore. She didn't want commiseration. She wanted nothing, not a spark of emotion, which would remind her of how much he had been loved.

"Can I—? Is there anything—?"

"No thank you. There's nothing you can do. There's the funeral— but I can see him off on my own now." She spoke as of some frightful chore, saying goodbye to a boring relative on a train.

CHAPTER
18

The Jade Sea

"**K**atey" was a six-ton Bedford truck and we were belting along the tarmac, out of Nairobi, on our way to the Jade Sea of Lake Turkana 500 miles and three days' drive to the north. Apart from John, our sensible New Zealand driver and two merry African cooks, there were sixteen of us passengers: half of them a group of clannish, childish British Kenyans who laughed irritatingly all the time—and what I could see already as an opposing team made up of two nervous Milanese spinster teachers, a genuine American Sixties hippy in a poncho and a slouch leather hat, a reserved young New York couple—rimless specs, a rampant beard—harboring anthropological interests, I suspected, a pale waif of a Scandinavian woman, wispy blond, unassuming to the point of invisibility, who looked ill at the outset, Walter, an amiably handsome, slightly roguish Italian computer specialist who might just have escaped from a Fellini movie, together with Eleanor—and me bringing up the rear as it were, in goal, someone as old as God by comparison with everyone else in the party. A mixed fruit cake, I thought, to say the least, with our rucksacks and overnight bags, sitting on tents and the rest of the gear, in the back of this once-weekly "Turkana Bus" where, for £120 all in, we were, we hoped, set fair for seven days camping out in the very wildest parts of Kenya, driving up to the lake and then back via the Kasiut desert in the Northern Frontier District.

The trip had been advertised in Nairobi as a safari into "Vanishing Africa"; that was the whole point of the "Turkana Bus." We were getting out of progress, going far north, dropping off the end of the escarpment, where the maps, the tarmac, and the cultivated land ran out and there was nothing but a few camel paths, a punishing track across the baking lava fields, through the red deserts and the warring, nomadic tribes: a bare, blazing land. Driving through the pastures and cornfields of the highlands again that morning we were leaving all Kenya's problems behind us, we thought—self-contained, self-supporting for a week with all our own food and camping gear. Thumping along in the big truck we were going into Africa before the fall—and even further into time, indeed, moving up to the fossil-strewn shores of the great lake where man was born.

Eleanor and I sat sideways on, jaunting car-style, at the back of the truck, next to the two Milanese spinsters: kindergarten teachers, special friends, dark-haired, communion-scarfed, with unsuitable slip-on clogs —Maria and Anna, in their thirties, one tall, one small, with barely any English. They looked dazed by this huge landscape among all us other Anglo-Saxons—a step too far beyond the Corso here. They were speaking in soft voices, to each other alone, as if saying their beads; for Walter, the mischievous Roman, sitting just beyond them, wouldn't deign to talk to them at all. He preferred talking across them, in broken English, to us.

"How when you want say 'Be shut up' in England?" he asked.

" 'Be quiet,' " Eleanor responded sharply, not fancying Walter much at this point. But the Italian women, knowing these English words at least, took them personally and ceased their whisperings. Maria had a small silver crucifix round her neck. She fingered it obsessively now. "No, I didn't mean you," Eleanor, next to her, apologized. But Maria, the small one, didn't understand, thinking she was being ticked off again.

The younger Brits, a group on either side at the front of the truck, screamed and joked and sang a Beatles song with their pony-tailed, cheeseclothed girls. There was something about ten years out of date in these young Kenyan British, living here on odd jobs, eternally messing about with their Minis, swilling Tuskers, and bombing the coast. England had had no place for them, apart perhaps from some minor public schools five years before; and a future there, with Mrs. Thatcher's work ethic, couldn't have appealed either. Yet they had no real place in Kenya either, knew little about the country, other than the car rally roads and tracks, the muddy ravines and hairpin bends, engines screaming through Maasailand. Kenya was just one big rally course with beer stops for them—followed by a mindless week on the coast recovering from these mechanical events. The empire had long gone that would have made them remittance men out here. Instead they aped Ben Hur in oily overalls and helmets, blind to the flame and thorn trees, concerned only with stopwatches and checkpoints. But even their souped-up Minis couldn't have made this trip, so that they'd taken a week off, in this bus, to bomb the lake.

Behind us, at the back, the academic New York couple listened willy-nilly to the original hippy in the slouch hat and poncho. "Man, this is wild, really wild. . . ." He was about fifteen years out of date. The Swedish woman, Christina, right at the end of the bench seat beyond us, was misery-me. Woebegone, eyes closed, head sunk on her thin bosom in a white shift-like dress, she might have been a sit-up corpse waiting for a wake. I wondered what she'd make of the real journey, over the rutted lava beds which the manager of the Safari Camp Services in Nairobi had described to me—for we were still on the asphalt here, in the cool highlands, where tomorrow, off the escarpment, the 100-degree deserts would hit us. Interesting, I thought.

The lush highlands began to run out and by late afternoon we'd come into lower, scrubby, empty country toward the northern end of the escarpment: endless thorn trees, sandy soil. The truck pulled off the road at five o'clock and we made camp in a sandy space surrounded by thorn bushes. Tent bags were distributed and the two cooks, Ole and Daniel, got out a trestle table, a big collection of pots and pans and a long griddle, setting it up over a ring of blackened stones where earlier fires had been made. The site was surrounded by rotten, whitened timber and the boys had a great fire going before we'd even begun to put up our small double tents: folds and poles, pegs and cords—to be straightened out, screwed together, hammered in, and tightened.

"Where?" Eleanor asked. "Where do we put this?"

"The fly sheet. Over the top—with a gap, in case it rains." We'd hired sleeping bags, unrolling them inside when the tent was finally up.

"There," she said. "At last—your tent under the stars."

"Yes."

"You're not going all glum again, are you?"

"No." I went over to help the two Italian women. Their tent was just a mass of nylon and cord lying in a jumble on the ground.

"Grazie, grazie," they said. Walter came over. He had a tent to himself, odd man out, relenting now with Anna and Maria. He spoke to them in Italian, smiling wickedly. The women looked startled. "Mamma mia," Anna said.

"What did you tell them?" I asked afterward.

"Bocca di leone," he said. "How you say it? 'Mouth of big lion?' Be careful out here, I say to them."

But Walter, surprisingly, was right. Before supper, John, our driver, briefing us, said among other things, "Oh, and don't wander beyond the camp site. Lion were seen in the area last week." And, sure enough, in the middle of the night, I started up, hearing several guttural roars in the distance. Eleanor slept through it, but with my movement toward the zipped tent flap, she stirred, then woke herself.

"What is it?"

"*Bocca di leone,*" I said. It was the name of the street in Rome where we'd stayed at the Hotel d'Inghilterra, just after we were married.

"Did you hear the lion?" I asked John over fried eggs and hunks of good bread round the camp fire next morning.

"Yes. Two of them."

Ole came into the circle then, carrying firewood from outside the camp site.

"Well?" John asked him.

" 'bout a hundred yards away. Some big marks."

"Of the *lion?*" I asked. John nodded, draining his coffee, while Ole put the firewood in the back of the truck.

"We'll have to get out and collect some more, before we hit the desert," John said. Later, before we set off, he told us, "Go sparingly on the tank of water in the truck. But drink any of your own orange and lemon meanwhile. It'll be hot this afternoon, off the escarpment, a long journey to Kurungu camp: prevent dehydration. . . ." The Swedish waif, hearing this, and looking no better for her night's sleep, glanced longingly the way we had come, the road back to Nairobi, hitchhiking dreams in her eyes. But very few cars or trucks had passed us since we'd left Gil Gil. The hippy, looking the other way, said, "Go, man, go!" I helped Anna and Maria with their tent again, while others in the party made last-minute sorties into the thorn bushes. Walter came up to me, his tent all neatly packed. "Did you hear the lion last night?" I asked.

"No." He looked about him in surprise.

"Just behind your tent—not a hundred meters away."

"You joke me."

"Not at all," I assured him. "Left their footprints—go and look."

"*Mamma mia.*" We all piled into the truck again, Walter not quite so cocky, seeing how he, too, had strayed a little beyond the Via Veneto. "Trouble," Walter muttered to us, as we drove off. "I want no trouble from one bad lion."

It wasn't until we got to Maralal an hour later—the last town on the edge of the escarpment where the road ran out—that the real trouble started, taking on a violent shape, exploding in the capital a few hundred miles behind us. There was that sure sign of impending disaster in the

Third World: they were locking up the shutters on all the tin shops right along the one dusty main street of the town. A few minutes later, outside the general store, we heard the news from the locals, a group of them crouched round a transistor. There had been a coup in Nairobi a few hours earlier; the Kenyan air force, it seemed, was now in charge; a new revolutionary government, broadcasting from the radio station, had taken over the country. Everyone was to stay indoors, or stay put wherever they were. All movement was prohibited, since neither the army nor the police would now accept responsibility for public order.

We were poised on the very edge of the escarpment at that point— a revolution running up behind us, an empty, pristine world ahead. To go or stay? The continentals, still in the truck, understood nothing of the news, while the others, the Kenyan Brits down the street just then looking at curios, hadn't heard it. Glancing round at the fly-blown tin huts of Maralal I thought a week stuck here would be like two weeks in Belfast. John obviously had the same thought.

"I'm tempted to run for it," he said. I nodded. We called the others back, the big engine revving urgently, and left the little frontier town, clattering north down the stony mountainside like the hammers of hell.

"Mamma mia!" Anna really meant it this time, when Walter had explained matters to her. Of course, we'd be safe enough, John told us, as far as the police and army—and the Kenyan air force officers— were concerned, since there weren't any ahead of us, apart from the small police post at Loyengalani, our destination 200 miles north on the lake. The only trouble might come from the Shifta, the brigands, the armed cow- and camel-raiding gangs that roamed this vast lake and desert area ahead of us. If they had heard the news from Nairobi they might well take advantage of it, seeing a truckload of camera-toting travelers, ripe for the picking in these completely isolated parts, where our own "Turkana Bus" was often the only vehicle seen in a week on this wild track.

"I banditi!" Walter leered, flourishing his arms at the Italian women. *"Garibaldi,"* Maria said, blessing herself, mopping her face, for we were down two or three thousand feet now, nearing the bottom of the es- carpment, approaching the spectacular Horr valley, and it was suddenly very hot, the land turning red, streaked with sharp, slate-gray lava fields, nothing but the long raw desert ahead of us.

Yet the razed landscape, we soon saw, wasn't entirely empty or with- out movement. An ostrich loped away from us, feet swinging like a giant hen, a sort of nightmare chicken, disappearing behind a stunted acacia tree; dik-diks, terrier-sized antelopes, skipped delicately through the few thorn bushes; hornbills flapped up into the searing light on one side of the stony, rock-strewn track, while dust devils gathered force, darkening the whole sky on the other, spinning malevolently up from the horizon.

A white priest in a Land Rover and two soldiers in a jeep rushed past us, going in the opposite direction, taking no notice of us. Making for safety, we wondered? Was there more danger ahead than behind us? The desert, we saw, contained all sorts of unexpected life. We scanned the hills about us nervously, waiting for the brigands. Walter was enjoying himself. But Anna and Maria, crouching down, had hidden their Kodaks, while the laughter died at last among the juvenile Brits. Normally we would have paused for breaks and meals. But instead we drove all that day to our evening camp site without stopping, a thumpingly slow journey, maneuvering round the sharp rocks on the lava track, groaning down across dried-out river beds or moving through sudden vicious winds in the desert proper that blew the sand up from the wheels, covering us, caking us from head to toe in a yellow choking mist. The jokes died then all right. It was genuinely tough going. And because of this we soon forgot the bandits and quite forgot the revolution behind us. Instead a sort of silent, desert-dry exaltation dawned on us.

That day, I think, we all became awed by, completely absorbed in, the gigantic ferocious landscape unfolding in front of us. Revolution meant nothing here—and man himself very little either. This was true wilderness, where you could put away all earthly things. And still driving through it in the late afternoon, sweat-caked in yellow sand, still punching our way up and down between the lava hills at five miles an hour, I began to think we'd be stuck here for the full forty days.

But then, an hour before sunset, the green oasis of Kurungu came in sight. The camp, surrounded by a grove of great hovering acacias, lay between two tree-covered mountains that reared up out of the valley, with the white wash of a small, water-falling stream just visible, running down the side of the western hill: water, a sandy circle beneath the flat-topped trees, a thorn stockade built right round the site, with a gateway that led out into a bamboo grove and beyond that the river twisting in small shallow pools through a dappled evening light. This was a permanent camp for the Safari Camp Services, where trucks were stationed, with water and fuel tanks, and beyond the stockade a small tented hotel with a cabin bar and terrace for more permanent guests. Our tents up, we bathed in the stream, in twos and threes, flopping about in the deep pools, before going on for warm beers on the terrace before supper. The fridges had broken down, and a truck bringing new ones with bottled gas had caught fire some way south a week before. It was still hot and cold beers would have been nice. "Let's hope the fridges are working at the lake," John said. "This heat is nothing."

We went back to the stockade for the evening cook-up over the huge stone fire circle in the middle. The food was good—celebrating our deliverance from the *banditi:* big steaks, chips, salad, hunks of bread, blue smoke spiraling up into the acacia branches where things rustled and twittered high above us. We sat on tiny painters' stools in the firelight watching the last glimmer of violet fade from the sky above the mountain, listening to the faint warble of the stream, tired, content, true travelers. Here, with the camp radio affected by the magnetic hills, they had had little news of the coup in Nairobi. And John was only able to hear a few words when he got through to HQ on the transmitter that evening. There'd been much killing and looting in the capital: the situation was uncertain. He'd heard no more.

"I never heard properly," I said to Eleanor that evening. "What did your father say—when you called him?" She'd phoned him on our last night at the Norfolk.

"I told you. He was surprised, my being in Nairobi."

"With me."

"Just a friend, I said. Didn't say who—or what or why."

"No. And—"

"That we were going on to the coast, up here, that we'd been in Mara."

"That I was a man, I suppose?"

"Oh yes, that you were a man. But don't go on. I see all the problems, just as well as you do."

"You didn't the other night, over those drinks."

"I didn't want to. But one has to be realistic: you're not going to suddenly leave home and live with me. And I'd hate any sort of hole-in-the-corner business with you—odd days in London, nights, lies: that kind of now-and-then relationship. I've seen it before, with my mother, I told you: evenings outside the Kensington Public Library, sad little dinners in some Italian place round the corner. And the pain of it all, sooner or later. That shouldn't be for anyone."

"No."

"That's just madness—in the end—starting out on that."

"The voice of experience there."

"My mother's. Not mine." I was surprised at her equanimity all the same. "On the other hand," she went on in exactly the same level tone, "I don't see how I'm not going to want to go on seeing you."

"No. Nor me."

After supper some of the local Samburu tribesmen danced for us in the bright moonlight outside the stockade gate, jumping up and down in stiff verticals, feet away off the ground, uttering strange cries, staffs in their hands, the rhythm accelerating, subsiding, rising again—thin, bone-jangling, half-clad, chocolate figures against the white-night bamboo grove; those painfully exultant whoops, strangled gutturals—men with two or three wives, I was sure, taken without a qualm. I sat there, thinking of the Kensington Public Library and some little Italian place round the corner.

Next morning we drove for hours along the gradually rising lava track, toward a line of jagged, slate-colored mountains on the horizon. Approaching them, we were soon in first gear, twisting slowly upward round hairpin bends for nearly an hour. Then, just before noon, getting to the top of the pass and rounding a vast shoulder of black rock, we saw a line of faint blue in a great valley beyond: not the lead-blue sky, but the white-flecked, sapphire tint and flash of water, which gradually expanded as we ran down the other side of the mountain until finally we got to the shoreline and there was nothing in front of us but the huge lake.

It wasn't jade that morning, but lilac blue—since, as John explained to us, the color changes from one to the other depending on the strength and direction of the wind, which moves the green algae in the lake either up or down in the water, thus giving it the different colors. But it was certainly a sea. Nearly 200 miles long and up to thirty-five miles wide, it's surrounded by malignant old volcanoes, filled with crocodiles, and scorched year round with a fierce dragon's breath wind—out in force when we arrived, tossing the water up into big whitecapped waves in the distance. An Austrian, Count Teleki, was the first European here in 1888, naming the lake after the suicidal Hapsburg Crown Prince Rudolph. Now it takes its title from the powerful, warring Turkana tribe who live on its Western shores. On our side, to the east, only a few hundred El Molo fishermen are indigenous to the area, the "Wretched Ones" in translation; a dying tribe, literally, whose bones and teeth bend and rot before they're thirty, debilitated over centuries by their vast fluorine intake from the lake water.

But that morning on the treeless, burnt black lava shoreline we had only the migrant birds for company—a huge array and variety of them, picking along the beach, almost at our feet among the little waves in the weed-filled shallows: pelicans, ibises, spoonbills, Egyptian geese, waders of all sorts. Shimmering a mile away out in the lake was the raised plateau of a large volcanic island, sheer cliffs down to the water: an inaccessible, mysterious landfall, where we were all of us Professor Challengers just then, gazing out onto a lost world—all of us except Anna and Maria, who, shoes off, were paddling about in the shallows picking up bits and pieces from the frothy tidewrack, throwing them over their shoulders, happy now, like Ferragosto holiday-makers released in the bay of Naples, their odd cries the only sound above the lapping waves in this wind-scorched silence.

"Well," the aging hippy said. "You've really *gotta* believe it!" Walter, his shirt off now, just in pants, bared his chest to the ocean. "I *am* believing it," he said, aggrieved. "Why I not believe it?" "Forget it, man. Forget it." The hippy fanned himself with his slouch hat. The poncho had long since disappeared. Then he took the hat to the water, filled it, put it back on his long curls, and stood there dripping, motionless, gazing out on the endless sea-glitter. We'd vanished into Africa finally here, swallowed up in this brutal, radiant landscape, the same primeval scene in front of us that had been here a million, two million years before, standing now where man himself had first stood up.

We made camp with our tiny tents later that afternoon ten miles up the shore, at the palm-fringed oasis of Loyengalani, where there was an airstrip and a smart fishing lodge just beyond our site where rich people like Prince Charles and Gregory Peck stayed, flying up from Nairobi to have a go at the 300-pound Nile perch that lurk in the deeper waters of the lake. Our accommodation was less salubrious and the little lamed Indian in the camp bar, running short of fizz and beer in this wild spot, was mean with the cooling beverages. It was hot, too—an oven-damp heat, with swarms of flies that tortured you quickly, so that soon we were all down to the lava-pebbled beach where the crocs had been frightened away, we'd been told, and were swimming out into the hot bathwater, which had turned jade now with the wind dying in the afternoon, the algae rising to the surface so that your legs were bottle green in the rising vegetation and you swam like Jeremy Fisher—fast, toes well up, frightened of all sorts of potential nips, or much worse, from beneath you.

Maria and Anna kept well inshore, wading, not bathing. "Tee-hee." "Ha-ha." Their voices rose and fell between the flapping waves. Walter bounced up and down on the sandy lava bottom, then dived underwater, swimming right up to the chortling women, surprising them at the last moment, shooting up like a missile by their white-skinned legs.

"Mamma mia!"

"I am a cockodile," he leered at them, testing their English. "Tee-hee. Ha-ha!"

The Kenyan Brits and their girls swam further out, languidly or in racing crawls, still laughing irritatingly. I wondered if a croc might get one of them.

The lame Indian told elaborately wearisome stories later that afternoon, when he deigned to open his bar tent on top of the oasis, beyond the pit latrines. "When I was in the Sudan, now," he said, having rationed us to one cold beer each, "I gave them what for, I *can* say. . . ." He was a Nairobi trader, one of many brothers, who had the bar franchise here. Not an old-timer, he looked in his mid-forties, but prematurely wounded and wizened, dragging his club foot behind him as he went to and fro with his precious store of Tuskers, carrying his everready archaic British slang along with him. He was regaling the young Kenyan Brits at this point. "They told me, those oafs up there in the Sudan, I couldn't get on the boat, see. Well, I had to take my hat off to them—for trying. But I said, 'Look here, you fellows, I already *paid* for my ticket'—wasn't going to take anymore malarkey. But still they said, 'You have to go back.' Well, I wasn't going to give them another half-dollar either, see, and I thought these blokes, well, I was going to have to teach them a lesson. So I said, 'You let me on this boat right away, chop-chop, or there'll be hell to pay, merry *hell*,' I said. I gave them what for, I can tell you."

He had an African pot boy with him who washed up and dealt with the empties: a huge, shapeless, short-haired child moving cumbersomely about behind in the shadows, with a whitish skin—he might have been albino. But when the monstrous figure came into the light I saw it was a young woman, grossly overweight, lame on both feet. The Indian spoke to her like an animal and she took away another load of empties. What a life—for both of them—among the constant flies, the raw-edged, sand-filled, sweat-damp wind, dispensing a few warm beers once a week in this ultimate exile, for there was nothing north of here until you got to Khartoum 500 miles away. It was the trading instinct that had brought him so far afield and there was something to admire there, I suppose. But he knew the price to be paid for this money-grubbing endeavor, this long commercial exploitation by his kind among the locals. He spoke of the events in Nairobi. "The blackguards," he said. "They are not interested in political revolution. They will rape and loot and murder us Asians now, with a free hand. That is all they want. That is what they will do." In the event, as we discovered later, he was absolutely right in this.

I looked out of the tent, beyond the thorn bush stockade round our camp, to where the local Samburu—solemn children, twittering girls, and a very old man—were attempting to sell trinkets and bits of rock to some of our number, the cheeseclothed girls and the two Italians. These locals were not allowed within the camp site—stretching their arms through the thorns, ever-insistent with their beads and necklaces. They haunted the perimeter long after all their potential customers had disappeared—attentive, hopeless sentries, jangling their bits and pieces. Even when it was dark and we were round the fire once more at our supper, we could still hear their voices, calling to us softly as we ate.

"Yes, it's a tourist economy up here now," John said. "That's all there is really. And sacks of American flour from the Catholic mission. And far too many people to feed in the village. Samburu and Rendile, not the El Molo, pushed up here by the Turkana these last few years —raiding, killing all the time from the south end of the lake. One may complain about it—end of the old ways and so on. But that's irrelevant, really. It's a question of living or dying for most of these people up here, always has been. Tourists help them live. They're not concerned about their 'old ways' anymore. They've lost all that. They're just anxious to keep away from the Turkana. The Turkana did for them, not the tourists. They're refugees."

Refugees? The word seemed too modern a description for what struck me then as really a very ancient plight in these parts. What was happening here now had surely happened for several million years—in this brutal world where man had first triumphed over the other animals round this lake, and was simply continuing to do so, among his own kind now, the strong forever lording it over the weak.

The wind off the mountains died in the evening. But by one o'clock in the morning—when we'd barely slept anyway in the fetid, breathless heat of the small tent—the dragon's breath got up again like the start of a hurricane, long solid blows and sudden tremendous gusts, a withering midnight storm that threatened all the tents, seeping through the cracks, covering us in fine sand, turning our damp skins a harsh sandpaper, grating beneath our arms, between our fingers, over our lips. We tried to hide, head down inside the sleeping bags. But that was worse.

We sat up, opened the tent flap a little, hoping to cool ourselves in the hot storm. Nothing worked. We got up, dressed, left the tent and the stockade, and walked down toward the lake, moonlit, wind-tossed in the distance beyond the airstrip and the lava pebble beach. At the edge, by the fishing boats pulled up on the shingle, we washed the sand off our skin, doused our faces with handfuls of water. It was cooler then, but not much, for the water was still bath-warm.

"Richard Leakey works just north of here," I said, looking up the dark lake. "At Koobi Fora, where he found all those oldest hominid fossils a few years ago. I'd like to get up there."

"What a place to live."

"For him—or them, the old bone people?"

"Both."

"They came down out of the trees somewhere round here: four feet, then stood up on two, finally became human. Took a few million years, I suppose. Then hunter-gatherers for another million or so, going further afield, south to the plainslands, Olduvai Gorge in Tanzania and places, where Leakey's father found a lot of later old bones before the war."

"You really think—we actually began here?"

"Richard Leakey thinks so. Though some American rivals think it was in Ethiopia. They found 'Lucy' there—part of an older skeleton, maybe. But Ethiopia's not far away. Somewhere round here, yes: we stood up and started out—long trail of upright destruction."

A thin, phosphorescent hue flashed over the waves, here and there, far out; the wind rose and fell in our hair. We could barely see each other as clouds hid the moon. Eleanor laughed above the storm. " 'Our Father who art in Heaven, hallowed be Thy name. . . .' " She began to intone the prayer darkly over the waves.

Next morning there was a photo-call out among the remnants of the "Wretched Ones" at El Molo Bay ten miles up the lake, where they lived on a scorched beach in several dozen leaf and stick huts, like igloos, surviving on small, sun-blackened fillets of Nile perch, but supplementing this now with a cash income by charging the few tourists like us to photograph them. In fact, and perhaps as a result of this recent cash flow, they didn't look very wretched at all—rather a plump, marvelously dusky lot: the young child brides ogling us, laden down with their foot-deep, bead collars, each strand representing a conquest—while their elder mamas did business in curios and trinkets: hippo teeth, bead bangles, and harpoon heads.

Apart from their palm log rafts they had a real fiberglass fishing boat now, with an outboard motor. And another deal was soon made, among half of us at least, including Anna and Maria, for a trip round the island in the bay. The El Molo headman came with us—a splendidly piratical gent, sitting up in the bows with a red bandana hanky round his throat, carrying two harpoons—brought purely as a tourist show, I thought, until we neared the island and we saw the crocs basking along the shoreline. Then the helmsman suddenly accelerated, driving the boat straight toward the beasts, and the rest all happened in a flash. The headman was on his feet, harpoon raised. A croc lolloped into the water with a great splash. At the same moment the boat tipped in a shower of spray and the harpoon flew downward, deep into the green swirl, and by then we were all gasping, the Italians in frenzies of alarm, shrieking invocations. Another croc followed into the water, its great green shadow diving quickly down, and a second harpoon followed it. But both missed. We pursued the crocs round the island for another hour, without success—but man definitely the hunter-gatherer now. And I have to admit I came to enjoy it, the old blood lusts rising all too easily, civilization seen clearly as only a veneer in this kill-or-be-killed world. Yes, suddenly I was longing for it all—these vicious ends to things, where there was no argument about right and wrong.

Late that afternoon we went with the three Italians to visit the smart new concrete church with stained glass windows—and the Italian mission beyond in another stockade, but made in firm wood this time, with locked gates, where there was a single petrol pump, piles of bagged flour, and a big verandahed bungalow in the middle. The young priest, in slacks and an open shirt, was listening to news of the attempted air force coup on an expensive short-wave transistor when we arrived. "The government is back in control," he said, giving us glasses of deliciously chilled and filtered water from a patent device. "But the army seems to have taken great revenge, as expected. Hundreds just executed in the streets." His English was good. "We heard that on our transmitter earlier, talking with base in Nairobi. The official news doesn't give any such detail."

Then he spoke in Italian, unconcerned, not the least surprised to be suddenly confronted with three compatriots, turning up out of the blue. Another, older priest came in a few minutes later and the five of them chattered away, leaving Eleanor and me to our own devices. The big room was simply furnished: tables, a lot of easy chairs with antimacassars, a few African curios, some naïve holy sculptures and pictures, a collection of very detailed, large-scale maps of Kenya as well as of the immediate lake area. These Italians knew their way around—the only

Europeans living permanently in this vast desert. The mission had been here for nearly twenty years, I gathered. In that time a school, a clinic, a big church had been built at Loyengalani, together with outlying mission posts elsewhere, along the lake and back in the hills. The Italians, in fact, had taken over civic responsibility for this oasis village: feeding the El Molo and the other refugee tribesmen, supplying flour, petrol, medicines, text and hymn books—in return for Christ, I supposed. And of course, I thought as well, with these civilizing services, they had made it impossible for the locals here ever to return to their old ways, to grow or catch anything for themselves. The tribesmen, even in this remote moonscape, depended now on handouts of unsuitable white American flour and penicillin from London. They were better off, of course. Or were they? It was Harry's African question all over again. But here in Kenya—with the good roads and tracks even up to this wild place, together with plenty of fuel—these ready communications would ensure that everyone was civilized quite soon. No one would escape: all would believe in Christ in the end, all walk upon the waters. In Zaïre they might well become happy savages again, buttock steak and missionary stew for dinner. But in Kenya all that would have to go by the board sooner or later. Here, where man was born, everyone would end up in a dark suit going to church on Sundays.

That night the heat and wind in our tent was as bad as ever, and two or three of our party, including the Swedish waif, had come down with bad gastric troubles—enteritis, diarrhea. I'd given each of them the special stomach-caulking pills that had cured me in Rwanda.

"Those pit latrines don't help," I said. These were two deep and noisome holes, curtained off by thorn branches on the outskirts of the camp. The smell from them, and the collar of feces round the surface edge, was grim.

"Another night here—would be too much," Eleanor said, her head out of the tent flap trying to cool herself, her naked flanks twisting on the sand-covered sleeping bag. I ran my damp hand down her back, picking up the little grains that had stuck there in the valleys of her spine.

"Well, this is what it's all about, isn't it?" I told her. "What I wanted out here, the tough times, tents under the stars."

"Splendid romantic notion. I'd give anything to be back in the Norfolk."

"Come on—'Nothing venture.' . . ."

"Yes," she said after a long pause. "I thought you didn't have much of that spirit. I must have been wrong."

Eleanor was morose, flagging; perhaps she'd be next for the tummy bug. We seemed to react against each other, in producing opposite moods, like figures for rain and shine in a Swiss weather-house. When I was up, she was down—until some new climate between us reversed the position. We were not so often on a par together, as lovers are supposed to be. I wondered why. Because we weren't lovers in that expected way at all, I thought, and we tended, unconsciously or not, to punish each other for that. It grated on our better natures, this uncertainty, like the sand-filled wind on our skin, reminding us that soon, in Kenya or at home, there were still awkward decisions to be made: pallid bed-sitter meetings or a clean break? Or something else —the sort of life we could have lived together? This last was the key to the whole business. Here was where character had to operate, not love, which was the least of our problems: my character, not hers.

Nothing venture. That was exactly it. I said in the darkness, "I wish I had the strength of mind—to make *up* my mind, not just organize safaris about Africa."

"Yes." She rolled over on her back. "But then you wouldn't be you, would you? And I wouldn't be with you then, would I?"

A felicitous excuse, I thought. But it made us both feel better then, on a par again, at least for that night.

The following day, far out eastward, taking another route back through the middle of the Kasiut desert over a camel track, we stopped for lunch beneath some thorn trees, the remains of an oasis beside a dried-out riverbed. And this was real heat now, though it was dry: skin taut, lip-cracking heat—mirage-making, where nonexistent palm trees and hills danced on the horizon. We lit a fire to brew some tea, the last of our wood, for there had been none at Loyengalani. The smoke rose. But nothing else moved.

When I saw the figure, in the very far distance, I thought it was a mirage: a shimmering figure, risen well above the earth, dancing in the air, suspended, coming gradually toward us. Slowly the vision sank to earth. It was a man, a young, stocky Samburu tribesman, a herdsman without his flock, who had seen the smoke from our fire far off and made toward it: loincloth, a red blanket over his shoulders, a deeply scarred and decorated face, carrying two small throwing spears against the lion. He didn't say anything. Ole and Daniel spoke to him. But he didn't understand. He brought his hand to his mouth, staring ahead, not seeing any of us. And he was shaking now, under the shade of the thorn tree, minute trembles quivering up and down his whole body. Ole took him to the water tap at the back of the truck and gave him a cup. He looked at the cup—then at the tap. But it obviously meant nothing to him. Ole showed him how it worked, a thin stream of water falling on the ground. He put his head under it, turning up his mouth, drinking it like rain. Afterwards he had food—some of the tuna sandwiches and tomatoes we'd had for lunch. And he'd never seen this sort of food before either. He picked it up from the plate and looked at it, before mashing it together in his palms, feeding himself with it in a mushy paste, like an infant, standing by himself beyond the tree trunk. As soon as he was finished, gathering the red cloak about him and picking up his spears, he lolloped off into the desert again, back the way he had come, in just the same slow dance steps, so that soon, out in the blaze, he started to shimmer, then rise above the ground, a red speck in the light, where he stayed suspended high up in the air for a long time, a trembling mirage once more, before he disappeared.

We all watched him go, in awe, this image of real self-sufficiency, which yet to me, at least, suggested an impossible loneliness, a terrible division between men—between him and us. I saw no noble savage here, simply the profound isolation of people, one with another: my own isolation, given back to me here, reflections of this mirage man lost over the horizon now.

I said to Eleanor, "We must see each other later on. We'll have to."

She looked at me, shading her eyes, her hair caked in yellow sand, dry sweat streams running through the same powder down her cheeks and neck.

"Yes," she said. "We have to."

When we got back to Nairobi late the following day—the shop fronts all smashed in, the glass crepitating beneath our feet—the revolution there seemed a small thing. My eyes were still glazed with a vision of jade and sapphire, a red cloak dancing away over the desert. Bones aching, skin desert-burnt, with a half-inch beard, I had returned from man's first world, the scorching wilderness where the real revolution had taken place.

19

Coast to Coast

*T*he train out of Nairobi for Mombasa had sixteen carriages with an ancient dining saloon in the middle, and no egalitarian concessions in the rolling stock. You could travel half a dozen different ways, from hard class to comfortable twin-bunk sleeper. And pretty soon after leaving we'd explored the fifty shilling, four-course menu and were tucking into braised veal chops with a bottle of Mâcon, looking at the antelope scattering away into the sunset, easily outpacing the train rumbling across the Athi plains at hardly more than jogging pace.

Nearly three months from the Atlantic we were getting near the other coast at last, the Indian Ocean, fourteen hours away at this sedate speed, even downhill, off the plains. But we had no complaints. When you get inside the Mombasa train these days, with its chocolate-and-cream paneling and smell of chicken curry, and sit down among the heavy plated cruets, the old commercial hotel cutlery, and dented Birmingham teapots, you're traveling back as well as very slowly forward: back about fifty years, almost into the Nairobi Railway Museum, to an era when rail companies knew what they were doing, when you traveled hopefully *and* arrived.

" 'Sausages and mash,' " Eleanor said, liking the chops, sitting opposite, at a table for two next to the window. "I wonder what happened with Petal?"

"Nothing we could do. She wanted to be alone. And I suppose people like her, who lived here in the old days—they're used to that. What can we mean for them? Or 'Africa Now'? Not much. We were never part of Happy Valley. And Africa only needs our money today."

The train approached a long curve in the track, the lights on, a gently swaying necklace against the eastern dark, so that soon, with the vast length of it, looking out the window, we seemed to be coiling up on ourselves, going round in a circle. The wheels groaned against the rails, sighing and squeaking before starting to vibrate hollowly: we were crossing an iron-girdered bridge, the raised stanchions flipping past us in the shadows. The lights flickered in the saloon, our speed down to less than walking pace. On firm ground a minute later we resumed our jog trot, the carriages swaying a little, glasses and cutlery tinkling once more. The African steward came down the aisle, an old huge-girthed man with heat-flushed eyes, balancing two plated vegetable dishes in one hand while he plied a spoon and fork like tongs in the other. His great bulk filled all the space between the tables and when he leaned over to serve he was like a tree trunk bending. But he never faltered or stumbled with the carrots and mashed, which his pudgy hands delivered each time with the precision and delicacy of a piano player. He was part of the train, like a wheel spring or a bogey, so long adapted to its movements that his actions and reactions were automatic, unconscious. The diners were all white, middle-aged American and British tourists, taking advantage of this unique train service: four-course meals, old linen tablecloths, good wine, stewards making your bunk up for the night a few carriages away.... This wasn't typical African travel these days certainly. All this was from years before—Petal's years out here, and Willy's and all the other old-timers. They would have made exactly this same journey often enough—down to Mombasa, on leave for England with their cases and steamer trunks, their Somali servants in the hard class waiting to help them unload the other end, taking their stuff from the station on hand carts over to the harbor, to the *Empress of Britain* which would dock in the Pool of London a fortnight later. Or perhaps they'd have gone via Marseilles and taken the train north to Paris for a week, before crossing the channel to some villa near Bagshot or a flat rented in Mayfair for the summer. Then their return, on this same train, up to Nairobi, three months later: a few days there, a few cocktail parties, all the lost gossip renewed at the Norfolk and Muthaiga before they finally made it back to their farms in the highlands. Discredited people now, of course—all of them lumped together with the old Happy Valley crowd and all seen as irresponsible, promiscuous, drunken, racist, imperialist.

What a flat, lackluster world we'd come to live in. Of course the African bigwigs today and the millions out here on their package tours were people of the highest morals, the most liberal, farsighted principles. And you didn't shoot the animals or drink gin slings from one noon to the next out here anymore. You poached the wild life with machine guns instead—and let it be poached—and set up an industry of tarts and porno magazines and casinos, senseless safari boutiques and expensive native curios probably made in Taiwan. All this was entirely appropriate because it was thoroughly democratic, everyone could do it, get in on the act—except most of the ordinary Africans, of course, who were landless, famished—worse off if anything, than they had been under the whites. What hypocrisy it all was. But that was very much the order of these days, too. I'd have given quite a lot that evening to have shared a few drinks with some old remittance man from these parts, some ghost of Happy Valley: someone who didn't have to lie, who saw this country as it really was, yesterday and today. This was their train all right—the very same dining car probably, perhaps even the same steward, the old man, portly, benign, offering us some more carrots and mashed at that moment.

"Thanks."

"No thanks."

As if in answer to my thoughts, the spry little man walked down the aisle just then, taking a seat straight away at a table for four next to us, waiting for the second service. The old steward came soon afterward, pointing out that the table was booked, that it was for four people, that the second service hadn't yet started. . . . The Englishman smiled, raised his hand, spoke to the steward in fluent Swahili for a minute. The steward smiled then and the two of them talked animatedly for another minute. "*Moja ingini,* another beer," the Englishman said finally and the steward left. He was small, late sixtyish, rather insignificant-looking at first glance. But when you looked closer, especially at the big dancing eyes, alert orbs, the sun-frazzled leather skin, deeply creased cheeks, the totally relaxed body—when you heard his easy confidences with the steward —you could see he contained worlds: an African world. The narrow, tanned head, thin bleached hair neatly combed, his intimate Swahili— here was another old-timer, I was sure: something casually military about him in his sleeveless khaki husky, pullover, open check shirt, and slacks. The last of the bottle of Mâcon gave me the courage to lean across and introduce myself.

He looked up sharply, giving a studied imitation of surprise, then said, "Well, how do you do? Sandy Wheeler—vaguely at your service." He played with an unlit cigarette in long, supple fingers: cricket spinner's fingers, moving the tube about like a bullet from hand to hand. His beer came and we moved over to his table.

"So you know Petal, do you?" he said later. "And Willy. Yes indeed. Know—and knew—them both. Just spent a week at the Muthaiga, after Willy's unfortunate demise. Attended the obsequies. Quite a party afterward. He'd have enjoyed it. But that was the whole point. He was there in spirit—very *much* so, I may say."

The accent was clipped, chirpy English Midlands, always with a ripple of ironic laughter running through it. But a kind irony. Behind the bluff, military exterior there was something sensitive here.

" 'Drinks at the very, very soonest,' as Petal always says. Well, we did. Ah, yes, the wompo flowed. Very lubricating. All ended up very far gone."

We swapped stories, truths and hopes, traveler's tales—past, present, future, throughout the second service. Sandy had been an army major in Kenya and in the desert wilds of Somalia, before and during the war; and after that a white hunter all over East Africa for many years, until the sport had been outlawed ten years ago, when he'd run a game lodge for a while, finally retiring to the island of Lamu, England well lost for him by then. "Could have got other work here, of course, if I'd cashed my chips in and become a Kenyan citizen. But damned if I would— changing horses in midstream. Though in my case, I fancy, it would have been with one foot on the far bank. Never mind. Point is I'm English, do you see? Not Kenyan. Family actually goes back quite a long way. Well, these citizen chaps here now—they don't seem to grasp all that. Doesn't matter. My pension will see me out. Though there are still some irons in the fire. Met a man in the Club, had an idea I might do some PR work for a game lodge. Bring back a little of the old flair —sadly lacking, I may say, these days out here." There was a twinkle then, the eyes very merry. We had some more Tusker as the train rattled slowly through the night, and he told us some splendid stories of the old days on his hunting safaris.

"Well, there I was, right up in the middle of the shag, doing a spot of Egyptian PT after lunch in the tent, when she jumped me, do you see? Naked no less, a sight for sore eyes. . . . Well, some of the clients, the women, were interested in birds. So, first thing next morning, well, there she was again, shower curtain partly open. So I got the glasses out, do you see? And said, 'Ah, what's this I spy? The Rosy Breasted Crumpet Bird'—do you see?"

We did. And there was more: a witty, scabrous, loving, sometimes tragic scrapbook of a life spent in and out of the shag—the desert, the bush—forty-five years fighting and hunting in all the East African wildernesses. "Well, the bullet took the buff on a horn, ricocheted, do you see? Came back almost at right angles. And that was that. Never knew what hit him . . ." And finally: "You must come and visit in Lamu, when you get there. My humble abode: just behind Petley's Inn. Can't miss it." We agreed that we would meet.

"Africa, Africa . . ." I said in the top bunk that night. "That was it. He knew it all. *Africa Addio.*"

"Rather a romantic notion." Eleanor was almost asleep below me.

"Yes—but it was."

The sea stormed over the coral reef half a mile from the Mombasa Beach Hotel—tossy froth from the huge waves running inshore to where we swam in the shallows. Dark blue far out, pearl on the coral, jade shadows moving toward us like great shoals of fish as we trod water, crystal beneath our feet where each toe stood out against the sandy bottom—the ocean's color made up the whole world for us just then as we turned in the water, looking back on the dazzling white beach that ran beneath the hotel. Coast to coast—we'd made it. So we danced in the water for half an hour and lay on the sand afterward, tired, saying nothing.

Further down the reef a large freighter had run aground, wrecked, the hull already rusting, great waves lashing it on the windward side, stalled forever, it seemed. I gazed at it. Journey's end. Eleanor hadn't noticed the ship, I thought, face down in her towel, basking, her back a veneer of sun oil and fine white sand.

"I know what you're thinking," she said at last.

"You always do."

"You're looking at that wreck out there. And thinking it's all nearly over now. And you're really quite pleased."

"About the journey—yes. We made it. Of course." The beach was almost deserted. It wasn't the high season. Eleanor wriggled her toes in the sand, burrowing her feet into it suddenly, as if trying to anchor herself to the beach. "I'm not pleased about the wreck," I added.

"Wrecks are where you put them, like hills. It might be a mirage."

"It's not. It's real. You can see the waves quite clearly—hitting the sides."

"Very literal of you."

"You said I was 'romantic' last night."

"Yes. But about the past. In the present you're terribly down to earth. I'm the opposite, because—"

"You haven't had much of a past—in time, I mean."

"Awful interrupter sometimes. . . . No, because I see things—with more hope than you do."

" 'Youth at the helm.' Of course. So you can put hills and wrecks just where you want them. Later on—it may not be so easy."

"Good schoolteacher stuff."

"Come on. I've specially avoided that with you. No need for it anyway. We're equals, I've told you, apart from age."

"Are we really, though?"

"Yes—so that the age doesn't matter."

"Well now, we're going to have to pretend we're very different then, incompatible and so on."

"Why?"

"Because it'll be easier that way—when we don't see each other every day, when we won't see each other at all. We'll find lots of excuses and justifications for that. We'll have to."

"That's not very hopeful of you. You said you could move mountains."

"Not you, though."

Her voice was entirely matter of fact, colorless. I looked away from the wreck, touched her sandy arm.

" 'Africa Addio,' " she said, lively now, suddenly sitting up, gathering her things together. "Not only for you." And she smiled, so that I thought hope had returned, and I said "What about trying that special restaurant tonight—'Maxim's,' beyond the pool? The menu looked good."

"Yes." But she was listless again, frowning, where it was clear she didn't care one way or the other. Then she ran her eyes down the reef and gazed at the wreck.

After lunch she went to bed in our room and stayed there, drowsing in and out of sleep most of the afternoon while I read some books and guides I had on the island of Lamu. And that evening we didn't go to Maxim's. Eleanor seemed drugged with tiredness, sweating in the humid coastal heat, barely able to stir herself. I felt something of the same lassitude myself. Journey's end: the fatigue of climax and anticlimax. Though there was more than another week to go before my plane left for London, it seemed we had left each other already. I tried to cheer her up by reading passages out of the guidebook to Lamu—playing the game, the pocket Africa game, we had played in her red room in Kinshasa. " 'Lamu,' " I said, reading a description of the town in the eighteenth century, " 'was a town pouched in silk and held together with gold and silver thread, complete with harems, hookahs, powerful sheikhs, booming cannon and delicate mosques, where nothing lacked in the arts of pleasure, faith or war.' "

"Oh," she said, turning over in bed.

"That all?"

"Sounds splendid. ...." She dropped off again. She no longer had any cards in this African game. Indeed, it was as if she had never come to Africa, had never been inspired by it: a child now, for whom the continent meant nothing. She had gone away from me—not forward, but backward, a child again now as she slept. When she woke I more or less forced her out for a simple supper on the main terrace restaurant.

"Now *you're* all glum." I smiled in the lamplight, waves murmuring nicely down on the beach.

"Tired."

She ate her prawn cocktail in silence, forking it slowly, delicately, like a duchess, peering into it deeply.

"There's more than another week to go," I said. "And Lamu *is* splendid."

She looked up. "Am I flying back with you?"

"If you'd like. ...."

"Is your wife meeting you?"

"No—not that I know of."

"Well—bugger it." She left the prawns half-finished.

"What?"

"Whether I fly back or not—with you. Hardly matters. Only to the fag end of August in my bed-sitter."

"You've got your lectures coming up haven't you? Work—"

"Yes, yes. Don't tell me: 'There's another life—life beyond Africa.' "

"Well, there is. Don't be stupid. We said we'd meet." I looked at her. But she wouldn't look back.

"I don't want to punish myself," she said at last. "You're the one who always wants to do that—coming out here for no real reason: just some trouble at home. Running away for nothing. You should have seen my parents. That was real trouble. You should take yours flying— flying jump—instead of moping about it. It's nothing. I don't want to see you later on, if it means seeing you with all that load on your back. I told you. It's all such a bore, that. Time-wasting. Leads nowhere." Then she looked at me—a surprised expression, as if startled by what she'd said. I said nothing. "Besides," she went on. "If it was *really* as bad as all that with you, like it was with my parents, you'd get out of it. You'd have to, to survive. And if it was like that, well, you could think—of living some other way."

"With you. I'd thought of that," I said flatly.

"Thanks."

"Well, it must have crossed your mind, too."

"Yes. It had." She was equally flat. "I'd thought of that. But I knew what you'd say: 'Nothing's ever so cut and dried—nothing so simple.' So I didn't think about it for very long."

"Well, it's not. It's never simple, leaving people. Most difficult thing, probably. And it cuts both ways—with you as well, I can promise you."

"Of course. That's exactly what I knew you'd say. So what's the point of my going up to Lamu? Just prolonging it all—when it's over anyway. You see, you've got all the cards. I have none. I'm bound to lose. So why not get it over with?"

She was old again now, the wise child, for she was right. Oh, I had her to lose—and she was a whole pack of cards, most of them winners. But I couldn't open that pack, mint fresh and waiting to be played with, throughout the rest of my life. That was what I was losing—the whole war in return for victory in a brief holding operation. I didn't suppose she knew that and I wasn't going to tell her. I just said, rather limply, "Well, you know what I feel about you."

"Yes," she said. "I do. Just the same as I feel. That's what makes it so much worse. I'll take the train back to Nairobi tomorrow."

She was very firm and calm and something turned over in my stomach which wasn't the food. She was leaving. I was losing her. This was what was happening.

"Are you sure?" was all I could think to say.

"No. Not at all. Last thing I want. But I must." She turned, as if to call the waiter, looking everywhere about the terrace restaurant, searching for an exit. When she finally looked back at me she bit her lips, before turning away again.

"Where will you stay? And a flight, money—?"

"I've enough for a night in the Norfolk, if I don't get a plane out to London that same day."

"You're angry—"

"No, no—I'm not," she said urgently. "We've got to the coast. That's all there is—and it's been wonderful. But anything more would make me angry. Any more of you—but not having you, knowing I can't, knowing that, in the future."

"But—"

"More of you now, but not then—don't you see, I'd be drinking again up in Lamu for a start, just like it was with Robert? Being with you now, I don't have to drink. But I would in a day or two. You taught me not to drink. You cured me of that. But I couldn't cure you."

"Of what?"

"Her. Home, all that. Childish of me to think I could. But I'm not anymore. You cured me of that, too," she added shortly.

She fingered the gold choker round her neck, wearing it again, with the white, loose-weave cotton cocktail dress she had first taken out in Harry's bungalow in Kinshasa. She had held it up against her then with the surprised innocence of a girl, a Joan Hunter Dunn off to a first tennis dance. Now she wore the dress with the choker like a woman, tired at the end of the season where there would be no more dances. The drink, the irresponsibility, her youth seemed over. I had cured her of all these things. Or had I, in fact, in some sense corrupted her? She was hard now, all the *tizzy* charm gone, where she had armored herself, perhaps forever, against emotion, against the hurt that lay in things she could not have. But I should never have offered them. So, in the end, I was to be just one more Robert in her life, the last one perhaps, where she would never again risk everything, in loving—simply settle for a convenient marriage among the Hooray Henrys of her class, the young stockbrokers and underwriters of the Thames valley: a conventional life, without heartache, where she would be one more typical ornament among the crowds in the paddock at Ascot or at Henley. Yes, I had probably confirmed her future here, a strictly adult direction, where I remained the child, unable to match her growth, or promote the life she might have had with me, unable to sort out my own domestic problems, sunk in indecision. She had decided. I hadn't the courage to offer her anything beyond bed-sitter assignations in Gloucester Avenue and a little Italian place round the corner. So she had made the right decision. But that fresh person I had first met and lived with, the child in her, the trousered dream—these things had disappeared in her choice. I had eaten them up. So that now it was I who couldn't look at her, as I searched around the terrace looking for an exit. After dinner she checked the train times for Nairobi the next day and I made a booking on a local flight up to Lamu on my own.

My plane left at midday, and so it was that I left her, since her train didn't go until evening and she intended staying on in the hotel for those few hours. She had my address in England and I had hers. We exchanged them after breakfast, among the remnants of toast and marmalade, like two cagey commercial travelers met by chance on the same route, with the same doubtful product to offer. She wasn't cold—or warm. She was going through a social duty and that made it the worse.

I would never have pleaded with her. But I longed for less formality—longed for an immediate transformation from lovers to friends, which could never have happened then, if it ever did. Of course, I ought to have been thankful for our steely high wire act that morning: we were tiptoeing away from each other over a chasm of despair, anger, hate. I got my bags together afterward as quickly as I could while the hotel called a taxi, surrounding myself, comforting myself with all the nervousness, the paraphernalia of departure—things which offered themselves as a balm against the trite phrases we shared, when we spoke at all. We'd slept with a Siberia between us the previous night and now we kept our balance with verbal commonplaces—as if we had been spotlit in the bedroom that morning, the lobby, out on the forecourt now: the world watching us on our tightrope, waiting for the fall, a crowd hanging on our every move, longing for disaster, a scene, a shouting match, sharp backhanders on the cheek.

"Yes, of course. . . ."

". . . see you."

"I hope it goes all right in Lamu—"

"I'll send you a card."

The taxi drew up, bags were bundled in. There was a last moment, like a great hurdle looming up. I leaned forward to kiss her. She withdrew for an instant, before I touched her cheek, before allowing my short embrace, where I suddenly felt her body shiver, wriggling against me for an instant in a little dizzy spasm.

CHAPTER
20

Africa of the Heart

The ocean made up my whole world again as the little plane rose: the blue water creaming against the endless coral reef, jade shadows moving inshore, then the long white beaches and the mud-green mangrove forests further up the coast. And when I crossed on the ferry from the airstrip on Manda island to Lamu, bouncing about on the hot waves, blinded by the sea dazzle—when I got to Petley's Inn right on Lamu waterfront and opened my first-floor terrace window, I knew—as the guidebooks had promised—that I was in a genuine tropical paradise. But more than that, as other older, wiser books had been telling me, I'd come to a place which people, not just climate, had made rich and strange—and without Eleanor, trying not to think of her, I threw myself into the role of tourist, historian, all-inquiring reporter: concentrating on this island at the end of Africa, where it would somehow blot out, supplant, the continent of light that I had lost with her.

Lamu, geographically, has never been more than a speck on the map, a tiny island oasis just south of the Somali deserts. But its history makes it much more important—a jewel at the base of this scorched horn of Africa. For it was here, in and around Lamu, somewhere in the tenth century, that the Swahili culture was born, a vitalizing mix of Arab and African tradition which first of all resulted in the distinct Swahili language and then, from about 1500 onwards, in an elaborately decorative Afro-Arab civilization. So that Lamu became a tiny glittering world on the edge of a vast darkness, kept alight, fed on the monsoon winds by the riches of India and Arabia: a most elegant stone and mortar town, filled with a mixed race of sailors, merchants, craftsmen, poets, with lovely carved doorways, metal and plaster work, inlaid furniture—"a town pouched in silk and held together with gold and silver thread. . . ." Lamu, for a hundred years and more, was a vigorous dominant city-state in fact, a sort of African Venice on the edge of the mangrove swamps which reached its heights in the eighteenth century and then, with the consolidation of Mombasan and Zanzibari power in the south, embarked on its long decline—an indolent pursuit which it has followed passionately ever since.

But as I could see at once that afternoon from my first-floor balcony the great trick, the miracle of Lamu—which makes it unique on this African coast if not in the world—is that very little has changed here since the eighteenth century. The jewel is still almost intact. The layout, the fabric, the decor of that golden age lay all about me, to either side and rising up the slopes behind the Inn: a seeming hodgepodge of buildings, yet with a secret order, where the raw coral, walled, or white-washed or mortar-blackened, flat-roofed, largely windowless houses—crammed together at all angles and heights across the yard-wide alleys—gave the place the air of a three-dimensional cubist painting.

In front of me, unfolding like some old Arabian maritime scroll beyond the seawall, was a collection of lateen-sailed dhows of every shape and size—not a modern boat among them—from large, high-transomed ocean-going boats to the much more numerous local *jahazis,* little arrogantly shaped craft with sharp perpendicular bows and eyes to either side, painted as stars or crescent moons. Equally arrogant-looking Afro-Arabs—thin-faced, hook-nosed loungers in faded red *kekoi* skirts and white embroidered skull caps—squatted on the seawall, legs akimbo, letting a faint breeze aerate their backsides, skirts flapping adventurously. Three donkeys, heads down in Indian file and dead set on some mysterious purpose, made their way up the middle of the sand track road. A road? Well, it wasn't. For there are no cars, no wheeled vehicles at all apart from a few wooden hand carts, on Lamu island. No, there was nothing in front of me just then which might not have been there a hundred, even two hundred years before—except, as I soon saw, the hippies. Bleach-haired, sunstruck northerners, eyes fixed like sleepwalkers, they moved up and down the seafront, dressed in the same native *kekois,* but from there up kitted out in their largely standard uniform: beads, beards, and leather begging bags.

The hippies, I knew, like some of the jet setters, rich remittance men, and richer widows, had discovered Lamu some years before. The latter were still taking their siesta, no doubt, in their refurbished thousand-and-one-night holiday homes. But these aging flower children had to keep on their long march, in every weather, always on the lookout for a potential "crash," the cheap pad or kip, the rice bowl, and the un-sweetened yoghurt. The aristocratic loungers on the seawall—mostly local guides and con men as I'd already discovered when I got off the ferry—looked at these equally brazen freeloaders with dumb distaste. They were birds of a different color, but not of feather. Neither could take advantage of the other. There could be no financial exchange or gain between them, no expensive trips in a *jahazi* to see the Arab ruins on Manda island opposite. The hippies, with tuppence on them, were looking for the sun; while the con men, among the rich visitors here, were hoping for the moon.

I wasn't rich or a hippy. But I was a single foreigner all the same. So that when I went out and about later that afternoon, and had again been offered, and had refused, all sorts of decent and indecent proposals right along the seafront, I soon recognized a tension in the air between the black and white tribes here: envy, avarice, a mix of all sorts of vivid expectations, sexual and commercial—of hopes dashed on both sides, a growing disappointment and ill-humor rising in me. There were snakes in this Eden.

In the late afternoon I went back to my room and took a bottle of gin I'd brought with me out to the first-floor terrace. I hadn't bothered unpacking yet. There seemed no point. There was no joy in that anymore—and I'd exhausted my guide and history books. The channel in front of me turned royal blue in the short twilight, an evening breeze frisking the waves and the palm trees outside the Inn, where I could still see the con men plying their trade among some ordinary tourists who had gone out to take the air before supper in the restaurant on the top floor of Petley's: offers of *jahazi* trips on the morrow to the bourgeois couples—limitless sexual provender, no doubt, to the few single strollers they trapped. I drank the warm gin like water; there was nothing to prevent me drinking now. Perhaps I'd cured Eleanor of drink—just as, lurking at the gateway, she had led me into life. But now the positions were reversed. It was she who had gone on through that door, which had just been closed to me, and so I drank. It was I who needed the cure now.

I saw how repose had trapped me. The history of the island, from books and guides, traveling to and around it, had kept me occupied. Now at the end of the day, sundowner time, she was not there. Over two months before I had told her how I had never traveled with anyone on these trips, how this destroyed the sharp, uncomfortable edges of travel, where one needed that painful, unencumbered vision, if one's own real feel of a place was to emerge. But we had managed our travel together all too well, I realized then. Africa had become a dual vision which we created, shared. I had seen it through her eyes, her remarks, and she through mine. Now I was looking at everything with one eye short. I couldn't feel the place anymore. It was there, all of it—the palm fronds, the tide running in, wine-dark channel, the sandy lamp-lit track, paradise island—but it was all in one dimension, without resonance, interest. There was no future in it—just a job to be done, like the history and guidebooks had, where I would extract a passable broadcast from this travel poster setting. Before, what I had seen in Africa had not been through rose-tinted glasses—that was how I was seeing it now: the falsely romantic. With Eleanor, where the romance was real, I had been able to see the reality of the country. Far from taking away my judgment of places, people, things, she had given me the peace, that added dimension of sight, companionship, love, with which I was able to see everything twice. That was what love was like. Later I ate alone upstairs. They had lobster and Frascati. I didn't bother with the lobster. Next morning, with a hangover and half a dozen cold Tuskers from the bar fridge, I set out to look for Sandy Wheeler.

The hotel manager had given me vague directions. "Ah, yes, the Major. Go straight back from here, then left, straight, then right. . . ." But within minutes I was hopelessly lost in the tiny alleyways that led up the hill behind Petley's. I asked an old man in a doorway. "The Major?" He pointed toward a tall, almost windowless, four-square, tower-like building further up the hill; old lichened coral walls jutting like the ramparts of a castle into a tiny square. The doorway was in a dark porch on the other side, facing up the hill: big hardwood double doors, intricately carved in the local manner. I knocked. A minute later bolts were drawn, chains rattled and a dark face peered out at me. "Major Wheeler?" I asked.

A thin, uncertain African youth led me into a low, dark hall, then up a winding stone stairway set into the very thick walls, round and round until light gradually touched us and we emerged right at the top, on a battlemented roof, where across on the windward side a little penthouse, a bed-cum-drawing room had been set up under a palm leaf awning— and there was Sandy, naked except for a spotted bandana cravat and faded red *kekoi* skirt, taking the morning airs, reading an old airmail copy of *The Times,* stretched out in a latticed wood steamer chair, surrounded by a great clutter of books.

"Ah." He lowered his reading specs. "You, indeed! Welcome to the humble abode."

It was far from being a humble abode—this lovely eighteenth-century tower—a sheikh's house, he told me, which he'd rented some years before on his "retirement." It was a splendid place, quite unspoiled, the original plaster and woodwork still intact where nothing seemed to have been tarted up. The view out over the coral houses and palm roofs beneath us was something to start with: very *de haut en bas,* where, looking downward, one saw the crazy cubist patterns in three dimensions. Then there was the channel, jade-blue in the dazzling morning light, with the mangrove trees a dark green margin to the water on the other side by Manda island. The colors were bright but not electric: indolent color, carelessly applied but absolutely sure in tone. We were quite high up so that an ocean breeze caught us, rustling the penthouse fronds and drying the sweat on my brow straight away.

"Excuse the skirt." Sandy had stood up. "Only worn indoors, you understand." I offered him my brown bag of Tuskers. "Ah, drinks at the very, very soonest. Why not? Mohammed!" He called his boy. But there was no reply. "Wretch has gone out. He and I have been having something of a tiff this morning. Asked him to get some limes in the market—I make my own brew here. Came back with everything else but. Still, we'll give the Tusker a run-in—you can try some of my wompo later. And your good woman?" he asked. "Back in Petley's?"

"No, in Nairobi by now. She decided not to come on up here. Another little tiff."

"Ah. . . ." Sandy pondered this fact, without remarking on it further, as if it was, for him, a familiar pattern of feminine contrariness. Then, from among a collection of old photographs, cricket caps, and other colonial mementoes on a shelf behind, he rooted out two pewter tankards and the Tusker frothed. I gave him my initial impressions of the island—the hippies and the local con men.

"Yes," he grimaced. "Rather far gone around here—like Shela at the other end of the island where the rich foreigners hang out. In all—bum boys, hippies, trendies, superannuated jet setters, Lotharios, widows, queers—rich and poor: piss pots of every sort. That's the only problem here now."

He lowered half his Tusker, then cast an ear toward the stairway. "Mohammed!" he shouted, though I'd heard nothing. "I really must get those limes. My friend Arthur, another old-timer out here—it's his birthday soon: getting up a special brew of wompo. We're the last of the old hands, I'm afraid. The other whites, I'm sorry to say, these newcomers—they're well on the way to ruining this place. Mind you, the locals have always been smarter than the Europeans here. I won't say these new folk have corrupted them. No. Just antagonized them—

turning Lamu into an unpleasant sort of permanent holiday camp. These frightful people live here mostly. Not tourists, you see. Just either very rich or very poor whites—but both on the make, out for anything they can get."

He eased his cravat and we broached another Tusker. "The rich come to buy up the old seafront houses down in Shela which they tart up like Turkish whorehouses—while the youngsters are laid out in some squalid room smoking pot or whatever. Well, of course, both these pursuits annoy the locals, and naturally they come to take advantage of the situation, any way they can. Because they're on the make, too. Always have been. But then it's their island and they reckon, quite understandably, that they should be first in line for any pickings going. Net result is an undeclared war between everyone involved. The rich hate the hippies and the feeling's mutual—and the locals despise them both. My own response is simple: I keep well clear of them all. And that suits me fine. Even cut off here way up the coast I'm still in East Africa—where I've always wanted to be. I'd like to see more of the plains, of course. Oh yes, I miss that badly—the old shag, up-country. Love to get a look at that more often—a little losing myself with a crate of wompo out in the Rift somewhere. All the same, I like it here well enough. You won't ever find me in Surbiton or South Ken, that's certain. But come—I must see if Mohammed is back. Show you the house *en route*. Mohammed?" He shouted down one of the stairways before we started to clamber down it ourselves.

This old fort-house, which had looked nothing much from the outside, was an elaborately conceived and decorated rabbit warren within. The small, narrow, whitewashed rooms, with their black mangrove pole ceilings, on the first and second floors, had mostly been inset, built as part of the very thick walls—with the partly open stone staircases winding up to them from an open courtyard beneath, which in turn was built not on the ground, but on the roof of the ground floor, where in the old days, the servants and slaves, hidden away, had lived in a windowless gloom. The house was like a square funnel, opening out into the world above, where you lived on the rim, slept in the wall just beneath, with all your other needs and fancies—your harem, Chinese porcelain bowled latrine, kitchen and servants' quarters—all tucked into little stone rooms, like shelves or drawers beneath you. It was a marvelously well designed place, precisely adapted to Lamu's steamy climate and all its old social and domestic conventions. And Sandy, 200 years later, was equally well adapted to it—Sandy, who apart from his hunting trophies, pewter tankards, and old cricket caps, had kept the place exactly as it had been. This was why he lived here, why he'd always lived in East Africa, I thought: not to change or "civilize" the land, upset the balance, lay down the concrete, to gain, to take things out of it, to set himself in any way apart from it by way of Turkish brothel decor. His ambition seemed to be just the opposite—to be one with the country, as he was in this old tower now, as he had been for forty-five years previously up on the plains and in the deserts.

"Mohammed!" he yelled when we got down to the dark of the hall. But there was no reply from the kitchen. "Little blighter. Won't get my wompo on the brew at all today at this rate. Well, you've seen *mon repos*. I suggest we adjourn again upstairs—try a little more Tusker."

Sandy stretched himself out again, wriggling his bare toes at the end of the steamer chair, then reached for a cricket ball on the shelf behind him and spun it from hand to hand: an old ball, a band of engraved silver set along the seam. He threw it to me.

"Took most wickets in an innings with it once, at school. Little memento."

I spun it from hand to hand myself. "I played some cricket out in Kinshasa—of all places. But I've missed all the games at home this summer."

I told Sandy of home. "I see," he said judiciously. "So the good lady with you—simply a friend. . . ."

"*Was* with me."

"Yes, well, there you are. No cricket in Lamu, I'm afraid. Just the *dolce vita*. Though I once had a splendid game a little further north of here, in Somalia during the war, with an Irish friend of mine, back in base after we'd been months in the shag. Just outside an old Italian fort, in the moonlight, both of us rather far gone. There was a smashed statue of Mussolini—used it as a wicket."

Sandy extended his memoirs once more—punishing months on end in the bush, tremendous relaxations and refreshments in the New Stanley grill or the Thorn Tree café in Nairobi on return, witty tales of derring-do. I listened to the stories, fables from another world, spinning the ball as I listened, gazing out on the blue-and-white patchwork of water and stone below us. . . .

Then I thought of playing cricket at home. Perhaps if I cut short my stay in Lamu I'd be back in time for a few September games—in Adlestrop, Chipping Norton or Great Tew. We opened the last two bottles of Tusker.

"Ah, yes," Sandy said, raising his tankard. "Wompo! Africa's impossible without it. You see, you don't drink to forget out here—you drink to remember."

We drank—and I remembered Eleanor: her smudged, sweat-caked face beneath the acacia tree in the blaze of the Kasiut desert, when we'd watched the Samburu herdsman disappear, lifting off in the white light, dancing into the horizon. "We'll have to see each other." "We must." The moment when we were no longer amateurs. How could I have let it all disappear, without protest, only twenty-four hours ago in Mombasa? I might still reach her, if she'd gone to the Norfolk, if she hadn't taken a flight out that day. "I have to telephone," I said a few minutes later. "Back at the hotel. What are the phones like?"

"Usually all right at Petley's. You may get through—to Nairobi?" I nodded.

It took me nearly an hour to get through to the Norfolk in Nairobi. "No," they said, remembering Eleanor. She had not checked in there. I might have tried the Mombasa Beach Hotel, in case she'd decided to stay on. I might have tried British Airways at Nairobi airport—I might just as well have been sighing for the moon.

That evening I asked Sandy down to Petley's and we had a lobster salad on the terrace restaurant looking over the seafront, the tide running fast now, pitch dark, with just the harbor lamps splashing yellow pools of light along the sandy road. It was the hour of release for all the local women of the town, strolling beneath the lights in groups of six or a dozen, laughing, tittering, shawled from head to foot in black cotton, like long cigars, just the white flash around their eyes showing through the dark letter boxes of their robes. The rich were having gimlets and martinis, no doubt, in their silk-cushioned seraglios—while the hippies had gone to ground, pondering their rice bowls. The town, at last, in this slight coolness of the evening, had been returned to its rightful owners. The pirate-faced men, joined now by the elders of the town, still gossiped in a long line, sitting on the seawall, eyeing their invisible wives or potential brides. Now that the foreigners had disappeared the tension had left the air. The locals were happy in the evening.

"Yes," Sandy said after I'd remarked on this. "Just how it should be. But it wasn't always. Always loved a fight here—nothing but in the old days. Mind you, I'm speaking of a few hundred years ago and more—out there on the seafront, when the Arabs boated down here, wave after wave, year in and out, massacring all the blacks. Awful tensions then, fearful bloodlettings."

"But the tribal antagonisms died out, didn't they? Two races eventually mixed, married, settled down—produced the Swahili culture, the language, all these marvelous houses, ironwork, doorways."

"Yes, indolent little paradise by all accounts—till the Europeans came pillaging down this same coast a hundred years ago. The Germans, the British—and now all these layabouts in the last few years. Really all over now. These rich sods and the hippies aren't going to mix or intermarry with the locals—leave nothing behind but the culture of the whorehouse: know nothing of Africa—and never will, other than how to find pot or fix the stock markets in London or New York to suit themselves." He speared another piece of lobster, finished a third glass of wine, gazed over the dark, lamp-flecked channel. "None of them will know it, as we did, as a loved and lived-in place."

"No. You've felt that—"

"Oh yes." He turned to me eagerly. "Oh yes. Nothing but. God's earth out here, if you ever came to know it properly. If you know the people. I'm sorry you're going back so soon."

"I don't seem to have managed very well in Africa," I said.

"I'm sorry your friend went back to London. . . ."

"It's not only that. I came here too late."

"Yes?"

"Yes. And without any real reason—when I came. Just a tourist."

Sandy looked at me curiously. "I wouldn't have said that of you."

I poured some more wine. "I was looking for an Africa that never existed—adventure books I read as a child. Henty, *King Solomon's Mines,* Allan Quatermain, Gordon of Khartoum. All that. Sheer romance. And it isn't. Never was."

Sandy shook his head. "Oh no—there were moments," he said, remembering. "Long moments. But as you say, you came too late for all that. Now, of course, you're right—bad to worse. Very far gone. See nothing for it." He leaned back, wiping his fingers. "This country, for example, wasn't 'free' in the old days. But the people were, by and large. Now it's the other way round."

"How—"

"Oh, the British here double-crossed the Maasai over their old grazing lands—to take one instance; and there was a lot of other unpardonable foolishness, God knows. But they preserved the freedoms, with the tribes, between them. Divide and rule, of course. But they kept the peace and most people had a square meal a day. Now everyone's at each other's throats, hands in everyone else's pockets—those of them that aren't far gone, that is. A sorry business," he added judiciously.

"On the other hand," I said, "they had to be free, just as we were bound to come out here in the first place: all that European technology, energy, invention, looking for space. The two things were bound to clash."

"No doubt, no doubt—"

"And perhaps we didn't properly educate them—in 'freedom.' "

"Perhaps we didn't. But that would have been our sort of freedom anyway, not theirs. Left them with a *very* pale version of Westminster, didn't we? And that's not their style at all in any case."

"What is?"

"Oh, a little local parley under the trees among the elders." He smiled. "But that's old-fashioned of me, no doubt."

I laughed in return. "No doubt."

"But I *saw* all that," Sandy went on slowly. "It worked. Knew these people better than I knew myself—months, years with them, in the old shag."

"You saw the past—and it worked?"

"Yes, indeed," he said firmly.

The next afternoon, walking along the vast, deserted ten-mile beach beyond Shela at the ocean end of Lamu, I saw a lone figure, miles away it seemed, coming slowly toward me, dancing above the sand, a mirage perhaps—as I'd thought of the Samburu herdsman in the Kasiut desert—in the shimmering heat haze. But the vision was real enough, I saw, as the figure came nearer. It was a tall African out jogging in a pair of smart silk shorts. He trotted straight past, without looking at me, without either of us speaking. And that was fair enough, I suppose. What was there to say? We both knew the arid, suspicious black-white dialogue too well already, I was sure. So there was nothing for it but for him to run past me and for me to go home.

Next day—cutting my trip short, crossing over on the ferry to Manda island to catch the flight back to Mombasa—the other ferry, with the latest tourist arrivals off the same plane, came toward us. It was crowded with passengers, I saw, as we neared each other in midchannel—Americans in bright shirts, camera-laden Japanese and younger people, half a dozen boys and girls laughing at the back, with Eleanor amongst them at one side by the gunwale.

Of course it was her—the blond helmet of curls, the tall frame, the red trousers, back in her pirate pants. We saw each other as we passed. She almost leaped out of the boat, shouting, waving at me.

"Where are you going? I came up to meet you. Come back! Come *back*! . . ."

"I can't." I waved my arms uselessly.

"You *must*. . . ." And she shouted some more. But already the two boats were separating, her voice lost in the stiff breeze and sea swell and soon she was just a wildly gesticulating figure, semaphoring a mysterious message, until she disappeared completely in the harsh dazzle.

I was tempted to go back, cancel my ticket—take up our life again in Lamu, lobster salads in Petley's with Sandy, a birthday party with his friend Arthur, filled with home-brewed wompo, a little band once more, as it had been when I'd first met her in Kinshasa. I was tempted, but I knew I wouldn't. Eleanor was among her own sort of friends again—young, happy, a little crazy. Thank God I'd been wrong. She'd recovered. I hadn't pushed her prematurely into a dull marriage and the paddock at Ascot. I hadn't soured her life—she wanted me back, we could have been together once more. No, she was bright again, shouting, waving, imperious, all in a tizzy, all that I had loved: Africa of the heart, my search since childhood, found at last and lost.